ADOBE®
PHOTOSHOP® 6
DIGITAL
DARKROOM

ADOBE® PHOTOSHOP® 6 DIGITAL DARKROOM

PRIMA TECH
A Division of Prima Publishing

LISA LEE

A Division of Prima Publishing

Prima Publishing and colophon are registered trademarks of Prima Communications, Inc. PRIMA TECH is a trademark of Prima Communications, Inc., Roseville, California 95661.

Publisher: Stacy L. Hiquet

Marketing Manager: Judi Taylor

Associate Marketing Manager: Jennifer Breece

Managing Editor: Sandy Doell

Acquisitions Editor: Jawahara Saidullah

Developmental Editor: Kate Shoup Welsh

Project Editor: Heather Talbot

Technical Reviewer: Bob Breece

Copy Editor: Kezia Endsley

Interior Layout: Bill Hartman

Interior Design: Stahl Design Inc.

Cover Design: Prima Design Team

Indexer: Katherine Stimson

Proofreader: Lisa Shaw

Adobe, the Adobe logo, Acrobat, the Acrobat logo, Adobe Premiere, After Effects, FrameMaker, PageMaker, Photoshop, and PostScript are either registered trademarks or trademarks of Adobe Systems Incorporated in the United States and/or other countries.

THIS PRODUCT IS NOT ENDORSED OR SPONSORED BY ADOBE SYSTEMS INCORPORATED, PUBLISHER OF PHOTOSHOP.

Important: Prima Publishing cannot provide software support. Please contact the appropriate software manufacturer's technical support line or Web site for assistance.

ISBN: 0-7615-3163-7

Library of Congress Catalog Card Number: 00-106665

Printed in the United States of America

00 01 02 03 04 GG 10 9 8 7 6 5 4 3 2 1

This book is dedicated to my dad, Ron Lee, who taught me how to take and develop photographs with a 35mm camera.

This book is also dedicated to the memory of Lucy Jen, my grandmother, who treasured great photography, art, and movies.

ACKNOWLEDGMENTS

This book would not be possible without Neil Tucker, Dan Bomze, Peter Ford, Paola, Tyler, Ficus, and Hiroshi, who were kind enough to let me include their photos and pictures in my book. Also, thank you Joe Britt and Sairam Suresh, for letting me use some of your digital pictures.

Thanks to Thomas Knoll and the Photoshop development team at Adobe. Thanks for making a revolutionary software product. Also, I'd like to acknowledge Nikon, Kodak, Olympus, Sony, and Fuji for making great digital cameras and bundling them with feature-filled Macintosh and Windows software.

Special thanks to Marta Justak for introducing me to the folks at Prima Tech. Thanks to Jawahara Saidullah for giving me the opportunity to write this book. Also, thanks to all the folks at Prima Tech who contributed to the editing, layout, and design of this book.

Finally, thanks to my family, friends, and co-workers for all their patience and support.

ABOUT THE AUTHOR

Lisa Lee is the author of *Fireworks Fast & Easy Web Development, Easy iMac, Easy iBook, Easy Linux, Guide to Mac OS 7.6* update, *Upgrading and Repairing Your Mac*, and co-author of *Teach Yourself Mac OS 8.5 in 24 Hours*. She has also contributed to many computer books, as both an author and a technical editor.

A former Apple and Microsoft employee, Lisa is currently working at a startup company, Danger Research (www.danger.com), in Palo Alto, California. She brings more than six years of Web building experience, and two dozen years working with traditional and digital cameras to *Photoshop 6 Digital Darkroom*. You can download and view the photographs used in this book at her Web site, http://www.flatfishfactory.com.

CONTENTS AT A GLANCE

CONTENTS

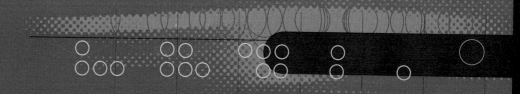

INTRODUCTION

PHOTOSHOP 6 DIGITAL DARKROOM FROM PRIMA TECH IS DESIGNED FOR
THE CASUAL OR AMATEUR PHOTOGRAPHER WITH AN INTERMEDIATE TO
ADVANCED LEVEL OF COMPUTER AND GRAPHICS APPLICATION
EXPERIENCE. IF YOU'RE LOOKING FOR A GUIDE TO PHOTOSHOP, THIS ISN'T
IT. I DON'T SPEND ANY TIME COVERING COLOR THEORY, PRE-PRESS,
PRINTING, OR TOOLS LIKE THE HISTORY BRUSH. INSTEAD, I START WITH A
CRASH COURSE ABOUT HOW TO TAKE A GOOD PICTURE, AND THEN TRY TO
SHOW OFF SOME BASIC AND ADVANCED TASKS YOU CAN PERFORM TO
CREATE SPIFFY-LOOKING WEB-READY PHOTOGRAPHIC IMAGES. I'M
ASSUMING IF THE IMAGE LOOKS GOOD TO YOU, USING YOUR EYES AS YOUR
GUIDE, THEN IT'S OKAY FOR YOUR WEB SITE.

Although many of the tasks in this book are fairly easy to follow, I don't recommend this book to a new computer user or someone brand new to graphics applications, photography, Photoshop, or Web design. All this information and new technology may be a bit overwhelming to grasp all at once.

Also, digital pictures are the focus of this book. Most pictures were taken with 2-, 3-, or 4-megapixel cameras. I used several different digital cameras to create the images in this book. However, Nikon's Coolpix 990 is the camera I use most frequently. You can download these images from my Web site at www.flatfishfactory.com.

WHO SHOULD READ THIS BOOK?

Naturally, I'd like to think this book would be helpful to anyone wanting to learn how to work with digital pictures with Photoshop. If you're adventurous and learn quickly by following visual, step-by-step examples, you'll probably appreciate this book. These examples are just one of many possible ways you can use one or several features in Photoshop. If you're looking for technical explanations and discussions on color theory, you'll be disappointed.

This book is for digital camera owners, and those who work with digital pictures and also know how to use a computer. It's also for those who are new to Photoshop 6, and preparing pictures for the Web. If you don't have any experience with photography or computers, I strongly recommend reading other books to learn more about photography, graphics, digital cameras, Photoshop, and the Web, in addition to using this book. If you are familiar with Windows or Macintosh computers, and have dabbled with digital cameras, Photoshop, and Web graphics in the past, this book is for you!

HOW THIS BOOK IS ORGANIZED

There are four main sections to this book. The first section is an introduction to digital cameras and shows you how to install and configure Photoshop 6. The second section introduces you to the Photoshop workspace and covers the basics of working with layers, masks, and channels. The third section is a more advanced section about how to experiment with layers, masks, and channels, and shows you how to create animation or automate tasks with digital pictures. The fourth section shows you how to create two Web photo albums and provides some simple examples for creating and customizing your Web pages.

The chapters cover basic to advanced topics to show you how to do simple tasks, like straighten a photo, to more sophisticated tasks, like combining images from different pictures. Skip to any chapter if you want to use this book as a reference, or walk through it chapter by chapter to try out different combinations of features in Photoshop.

The figures in this book were created with the Macintosh version of Photoshop 6 although the Windows version looks more or less identical. Keyboard combinations refer to Windows and Macintosh keys. For example, Ctrl/Command+click represents Ctrl+click if you're using Windows, and Command+click if you're using a Mac.

Finally, I welcome comments from my readers. Let me know what you like or don't like about this book. My e-mail address is lisalee@spies.com.

CONVENTIONS USED IN THIS BOOK

 Tips offer hints, explain more about a special feature, or tell you how to use a shortcut to boost your productivity and make work fun.

 Notes provide additional information about a feature, or extend an idea on how to use a feature.

 Cautions warn about pitfalls and glitches in the application or procedures. Many of the cautions are platform specific while others can occur on either platform running Photoshop.

WORKING WITH DIGITAL PICTURES

PHOTOSHOP IS ONE OF THE MOST DYNAMIC, HIGH-END IMAGE EDITING APPLICATIONS AVAILABLE TODAY. HOLLYWOOD PRODUCTION STUDIOS USE IT TO EDIT HIGH-RESOLUTION DIGITAL IMAGES FOR FEATURE FILMS SUCH AS THE STAR TREK SERIES. WEB DEVELOPMENT STUDIOS AND PEOPLE LIKE YOU AND ME USE IT TO CREATE GREAT-LOOKING DIGITAL PICTURES FOR WEB SITES.

BEFORE YOU CAN START EDITING DIGITAL PICTURES WITH PHOTOSHOP, YOU MUST CREATE SOME DIGITAL PICTURES. DIGITAL PICTURES CAN BE CREATED FROM MANY DIFFERENT SOURCES. DIGITAL CAMERAS ARE PROBABLY THE MOST OBVIOUS SOURCE OF DIGITAL PICTURES. TWO-, THREE-, AND FOUR-MEGAPIXEL CAMERAS OFFER AN EASY WAY TO GET A PICTURE INTO A COMPUTER AND ONTO A WEB PAGE. FILM, PAPER, AND PHOTO SCANNERS CAN ALSO CONVERT TRADITIONAL PHOTOGRAPHS OR 35MM SLIDES AND NEGATIVES INTO DIGITAL IMAGE FILES.

THE FIRST PART OF THIS BOOK CONTAINS A BRIEF OVERVIEW OF HOW TO USE DIGITAL CAMERAS, AND BRIEFLY EXPLAINS HOW TO CONVERT TRADITIONAL PHOTOS INTO DIGITAL FILES. IF YOU ALREADY HAVE DIGITAL PICTURES READY TO USE AND HAVE ALREADY INSTALLED PHOTOSHOP 6, MOVE AHEAD TO PART 2, "PHOTOSHOP 6 BASICS." IF YOU HAVE INTERNET ACCESS, I HAVE PROVIDED SOME DIGITAL PICTURES ON MY WEB SITE AT HTTP://WWW.SPIES.COM/ LISALEE/DIGPICS, WHICH YOU ARE FREE TO USE.

CHAPTER 1

TAKING PICTURES

THIS FIRST CHAPTER IS A SHORT COURSE ON HOW TO GET FAMILIAR WITH
THE FEATURES OF A CAMERA AND TAKE PICTURES. TO FIND OUT MORE
ABOUT HOW TO SHOP FOR OR USE A CAMERA, VISIT
HTTP://WWW.PHOTO.NET, OR PURCHASE A DEDICATED BOOK ABOUT
PHOTOGRAPHY. IF YOU'RE LOOKING FOR PHOTOSHOP INFORMATION, YOU
WON'T FIND ANY IN THIS CHAPTER. SKIP AHEAD TO CHAPTER 2, "GETTING
STARTED: INSTALLING PHOTOSHOP 6 AND OBTAINING DIGITAL IMAGES," TO
LEARN HOW TO INSTALL PHOTOSHOP 6.

WHETHER YOU'RE USING A CAMERA OR A SCANNER, THE MOST IMPORTANT
THING TO REMEMBER WHEN WORKING WITH DIGITAL PICTURES IS THAT THE
QUALITY OF A DIGITAL IMAGE IS ONLY AS GOOD AS THE QUALITY OF THE
ORIGINAL PICTURE. ALTHOUGH 35MM CAMERAS CAN TAKE GREAT PICTURES,
THE WEAK LINK IS OFTEN THE QUALITY OF THE SCANNER OUTPUT. I
EMPHASIZE HOW TO USE DIGITAL CAMERAS, INSTEAD OF 35MM ONES,
BECAUSE DIGITAL CAMERAS PROVIDE A STRAIGHTFORWARD WAY OF
BRINGING A HIGH-QUALITY DIGITAL IMAGE DIRECTLY INTO YOUR
COMPUTER.

ABOUT DIGITAL CAMERAS

The first digital cameras appeared on store shelves approximately seven years ago. They cost close to $1,000, and offered a 640×480 fixed resolution, with no capability to focus. Storage media were fairly expensive, with 1–2MB of storage space costing $100 to $200. Today, you can purchase a 4-megapixel camera—which can take a 2,400×1,800 pixel image (or 2,048×1,536 pixels for a 3-megapixel camera, or 1,600×1,200 pixels for a 2-megapixel camera) for less than $1,000. Today's 2- and 3-megapixel digital cameras truly rival the features and image quality originally created by 35mm cameras.

Film, lenses, and camera settings on traditional 35mm cameras are replaced by a CCD, software, and a storage disk, such as compact flash, smart media, or a miniature hard disk on a digital camera. The CCD (Charged Couple Device) is the essential chip that makes a digital camera a camera. Most low- to medium-range cameras have a single CCD. CCDs were originally used in video cameras, which initially supported a 640×480 resolution.

High-end cameras can use up to three CCDs to process red, green, and blue light. A camera using three CCDs dedicates one CCD to process a red, green, or blue channel. The camera combines the images from each of the CCDs into one image, which is stored as a file on the camera's storage card. High-end cameras also usually use larger lenses. High-end cameras can create high-quality digital images because the larger lens brings more light to the CCDs, which in turn can bring more image data to the image file created by the camera.

Digital cameras are similar yet different from the traditional 35mm cameras. From a distance, it can be difficult to distinguish a digital camera from a 35mm camera. Both usually have a built-in flash, shutter button, and a lens. In most current models, both can automatically focus and determine whether you need to use a flash. Many medium- to high-end cameras also offer a range of manual settings that enable you to set the aperture, shutter speed, and exposure settings. It's easy to take a great looking, quick picture with both kinds of cameras, too.

Despite the similarities, digital cameras work much differently from 35mm cameras. One of the main differences is that digital cameras use a storage card instead of film to store images. The two most common types of digital storage media are Smart Media and Compact Flash. A digital camera will either use one card format or the other, not both. Smart Media cards can store from 4MB-32MB of image data, with the amount of storage space varying with the storage capacity of the card. Compact Flash cards range in size, including 8, 16, 64, 80, 96, and 128MB. Some of the first digital cameras, such as Apple's QuickTake cameras, used 1MB and 2MB Smart Media cards and captured 640×480 digital images. The digital picture ranged in size from 60K to 100K.

 Not all CCDs are alike. Cost is a better indicator of availability of the CCD, rather than the quality of the image it can create. Visit a few Web sites and compare picture quality between cameras you're interested in before purchasing one.

LOW-COST CAMERAS

Many kinds of CCDs are used in today's digital cameras. Less expensive cameras most likely use CCDs that are limited by the size of the image that can be captured, or by the amount of light it can process. However, most 2- and 3-megapixel cameras in the sub-$1,000 price range—such as the Nikon 990 and 950, Kodak, Canon, Olympus, and Fuji cameras—do a great job taking pictures in regular daylight as well as in low-light conditions. Two 3-megapixel cameras are shown here: Nikon's Coolpix 990 is on the left and Sony's DSC-S70 on the right.

HIGH-PERFORMANCE CAMERAS

More pixels means bigger file sizes and more processing time for a camera. However, digital camera performance is increasing as rapidly as computer processor speeds are. And as with computers, if you can't afford a good digital camera today, chances are you'll be able to in six to twelve months. This figure shows the Fuji FinePix 4700 on the left and the previous year's model, the MX-2700, on the right. The FinePix 4700 boasts a 4-megapixel CCD, whereas the MX-2700 can capture 2.3-megapixel images.

MULTIMEDIA
Many 3- and 4-megapixel cameras can capture MPEG1 video and audio at 320×240 pixels in addition to capturing still pictures at 2,048×1,536 pixels. What's next? I'm guessing MPEG2 support in the next-generation digital cameras

COMPARING DIGITAL CAMERAS

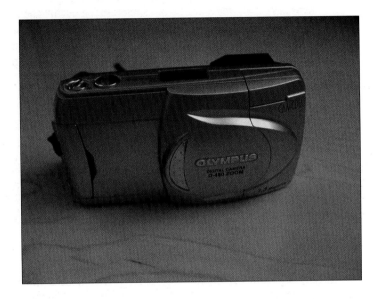

It seems like digital cameras are gaining so many new features each year, it's almost impossible to compare them, much less figure out what a good deal is. Some basic guidelines to use when comparing digital cameras are, in no particular order, features, cost, and quality. I tend to give the quality of the picture the most weight. However, depending on your preferences, you might choose differently. The Olympus digital cameras, like the D-450 Zoom shown in this figure for example, are popular because they look and feel very similar to a 35mm camera.

FEATURES

The features a camera supports are often related to the price of the camera itself:

✳ Most low-end cameras in the sub-$250 price range offer fixed or minimal zoom and slow focus, low-resolution images (640×480 pixels), no flash, and low-quality parts. You should compare prices and features, as well as image quality between two or more cameras, before actually purchasing one.

✳ Medium-priced cameras ($500–$1,000) offer zoom lenses, improved image quality, more focus settings, more flash settings, and an improved software interface. If you can afford a medium-range digital camera, you'll have plenty of models to choose from.

✳ Higher-end cameras (above $1,000) offer more of all the previous features, as well as larger camera bodies, some of which look almost identical to 35mm cameras. A larger camera body has two advantages. Larger camera bodies usually mean larger lenses. One of the biggest limitations of mid-range digital cameras is that the smaller lens and camera body sizes restrict the camera's ability to capture a broader range of light. Some high-end cameras can connect directly to a computer and download images to a computer's hard drive. Others, like the Fuji Finepix S-1 Pro, can work with both Compact Flash and Smart Media card as well as IBM's Microdrive.

COST

Although many low-end cameras are priced in the $100–$200 range, you can probably find one below $100. However, for a few hundred dollars more, around $400–$600, you can find a decent mid-range camera that can create larger and more realistic pictures. Three- and four-megapixel cameras are starting to appear in the $800–$1000 price range. If you can wait for next year's models, you might be able to get twice the camera for your money.

QUALITY

Low-end cameras, in the $100–$200 price range, typically have the poorest quality lenses and CCDs, and usually do not support the addition of filters or other lenses. Some mid-range cameras, however, offer this extensibility. Many mid-range cameras from Kodak, Sony, and Nikon take great pictures. Some models, such as the Nikon Coolpix 950, offer exceptional lenses at reasonable prices. High-end cameras usually support 35mm lenses. Clockwise from the left are the following mid-range cameras: Olympus D450-Zoom, Kodak DC280, Fuji 2700, and Nikon Coolpix 950.

 If you've already compared prices between traditional 35mm cameras and digital cameras, you'll immediately notice that digital cameras capable of using 35mm lenses are quite a bit more expensive than traditional 35mm cameras. The quality and size of the lens definitely makes a difference when you're taking pictures. If you already have a 35mm camera, or can't find a digital camera that fits into your budget, you can always scan slides or printed photos into your computer.

USING CAMERA MODES

Most digital cameras have two modes: a picture-taking mode and a picture-viewing mode. This section shows you how to use these camera modes with a few selected digital cameras. In many cases, your digital camera will have similar settings to those covered in this section. However, your camera's operation manual is the best source for finding out how to use your camera.

PICTURE-TAKING MODES

Most digital cameras have at least two modes: automatic shooting mode and playback mode. Some cameras have a camera connection, or picture download, mode. Most cameras usually have an automatic picture-taking mode, whereby the camera sets the shutter speed and focus for you. More expensive cameras also have a manual picture-taking mode, enabling you to focus and set the aperture, exposure, and shutter speed for a picture. Many of these types of cameras also enable you to add various filters and lenses. Some cameras even enable you to capture motion.

AUTOMATIC MODE

Not sure what a digital camera can do? To take a picture, set the camera to automatic mode, take some pictures, and check out the results in playback mode. Although automatic mode might not create the best pictures for low-end cameras, particularly in low-light shots, you can use automatic mode 90 percent of the time with most cameras and get amazing images.

The following steps use two digital cameras to illustrate how different it can be to take a picture in automatic mode. Depending on the camera you have, you might need to modify the following steps:

1. Put the camera into automatic mode. Some cameras, like the Olympus D-450, only work in automatic mode. Line up the line on the dial knob with the text and marker on the camera body to select a camera mode. The Kodak DC 280 is shown here. Turn the dial to change the camera's operational mode.
2. Press the power button.

3. Choose a flash setting. The Flash button, which usually has a lightning bolt icon on or next to it, is usually combined with a Flash icon in the status window of the camera.
4. Choose a focus mode.

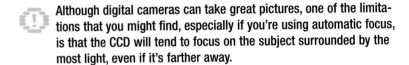 Although digital cameras can take great pictures, one of the limitations that you might find, especially if you're using automatic focus, is that the CCD will tend to focus on the subject surrounded by the most light, even if it's farther away.

5. Frame the subject.
6. Press the shutter button.

Keep a second storage card and batteries available for storing video. That way you don't have to watch how much space is available on your camera while taking regular pictures.

MANUAL MODE

Automatic mode is great for taking pictures of locations, events, and people in bright light. Low light, or artificial light, will probably require more experimentation to find the best settings for a particular location or event. In this case, you might want to put the camera in manual mode, which enables you to manually set the aperture, shutter speed, or exposure time, in order to capture a more color-rich or motion-sensitive picture. Medium to high-end cameras have manual settings that enable you to set up a digital camera similar to the way you set up a 35mm one.

If you have an older camera, using manual mode might introduce you to a world of confusing camera software. Today's 3- and 4-megapixel cameras, however, usually have an *M* on the mode dial to indicate manual mode. Turn the mode dial until the *M* lines up with the marker on the camera to put the Nikon Coolpix 990 into manual mode.

The basic procedure for taking a picture in manual mode varies from camera to camera; check your manual for details. Using a Nikon Coolpix 990, the procedure is as follows:

1. Set the camera to manual mode and then power it on.
2. Press the MODE button. *P* represents Exposure mode and enables you to select combinations of shutter speed and aperture settings. *A* represents Aperture mode, where you set the aperture size, and the camera picks the shutter speed. *S* represents Shutter Priority mode, enabling you to set the speed of the shutter while the camera sets the aperture. (These settings only apply to the Nikon Coolpix 990.)
3. Rotate the dial to choose a setting for the selected mode.
4. Press the shutter button.

 If the camera is in manual mode, you'll probably want to experiment with different shutter speeds, apertures, and exposure settings to see how the camera handles different settings under various lighting conditions.

When you take a picture in manual mode, you have control over the following:

❋ Focus, which determines the clarity of the image.
❋ Aperture, or the amount of light exposed to the CCD. A larger aperture (smaller f-stop numbers) decreases the depth of field and can create a blurry background. Smaller apertures increase depth of field and clarity between foreground and background elements of the picture.
❋ Shutter speed. Faster shutter speeds can freeze motion whereas slower shutter speeds capture blurred motion, but allow more light in.

Depending on your camera, you might also be able to add filters and lenses.

FOCUS

Sometimes a digital camera in automatic mode can't figure out what to focus on, even if it's right in front of the camera. Although digital cameras can have thousands of levels of focus, sometimes the CCD targets the brightest light at the center of the picture to determine what to focus on, as shown in this photo.

Press the shutter button halfway down to preview the focus mode of a camera. Cameras in automatic mode will adjust focus as your subjects move about. If you can't get the camera to correctly focus in automatic mode, set it to manual mode and manually adjust the focus of the camera. Digital cameras rely on light to determine what to focus on. Notice the person in the background is the focus instead of the person in the foreground.

APERTURE

The aperture in a 35mm camera determines how much light strikes the film inside the camera. On a digital camera, the aperture setting adjusts how light interacts with the CCD. View the aperture setting in the camera's software to get a general idea of how the CCD will behave. A wider aperture allows the most light to get in, and, combined with a fast shutter speed, is great for capturing sports action, or subjects such as lightning.

SHUTTER SPEED

The shutter priority settings, in addition to how they capture motion, affect how much light hits the CCD in a digital camera by adjusting the amount of time the shutter remains open. A faster shutter speed means less exposure time to the chip, whereas a slower shutter speed enables the camera to capture more color and light information. In some digital cameras, if the shutter setting is given priority, you set the shutter speed, and the camera will figure out the correlating aperture and exposure settings.

ADDING FILTERS

A few low-end, and some medium-end, digital cameras support adding filters to the lens. On the cameras that support filters, you can *neutralize*, or filter out, certain light qualities by adding a filter to a camera lens:

* **Ultraviolet.** Filter out bright light with the Ultraviolet filter.
* **Neutral.** This filter is most effective outdoors. It will filter out extreme bright or dark areas, thus equalizing the amount of light that gets exposed through the lens. Although this is a filter for light, it can help a camera capture a more balanced tonal range of light, reducing the likelihood of capturing overexposed or washed out colors in a photo.
* **Color.** If you're shooting in mid-day sun, adding a red or orange filter to a camera can create a warmer range of color tones.

 You can add similar effects to your digital images with Photoshop, although you might not be able to capture the same range of natural colors using software as you can taking the picture with a filter.

ADDING LENSES

Although most digital cameras can't share 35mm camera lenses, some cameras can share lenses across models, such as the Nikon digital camera series: the 900, 950, and 990. These models can use any of Nikon's Coolpix lenses, including macro, telephoto, wide-angle, and fish-eye lenses. However, you cannot attach any of Nikon's 35mm lenses to any of Nikon's Coolpix digital cameras. Although most people will probably own only one digital camera, if you want to shoot with multiple cameras or upgrade to a newer Coolpix model, you don't need to buy new lenses. This section highlights the macro and fish-eye lenses.

 If a digital camera has an extending zoom lens, like Fuji FinePix 4700, don't count on being able to use other lenses with it.

MACRO

This lens enables you to get up close and personal with your subject. Unlike other lenses, which require that you be at least 4cm (centimeters) from your subject, this one allows you to get as close as 4mm (millimeters). If you can attach a macro lens to your camera, you can take extreme close-up shots, like the rose shown here.

 Zoom in toward your subject when taking a picture with a macro lens. Some cameras, like the Nikon Coolpix 990, have specific manual menu settings for use with macro and fish-eye lenses.

 Avoid using the built-in flash with a macro shot. The flash will probably prevent the camera from capturing any detail from the close-up image.

FISH-EYE

A fish-eye lens is a super wide-angle lens. The lens extends out beyond the scope of a normal lens, up to 180 degrees, and has a more bulbous appearance than a normal camera lens. Around the edges of the image, straight lines are rendered as curves. Some digital cameras, like the Nikon Coolpix 990, have a built-in zoom. However, when taking a picture with a fish-eye lens, you want to zoom out, not in, to take full advantage of it.

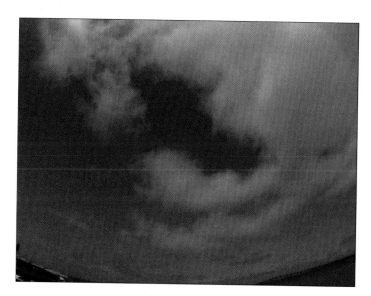

A fish-eye lens creates an extreme, wide-angle, distorted image by magnifying the center of the picture and shrinking the edges of the picture. The captured image is a little wider than an image taken with a normal lens. You can use Photoshop to merge a picture taken with a fish-eye lens with pictures taken with a regular lens to create a panoramic view of a skyline or horizon.

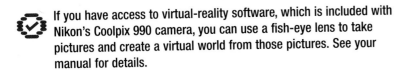 If you have access to virtual-reality software, which is included with Nikon's Coolpix 990 camera, you can use a fish-eye lens to take pictures and create a virtual world from those pictures. See your manual for details.

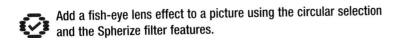 Add a fish-eye lens effect to a picture using the circular selection and the Spherize filter features.

MOTION-CAPTURE MODE

Many 3- and 4-megapixel cameras can capture MPEG1-quality video and audio. Although the size of the video is small in comparison to still pictures, sometimes it's more meaningful to capture audio and motion. You can import QuickTime movies into Image Ready and work with an individual frame or with the full video.

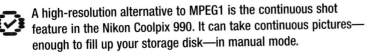 A high-resolution alternative to MPEG1 is the continuous shot feature in the Nikon Coolpix 990. It can take continuous pictures—enough to fill up your storage disk—in manual mode.

The basic procedure for capturing video (assuming your camera allows it) is as follows (the precise instructions for your camera might differ; check your manual for details):

1. Set the camera to record moving images, and then power it on.

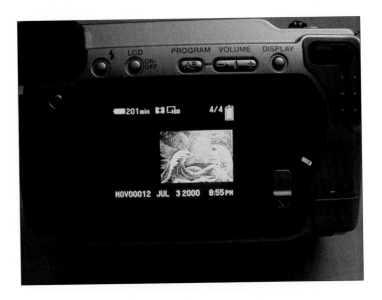

2. Hold down the shutter button and point the camera at the action you want to capture. Use your camera's LCD screen to view the action. The LCD screen is the real-time viewfinder located on the back side of

the camera. Move the camera, or follow your subject as it moves, to create your movie.

3. Release the shutter button to stop capturing motion, or let the camera run out of storage space.

 Although MPEG1 video is captured at 320×240 pixels compared to 2,048×1,536 pixels for a still image, it can fill up the storage card pretty quickly. Carry extra storage cards, or keep a laptop and PC card adapter nearby, so you don't find yourself having to erase something because you run out of space.

PLAYBACK MODE

After you've taken a few digital pictures, you'll want to view them. Here's how (note that the precise instructions for viewing images on your camera might vary from those listed here; check your camera's manual for details):

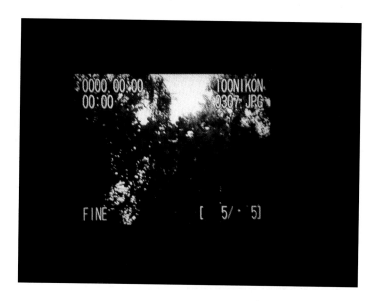

1. Set the camera to Play mode.

2. Press the up or down arrow buttons to view various images stored in your camera using your camera's LCD screen.

 If the camera has a cable to connect it to a television, you can view the pictures on a TV and use the camera to select images.

3. Press the grid button to view multiple images at once.

 Most digital cameras have a slide-show feature. Select the pictures you want to use for the slide show, put the camera into slide-show mode, connect the camera to a TV or projector system, and voilá! You have a slide show controlled by your digital camera.

IMAGE FILE FORMATS

A digital camera, much like a scanner, converts analog light information into digital ones and zeros, which represent the location and color of each pixel in an image. All this image information is stored in a single file. The information in this file can be stored raw, or uncompressed, thus preserving all the original image data.

The image can also be made smaller by compression. Compression involves storing iterative information in a file in one place, instead of several places in the file. The goal of compression is to reduce the size of the file without losing any of the original information. Some compression methods, such as a high-end JPEG file format, preserve most of the quality of the original image. However, other compression formats, such as low-end JPEG file format, often lose image quality during the compression process.

The term *file format* describes a type of file, such as a text or graphic file. The most commonly used Web graphic file formats are JPEG, GIF, and PNG.

Most digital cameras use the JPEG file format as the default for storing picture files on the camera's storage card. Some cameras, such as the Nikon Coolpix 990, allow you to capture raw or uncompressed images, which are then stored as TIFF files. Many of the latest 3- and 4-megapixel cameras also support MPEG1 audio and video files.

THE JPEG FILE FORMAT

As mentioned previously, JPEG, short for *Joint Photographic Experts Group*, is the standard file format used with digital cameras today. Although not all cameras take advantage of this option, JPEG offers various rates of compression. Compression rates are generally presented as plain-English options, such as "normal" and "fine" or "good" and "better."

The compression rate affects how large the image file will be. For example, with a 2-megapixel camera (1,600×1,200 pixels), a normal file is about 300–500KB. If you plan to take pictures for a Web site, this setting will work great for you. This picture, taken in Normal mode with a Nikon Coolpix 990, captures a clear, crisp image.

A Fine picture, on the other hand, is approximately 500KB–1.2MB. If you plan to print your images, this is the setting for you. If you have a limited amount of storage space, you'll probably want to use the smallest file size possible ("normal" or "good" rather than "fine" or "better"). However, if you invest in a large storage card, use the largest compressed file size possible to yield more detailed images. This picture, shot in Fine mode with the same camera, shows a little more detail than the previous photo.

THE TIFF FILE FORMAT

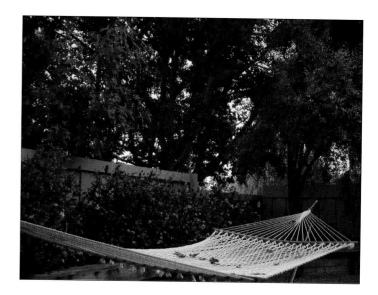

If you prefer to work with uncompressed image files, set your camera to capture uncompressed TIFF images (not all cameras allow this; check your manual for details). Be aware, though, that doing so will add lots of processing time to your picture taking. A 2-megapixel image, 1,600×1,200 pixels, can take up 8MB of storage space. Because this uncompressed file is rather huge (compared to JPEG files), it will take the camera a minute or two to write this image data to the storage card. In many cases you might not notice a significant increase in image quality.

 If your camera has a "fine" or "better" setting for JPEG images, take a few pictures with this setting and compare it to the TIFF versions. Unless you absolutely need an uncompressed image, the file JPEG image might be the better file format, enabling you to save more images in less time.

TAKING A GREAT PICTURE

Many books and Web pages discuss the best way to light, compose, and shoot a picture. The information presented in this chapter includes what I consider to be some basic picture-taking concepts, which you can take to heart or ignore. After all, it's not like you're wasting film.

LIGHTING THE SUBJECT

Light plays a big role in any picture. Light, and its counterpart, shade, can enhance or hide image clarity, color, and the overall composition of a picture. Here's a brief summary of lighting issues to consider before taking a picture:

* When taking pictures outdoors or indoors in natural light, try to shoot with the sun behind you or to the side of you at an angle to minimize washing out colors, or dramatic shadows.
* If the sun is behind the subject, try to counter its brightness by using the built-in flash on the camera.
* Try to keep the light source at an angle behind you in order to provide an even light over the subject. The most difficult pictures to take are low-light ones, or pictures taken with artificial light, such as a flash.
* If you take a picture with a flash, you are probably all too familiar with the red-eye effect. Red eye occurs when a picture is taken in low light, and the flash reflects off the pupil of the eye before the eye can adjust to the bright light. Most pictures with color and light-related inaccuracies can be corrected with Photoshop.

I must admit I don't have a professional photography studio. I prefer to take pictures of people and places in their natural state. But if you want to invest in additional flash bulbs and tripods, go for it.

The following steps illustrate when to consider lighting issues while taking a picture with the camera in automatic mode.

1. Set the camera to automatic mode and power it on.
2. Press the flash button and choose a flash setting.
3. Note the location of the light source in the picture. You might want to change the location of the camera, or move the subject to change the way the subject is lit. If your camera has a built-in flash, you can put the camera in force flash mode, using the built-in flash as a filler flash to handle shots in which the light source is behind your subject.

4. Press the shutter button. Lighting a subject from a side angle can create more dramatic effects compared to the same subject lit from above.

 For best results, hold the camera steady as you press the shutter button.

NATURAL LIGHTING

Taking pictures in the sunlight can be either extremely easy or somewhat difficult, depending on the time of day. For example, if you take a picture at noon, when the sun is directly overhead, you might need to move your subject into the shade to prevent the sun from washing out the image. However, if you take a picture at sunrise or sunset, you can capture a wider range of colors with a warmer light.

Although I don't usually put much thought into using a flash when I take pictures in daylight, here are a few things to consider when taking pictures in natural light. If you're taking a picture in the shade, you may want to force your camera to use a flash (also known as a fill flash) to make the subject of your photo stand out from the background. Light from a sunrise casts a bluish hue, compared to light from a sunset, which can have a reddish or orange tint.

TUNGSTEN LIGHTING

Tungsten, or halogen-generated light, can cast a yellow or orange hue on your subject. You can easily correct this type of light using Photoshop 6. For more information about correcting colors and adjusting light, see Chapter 5, "Correcting Images."

FLUORESCENT LIGHTING

Fluorescent light casts a greenish hue on your subject. Again, you can correct for this using Photoshop. For more information about correcting colors and adjusting light, see Chapter 5.

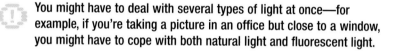 **You might have to deal with several types of light at once—for example, if you're taking a picture in an office but close to a window, you might have to cope with both natural light and fluorescent light.**

FRAMING THE SUBJECT

Ever taken a picture and mistakenly cut off the top of someone's head? In addition to keeping the subject in the camera's viewfinder, try to frame some of the background picture elements. *Framing* is the process of arranging the elements in a picture so that the subject is complementary to the other elements in the picture. Framing can be as simple as turning the camera sideways to change the angle or perspective of a picture or including a few trees to help frame some clouds. The following steps illustrate when and how to consider framing your picture during the picture-taking process.

1. Set the camera to automatic mode and then power it on. Set the camera to save the image at the highest-resolution available.
2. Use the built-in display to frame the subject. Alternatively, you can use the viewfinder to center the subject, and view the picture limits.
3. Hold the shutter button halfway down if you want to adjust the focus as you frame your picture.
4. When you're ready to take a picture, press the shutter button.

 If you're not sure how to frame your subject, include more information, rather than less information, when taking the picture. You can always crop the picture using Photoshop.

COMPOSING A PICTURE

Composition sort of takes framing a step further down the path of creative picture taking. Composing a picture is similar to composing a song, except instead of writing a song with notes, you compose a story with images. When I compose photographs, I try to tell a story. If there are no people in the picture, I try to balance light and shade, or highlight contrasting colors.

If you're not quite sure what I mean by "composition," try taking a look at some of the photos on my Web site (**http://www.flatfish-factory.com**). Pick one or two photos you like, and then try to decide why you like them. Consider these things when you compose your own photos.

Following are a few tips to consider when composing a picture.

KEEP THE SUBJECT OFF-CENTER

Try to keep the subject of the picture slightly off-center. Look for another picture element to include in the photo when you take the picture. Arranging the subject slightly off-center makes a picture more interesting and less two-dimensional.

THE RULE OF THIRDS

Putting a picture together can mean trying to figure out how to break up space. One way of looking through the viewfinder is to break up the space that you see into thirds. If you can see distinct subjects in each third of the picture, you're following the rule of thirds.

COMPOSING WITH COLOR

Another way to compose a picture is to place certain colors next to each other, as with the berries. The following steps illustrate the process of evaluating colors during the picture-taking process.

1. Set the camera to automatic mode.
2. Use the built-in display to frame the colors in the picture.
3. Press the zoom in and zoom out buttons to include or exclude other colors, or view alternative compositions.
4. Press the shutter button.

 You can also experiment with adding colors to pictures using Photoshop 6. See Chapter 7, "Creating Objects and Gradients," to find out more about adding color to pictures with Photoshop.

TAKING PICTURES OF PEOPLE

Whether you're in a studio or out on the street, the one thing to keep in mind when taking pictures of people is to keep the light behind you or to your side, and have the person face the camera. Having the light source stream in from the side of the subject can add interesting shadow effects and bring depth and texture to the picture. Try to keep the person or people in your picture comfortable and relaxed, focusing more on their faces than their clothes. Include more than one person in a picture if possible, and try to capture the moment. The following steps illustrate a simple process for taking pictures of people. A more elaborate process might involve setting up lighting in a studio.

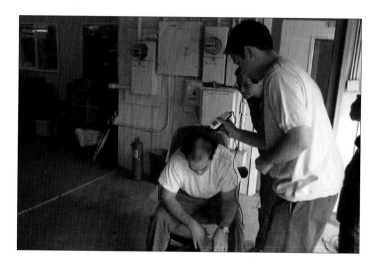

1. Set the camera to automatic mode and then power it on.
2. Stand to the left or right of the light source.
3. Frame the subject or subjects with the built-in display or viewfinder.
4. Press the shutter button.

 When taking pictures of people with a Flash, try not to stand too close or too far away from the subject.

CAPTURING MOTION

Digital cameras aren't always smart about how to focus on moving subjects. You will probably need to take continuous pictures to get the best shot of an athlete or performer. If the subject is moving quickly, you might need to set your camera to manual mode, and increase the shutter speed to reduce blur. The following steps explain how to take continuous pictures with a Nikon Coolpix 990. (Other cameras might vary. For example, the Sony DSC-S70 has a Movie setting on its mode dial.)

1. Set the camera to manual mode, and then press the Menu button. Press the arrow buttons to choose Continuous. Continuous mode enables a Nikon Coolpix 990 to capture up to 16 consecutive pictures.
2. Frame the subject in the viewfinder or built-in display.

3. Rotate the camera if the subject fits better in a portrait view. This
action shot was taken with the digital zoom option on a Nikon Coolpix
990.

4. Press the shutter button.

**Keep several storage cards and batteries on hand if you plan to
shoot continuous pictures. Fluid motion can range from 24 to 30
frames per second, and 3-megapixel images taken in Fine mode can
require over 1MB of space per picture.**

CHAPTER 2

GETTING STARTED: INSTALLING PHOTOSHOP 6 AND OBTAINING DIGITAL IMAGES

A DIGITAL PICTURE IS A SINGLE FILE, MADE UP OF A MOSAIC OF PIXELS STORED AS BINARY CODE. HARDWARE, SUCH AS A DIGITAL CAMERA OR SCANNER, MUST BE USED TO CREATE A DIGITAL PICTURE. THE PREVIOUS CHAPTER, "TAKING PICTURES," BRIEFLY EXPLAINED HOW TO CAPTURE A PICTURE WITH A DIGITAL CAMERA. THIS CHAPTER EXPLAINS HOW TO GET THAT PICTURE INTO A COMPUTER. IF YOU HAVE SLIDES, 35MM NEGATIVES, OR PRINTS, SEE THE SECTION ON HOW TO USE A SCANNER OR A WEB-BASED PHOTO SERVICE TO CONVERT TRADITIONAL PHOTOS INTO DIGITAL PICTURES.

MANY DIGITAL CAMERA AND SCANNER MANUFACTURERS INCLUDE OR INSTALL PHOTOSHOP PLUG-INS SO THAT YOU CAN DOWNLOAD OR SCAN IMAGES USING PHOTOSHOP. CHECK THE MANUAL OR MANUFACTURER'S WEB SITE TO FIND OUT IF A PHOTOSHOP PLUG-IN IS AVAILABLE FOR YOUR CAMERA OR SCANNER. WITH THIS IN MIND, THIS CHAPTER BEGINS BY SHOWING YOU HOW TO INSTALL PHOTOSHOP ONTO A WINDOWS PC OR MACINTOSH COMPUTER. BECAUSE YOU'RE WORKING WITH DIGITAL IMAGES, WORKING WITH A FASTER COMPUTER WITH ABOUT A GIGABYTE OF FREE HARD DISK SPACE BRINGS FASTER RESULTS USING PHOTOSHOP. THE REST OF THIS CHAPTER SHOWS YOU HOW TO TRANSFER DIGITAL PICTURES TO YOUR COMPUTER.

INSTALLING PHOTOSHOP 6

As you've probably guessed, you can't get started using Photoshop until the software is installed on your computer. Adobe's installer application for Photoshop 6 is similar to most Macintosh and Windows installer applications; if you already know how to install this type of application, skip ahead to the next section or to the next chapter after you've installed Photoshop onto your computer. ImageReady 3.0, Adobe's Web production application, is also installed with Photoshop 6. If you plan to use both applications at the same time, you probably need to have at least 128MB of available memory after starting up your Mac or PC.

INSTALLING PHOTOSHOP 6 ON A MACINTOSH

Photoshop 6 requires about 64MB of memory and 125MB of available hard disk space. A G3 or G4 processor is recommended, although Photoshop 6 runs on any Power PC Macintosh computer with Mac OS 8.5, 8.6, or 9.0 operating system. The monitor and video hardware configured with your Macintosh computer should be able to display an 800×600 pixel desktop with at least 256 colors (8-bit).

To install Photoshop 6 on a Mac, do the following:

1. Insert the Photoshop 6 CD-ROM in your computer's CD-ROM drive.
2. Double-click on the Photoshop installer application, and click on the Continue button on the splash screen.
3. Review the country in the Select a Country window. Click on the drop-down menu to choose a different country. Then click on Continue.

CUSTOM VERSUS EASY INSTALL

Install specific components of the Photoshop software package with the Custom Install option in the Photoshop installer application. If you're not sure what to install, choose Easy Install.

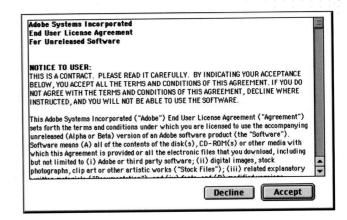

4. Read the license agreement in the Photoshop 6 installer window. Click on Accept if you agree with Adobe's license agreement to continue with the installation. Click on Decline if you disagree with the license agreement.
5. If you have no custom preferences for installing Photoshop 6, simply click on the Install button and skip to step 8.

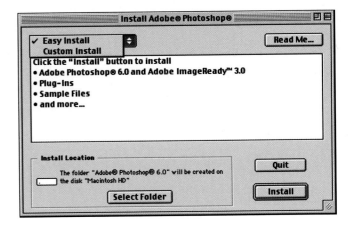

6. If you want to perform a custom install, click on the pop-up menu in the upper-left corner of the screen and choose Custom Install, as shown here.

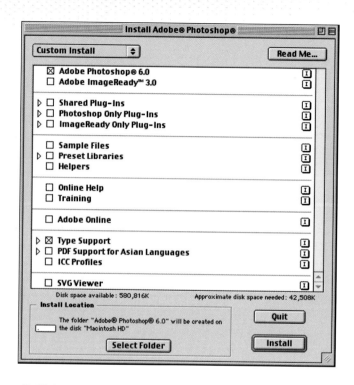

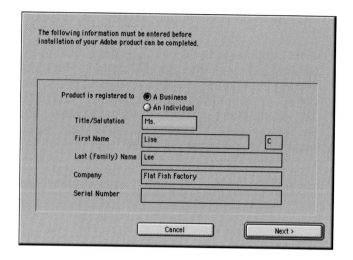

8. Enter the requested information, including whether the product is registered to a business or an individual, your name, your company (if applicable), and the product's serial number. Click on Next.

7. Click on the check box next to each software package you want to install, as shown. After you've selected the software you want, click on the Install button.

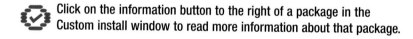 Click on the information button to the right of a package in the Custom install window to read more information about that package.

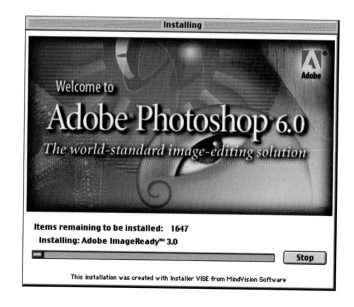

9. The installation begins. As you wait for it to finish, you'll see a progress screen like the one shown here.

10. After the installation process is complete, restart your computer.

Photoshop uses the hard disk to store most of its image-editing information. Although Photoshop will work with Mac OS virtual memory (set the VM to one meg more than the amount of physical memory), you can reduce any potential incompatibilities between Mac OS virtual memory and Photoshop's virtual memory, by going to the Memory control panel and disabling virtual memory prior to starting Photoshop.

INSTALLING PHOTOSHOP 6 ON A WINDOWS PC

Photoshop video, memory, and hard disk space requirements for a Windows PC are similar to a Mac. Photoshop 6 requires a Pentium class processor, Microsoft Windows 98, Windows Millennium, Windows 2000, or Windows NT 4.0 with service pack 4, 5, or 6a. Like the Macintosh computers, you'll need to configure a monitor and video card that supports at least an 800×600 pixel image at 256 or more colors, with at least 64MB of memory installed and at least 125MB of free hard drive space.

To install Photoshop 6 on a Windows PC, do the following:

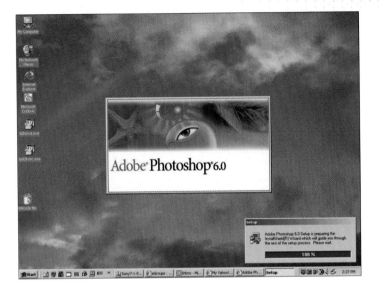

1. Insert the Photoshop 6 CD-ROM in your computer's CD-ROM drive. The Photoshop 6 installer application starts automatically if your PC runs Windows 98 or Windows 2000; you'll see a screen like the one shown here. You can also start the installer by double-clicking on the Setup executable on the CD.

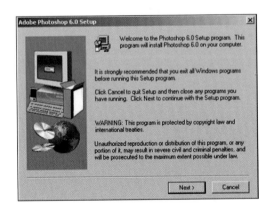

2. Read the welcome information, and then click on the Next button.

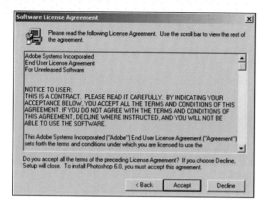

3. Read the software license agreement for Photoshop 6. If you accept the terms of the agreement, click on the Accept button. Otherwise, click on the Decline button to cancel the installation.

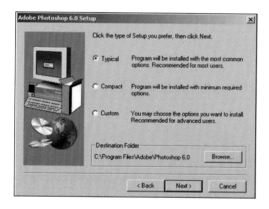

4. Choose the Typical option.

Choose Compact or Custom only if you have a limited amount of disk space.

5. Click on the Browse button to determine where you want to install Photoshop 6 on your hard drive. If you do not select a preference, Photoshop 6 is installed on your C: drive. Click on the Next button to continue with the installation.

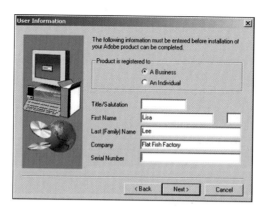

6. Specify whether the product is registered to a business or an individual. Then type your first and last name, your company name (if applicable), and the serial number for Photoshop 6.

7. Click on the Next button.

8. Review the Photoshop 6 components selected for this installation.

9. Click on the Next button.

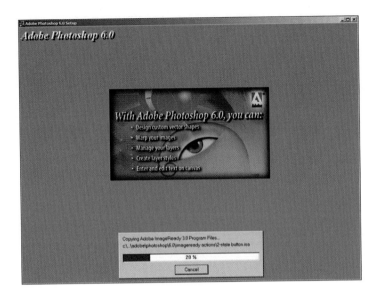

10. Wait for the installer to copy the files to your hard disk; click on the OK button to complete the installation. When the installation is finished, restart your computer.

INSTALLING PHOTOSHOP PLUG-INS

Adobe installs its Photoshop plug-ins to the Plug-Ins folder. The Plug-Ins folder is located in the Photoshop 6 folder on your hard drive. If your digital camera came with its own software CD-ROM, insert it into your computer and install the camera's software. If the camera comes bundled with a Photoshop plug-in, it will be installed with any other software included on the CD. The following steps show you how to configure Photoshop to work with additional plug-in files.

1. Choose Preferences from the Edit menu, and then select Plug-Ins & Scratch Disks.
2. Click on the Additional Plug-Ins Folder check box.

3. Navigate the hard drive and locate the Plug-Ins folder you want to use with Photoshop. If the Plug-Ins folder is on a CD-ROM drive, navigate to the Desktop, and then select the CD-ROM disc from the Browser for Folder window on a PC or the Choose an Additional Plug-Ins Folder window on a Mac. Select the folder containing the plug-in files.

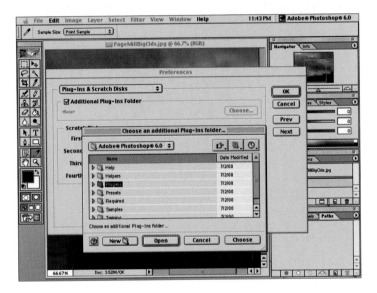

4. Click on OK/Choose to save the folder information to the Preferences window. Click on OK to save your changes and exit the Preferences window.
5. Alternatively, exit Photoshop. Then drag and drop any Photoshop plug-ins into the Plug-Ins folder located in the Adobe Photoshop 6 folder.

USING PLUG-INS

Adobe installs dozens of plug-ins with Photoshop. The previous section showed you how to install more plug-ins. To use a plug-in, first open an image file, and then do the following:

1. Click on the Filter menu to view the categories of plug-ins installed.

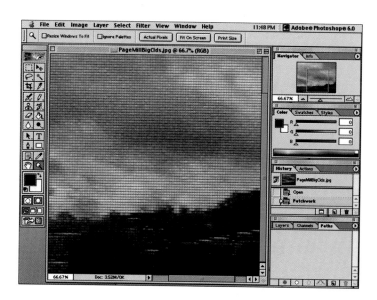

2. Drag the cursor over a category to view a list of filters, also known as *effects*, for that category.

3. Select a filter.

4. Adjust the Filter settings. Click on OK. Filter settings vary from filter to filter. If a filter does not have any custom settings, the effect will be applied to the image window. If this happens, skip this step. This example uses the Patchwork effect, located in the Filter, Texture menu.

5. View the effect of the filter in the document window.

 The most recently used filter appears at the top of the Filter menu. Press Command+F on a Mac or Ctrl+F in Windows to access the most recent filter.

OBTAINING DIGITAL IMAGES

With the right equipment, you can import all kinds of photographs—be it on a traditional film negative, on photographic paper, on a slide, or from a digital camera—to a computer. This section shows you how to download images from a digital camera, and reviews the general process of scanning and converting photos into digital images.

DOWNLOADING IMAGES FROM A DIGITAL CAMERA

Most digital cameras are bundled with several software packages enabling you to download, edit, and organize your photos. Almost all cameras include software that enables you to download files from the camera to your computer. You must install this software in order to be able to download your files. This section covers the basic steps you can follow to connect your camera to a computer and download images. Refer to your camera's manual for details.

Depending on what type of camera you have, you can either download pictures by connecting the camera to your computer via a cable, or by using a storage card adapter. Both are discussed in this section.

CONNECTING WITH CABLES

The first digital cameras supported a serial cable connection to enable cameras to download their files to a computer. The latest 3- and 4-megapixel cameras, however, support the faster USB cable and connector (some cameras also offer serial adapters, as well).

To download images from your camera to a Macintosh using a USB cable, do the following (note that the specific procedure for your camera might differ; consult your manual for details):

PHOTOSHOP PLUG-INS

Many digital cameras install Photoshop 6 plug-ins that enable you to download images directly from the camera into Photoshop 6. Choose Import from Photoshop 6's File menu to access the camera's Photoshop plug-in (this assumes the camera is connected to your computer).

1. Connect the larger end of the USB cable to your computer.
2. Connect the smaller end of the cable to the digital camera.
3. Start the download application on your computer. Choose a menu command in the camera's software application to start downloading the images from the camera to your computer (refer to your camera's manual for details).

 Some cameras allow you to view images only on your computer, and require an additional step to actually copy a file to your hard drive. Be sure to have plenty of batteries on hand if you plan to view lots of pictures.

Connecting a digital camera to a PC is more or less the same as connecting it to a Macintosh computer; USB ports are exactly the same for both computer platforms.

USING STORAGE CARD ADAPTERS

A faster way of getting those pictures off the storage card in your camera is to purchase a media card reader peripheral for a desktop computer. There are several USB storage card readers for both Compact Flash and Smart Media storage cards. Most readers work with either a Macintosh or PC computer.

	100NIKON		
22 items, 34.3 MB available			
Name		Size	Date Modified
DSCN0001.JPG		716 K	Today, 7:53 PM
DSCN0002.JPG		682 K	Today, 7:54 PM
DSCN0003.JPG		680 K	Today, 7:56 PM
DSCN0004.JPG		676 K	Today, 7:57 PM
DSCN0005.JPG		372 K	Today, 7:58 PM
DSCN0006.JPG		530 K	Today, 8:00 PM
DSCN0007.JPG		312 K	Today, 8:00 PM
DSCN0008.JPG		508 K	Today, 8:00 PM
DSCN0009.JPG		282 K	Today, 8:00 PM
DSCN0010.JPG		532 K	Today, 8:01 PM
DSCN0011.JPG		278 K	Today, 8:01 PM
DSCN0012.JPG		656 K	Today, 8:02 PM
DSCN0013.JPG		618 K	Today, 8:02 PM
DSCN0014.JPG		504 K	Today, 8:03 PM
DSCN0015.JPG		570 K	Today, 8:03 PM
DSCN0016.JPG		650 K	Today, 8:04 PM
DSCN0017.JPG		670 K	Today, 8:05 PM
DSCN0018.JPG		552 K	Today, 8:07 PM
DSCN0019.JPG		574 K	Today, 8:07 PM
DSCN0020.JPG		332 K	Today, 8:08 PM
DSCN0021.JPG		396 K	Today, 8:08 PM
DSCN0022.JPG		386 K	Today, 8:08 PM

When you insert a storage card into a reader (or insert a PC card adapter into a laptop), the pictures from your camera mount on the desktop, as shown next. You can copy them to your hard drive, empty the storage card, and then eject the storage card by dragging its icon to the Trash Can or Recycle Bin icon.

If you have a laptop computer, you can purchase a PC card adapter for the storage card, and access your pictures directly from the card. Simply insert the card into the PC adapter, insert the PC card into a laptop, and copy the pictures to your hard drive. When the image files are on your computer, you can remove the pictures from the storage card, eject the card from the laptop, re-insert the storage card into your camera, and you're ready to take more pictures.

Sony's latest digital cameras store pictures on a Memory Stick. Some of Sony's laptop computers have a Memory Stick port built into them, enabling you to simply insert the Memory Stick and access your pictures. If your laptop lacks this port, you can purchase a floppy disk or PC-card adapter for the Memory Stick.

CONVERTING 35MM SLIDES AND NEGATIVES TO DIGITAL IMAGES

If you have 35mm slides or negatives, you can pay your local photo shop to scan them onto a CD-ROM disc using a film scanner, or create a Photo CD. If you use this type of service, work with the highest resolution image available on the CD-ROM or Photo CD.

There are also several Web site services such as **www.kodak.com** and **www.shutterfly.com** that will also transfer slides, negatives, and prints for a fee. After your photos are on CD, you can load them onto your computer

and edit them using Photoshop. Other services will convert images and post the digital ones on their Web site where you can download them directly to your computer over the Internet.

If you're interested in buying a film scanner, the prices will likely change your mind; they can range in price from several hundred to several thousand dollars. Unless you have a large number of pictures, it's probably more economical to send those 35mm slides or negatives to the shop.

 If you have a 35mm camera, you can send your rolls of 35mm film to a Web business to have the pictures developed and printed, and also scanned and posted to Web pages. Some Web sites offer to develop and print a certain number of pictures for free. Visit **www.snapfish.com**, **www.ofoto.com**, **www.myfamily.com**, **www.shutterfly.com**, or **www.kodak.com** to find out more about each site's special offers and Web photo services.

CONVERTING PRINT IMAGES TO DIGITAL IMAGES

Chances are, you have several photo albums of pictures taken with everything from instamatic throw-away cameras to high-end cameras wielded by professionals. Fortunately, these pictures are not lost to you now that you've entered the digital world; you can use a scanner to convert these pictures to digital images and place them on your computer.

These days, you can buy several types of flat-bed and sheet-feed scanners and pay reasonable prices ($100 to $300). Film and photo scanners cost a little more (closer to the $500 price range). Although the traditional flatbed scanner offers the most consistent conversion of color and image into a digital format, you can purchase more inexpensive scanners, such as hand and paper-fed scanners.

Before scanning an image, consider using a scanner that can capture the highest resolution image. For example, choose a 36-bit scanner over a 24-bit scanner. A 24-bit scanner can capture up to 16.7 million colors for any given pixel, which is the same resolution of a Photoshop RGB image file. If a scanner captures an image at 36 bits, each pixel contains a wider range of color information. A larger, more detailed, image will be captured by a 36-bit scanner, even though your monitor won't be able to display more than 24 bits of color information.

There really isn't a way to compare a 3- or 4-megapixel camera's image file resolution (approximately 2,048×1,536 to 2,400×1,800 pixels) to a scanner's 24- or 36-bit capture resolution. One of the dynamic elements of a scanner (not found on a digital camera) is that you can configure how many dots per inch (dpi) are captured during the scanning process. A good general rule to use when taking a picture or scanning an image is to capture the image at the highest possible resolution.

A scanner performs two tasks, similar to what a digital camera does. First, the scanner captures the image placed on the scanner bed. Then it converts the image into a digital file that you can view or save to your hard drive. Low-cost scanners are similar to a copy machine, using one pass of a light source to capture and convert the photo image into a file. Higher-end scanners will have higher-quality CCDs and can support up to three passes of the light source to capture red, green, and blue channel information to produce a higher-quality image.

In order for a scanner to work, you must first install its driver software so the computer can control the scanner hardware. Most scanners are bundled with an application, such as a light version of Photoshop, that enables you to control the scanner, as well as view, edit, and save the scanned image. After the software is installed, you might need to calibrate the scanner to make sure the light source is properly oriented, and then configure the color management software to work with the scanner settings.

When you scan an image into your computer, try to set the resolution (dots per inch, or dpi) to at least 600 dpi. The dots per inch setting determines how many of the pixels in the scanner software will use to create the resulting image. Higher dpi settings tend to capture more image information. Lower dpi settings capture less information.

The scanner software might save the scanned image in a file format other than JPEG, GIF, or TIFF. If Photoshop 6 cannot open the file, try opening it with Adobe ImageReady, and then converting it to a Photoshop–compatible file format.

Don't want to fork out the dough for a scanner? You can always use your digital camera to take a picture of your photo print. Using your computer's RCA inputs, you can even bypass the usual rigmarole of downloading. Simply connect one end of the RCA cable to your camera and the other end to a computer's video input ports, and snap away.

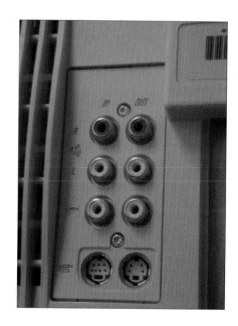

CHAPTER 3

VIEWING PICTURE INFORMATION AND SETTING PREFERENCES

WHEN YOU TAKE A ZILLION PICTURES WITH A DIGITAL CAMERA, IT
MIGHT BECOME DIFFICULT TO REMEMBER WHICH SETTINGS YOU CHOSE
FOR A PARTICULAR PICTURE, OR EVEN THE GENERAL PHYSICAL
CHARACTERISTICS OF A PICTURE, SUCH AS HOW BIG IT IS, OR WHY
AND WHEN IT WAS TAKEN. SOME 3- AND 4-MEGAPIXEL CAMERAS CREATE
A FILE ON THE STORAGE CARD CONTAINING THE APERTURE, SHUTTER
SPEED, EXPOSURE, FILE FORMAT AND OTHER INFORMATION FOR EACH
PICTURE TAKEN. USING PHOTOSHOP, YOU CAN ADD YOUR OWN CUSTOM
INFORMATION TO AN IMAGE FILE, AND ALSO FIND OUT OTHER INFORMATION
ABOUT A PICTURE ONCE YOU'VE OPENED IT. CLICK ON THE FILE MENU AND
CHOOSE OPEN, AND THEN DOUBLE-CLICK ON AN IMAGE FILE TO OPEN IT.

VIEWING AND CHANGING A FILE'S SIZE

If you plan to post your pictures to a Web site or print them, you'll probably need to know the dimensions of the original file. In either case, you'll probably be resizing a picture so that it can load quickly to a Web browser or a printer. When you open a file in Photoshop, you might only see a reduced or partial image in the workspace. Choose Navigator from the Window menu to figure out how much of the image is visible in the workspace.

To find out your image's dimensions in pixels, first open that image in Photoshop; then do the following:

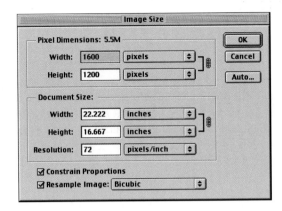

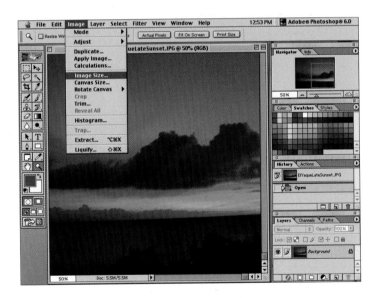

1. Choose Image Size from the Image menu.

2. View the Width and Height of the entire image in the Image Size window. The width and height data can be represented in pixels, or as a percentage of the original size of the image.

3. Type a different value into either the Pixel Dimensions Width or Height text fields if you want to change the size of the image in the image window. If the Constrain Proportions check box is selected, Photoshop automatically determines the secondary dimension of the entire image.

4. Click on the Resample Image pop-up menu to choose a resampling or interpolation method for the image. When this option is selected, Photoshop uses an algorithm to determine which pixels to remove or add to an image to resize the image to the selected dimensions. Click OK to save any changes you've made, or click Cancel to ignore any changes made to the Image Size window.

 Take the highest quality image possible with your digital camera. Whether you plan to create a thumbnail or the full 2,048×1,536-pixel image, it's always best to start with as much picture information as you can. After all, you can always take pixels away from a picture, but adding pixels to a low-resolution image is almost impossible.

Choose Document Sizes from the drop-down menu in the lower left corner of the image window. The actual and current uncompressed image sizes appear at the bottom-left corner of the document window. Even though a JPEG file occupies 1MB of hard disk space, the same file can grow up to 12MB when open in Photoshop. Photoshop stores this image data in its scratch disk space. See the section at the end of this chapter called "Configuring Plug-Ins and Scratch Disk Preferences" to find out how to select up to four scratch disks.

 View the dimensions of the image window by Ctrl/Command+clicking just left of the scroll area on the bottom of the document window. Title Width, Title Height, Image Width, and Image Height data will appear in a pop-up menu.

VIEWING A FILE'S TYPE

Most digital cameras create JPEG images as the default image file format. However, other file formats, such as TIFF, are also possible. No matter what format you use, however, Photoshop converts the image data and displays it in RGB (red, green, and blue) mode when you open an image file. Although the image data is represented in reds, greens, and blues, the original file remains unchanged on your hard drive. To determine the file's format, do the following:

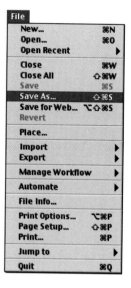

1. With the file whose type you want to determine open in the Photoshop workspace, choose File, Save As.

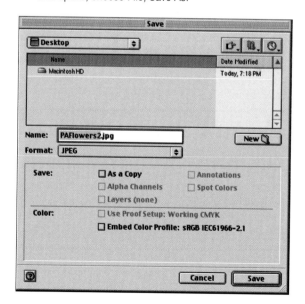

2. The file's current format is selected in the Format pop-up menu in the Save As window.

3. Click on Cancel to exit the Save As window without saving any changes.
4. To view the color mode of the image window, choose Mode from the Image menu. A check mark appears beside the selected mode.

> **(!)** Most digital cameras append three letters to the end of an image file to indicate the type of file it is. For example, if a file name ends in JPG, it's probably a JPEG image file.

> **(!)** Photoshop uses a color mode to determine the color model for how an image is displayed and printed. Most of the examples in this book use RGB (red, green, blue) mode. Some use grayscale mode. Color modes determine the number of colors that can be displayed in an image, and also affect the number of channels and the file size of an image.

VIEWING COLOR SETTINGS FOR A FILE

Most of the color-management controls in Photoshop are located in the Color Settings dialog box. Photoshop comes with seven preconfigured color settings. Each setting consists of a group of predefined color configurations designed to produce consistent color for publishing to the Web and other forms of publishing such as prepress output. You can choose a predefined setting or create your own custom combinations of settings. However, you must choose your color-management settings before opening or creating a file.

The Color Settings window consists of two main sections: workspaces and color-management policies. A workspace represents the default color profile for a newly created document, using the related color model. If Apple RGB is selected as the current RGB workspace, each new RGB

document created will use colors as defined by the Apple RGB gamut. The default color workspace setting for RGB files is RGB IEC61966-2.1. If you plan to share image files across computer platforms, use this color setting.

A color-management policy is a predefined color-management configuration that can be set in the Color Settings window. A warning will appear to let you override a default policy behavior on a case-by-case basis if you choose to use this feature for RGB, CMYK, or grayscale color management.

To view Photoshop's color settings, do the following:

1. Open the Edit menu and choose Color Settings.

Color Settings

Settings: [Web Graphics Defaults   ▢▢]

Working Spaces

RGB: [sRGB IEC61966-2.1   ▢▢]

CMYK: [U.S. Web Coated (SWOP)   ▢▢]

Gray: [Gray Gamma 2.2   ▢▢]

Spot: [Dot Gain 20%   ▢▢]

Color Management Policies

RGB: [Off   ▢▢]

CMYK: [Off   ▢▢]

Gray: [Off   ▢▢]

Profile Mismatches: ☑ Ask When Opening   ☐ Ask When Pasting

Missing Profiles: ☐ Ask When Opening

Description

Web Graphics Defaults: Preparation of content for the worldwide web (WWW).

[OK]
[Cancel]
[Load...]
[Save...]
☑ Preview
☐ Advanced

2. Click on the Settings pop-up menu to view the preconfigured settings installed with Photoshop.
3. Review the settings chosen for Working Spaces and Color Management Policies.
4. Click on any pop-up menu to view additional options for each setting.

 Press Ctrl/Command+Shift+K to open the Color Settings window.

SETTING YOUR PREFERENCES

Many of Photoshop's default settings, such as where the floating windows are located in the workspace when you start the application, and how files are named when being saved, can be changed in the Preferences window. On a Windows PC, preferences are stored in the Registry. On a Mac, they are stored in an Adobe Photoshop 6 Settings folder in the Preferences folder of the System folder. Preference settings are saved only when you exit or quit the application.

CHOOSING GENERAL PREFERENCES

Photoshop's General Preferences screen enables you to configure those features that affect any image window. For example, if you resize an image, the image sample pop-up menu contains a default value. You can change the default value for sampling or interpolating an image—as well as many other default settings—in the General Preferences screen.

The following is a brief summary of the General Preferences settings for Photoshop:

✳ Color Picker—Enables you to choose the kind of color picker window that appears whenever you want to select a foreground or background color for a drawing tool, stroke, fill layer, or gradient.

✳ Interpolation—Determines which algorithm Photoshop uses to resize an image. The algorithm resamples the pixels in an image to determine how to restructure the resulting larger or smaller image. Bicubic interpolation, which is the default setting, provides the best quality image.

✳ Redo Key and History States—Control how many times you can undo any number of previously executed commands or tasks in the image window.

✳ Export Clipboard—If you select an image in the window and choose the Copy command from the Edit menu, the image in the Clipboard is available to any other applications from the Paste command. This feature prevents the image in the Clipboard from being deleted when you switch to another application.

✳ Short PANTONE Names—Abbreviates the way PANTONE color names are stored. To use this feature with other applications, such as Quark, PageMaker, or Illustrator, these applications must be configured to recognize the naming conventions of the Photoshop files.

✳ Show Tools Tips—If you let your cursor hover over a tool in the toolbox, this feature enables Photoshop to display a small window containing the name of that tool, and the letter you can use as its shortcut.

✳ Keyboard Zoom Resizes Windows—If you use the Ctrl/Command+Plus or Ctrl/Command+Minus keys to zoom into or out of a picture, checking this check box will automatically resize the window to match the changing image size.

✳ Auto-update open documents—If you have the same image document (such as a Photoshop document) open in ImageReady and Photoshop, selecting this check box will update the image in Photoshop each time a change is made in the non-Photoshop application. Depending on the size of the image you are working on, this auto-updating feature can slow down Photoshop, as well as your computer system.

✳ Show Asian Text Options—If you have Japanese, Chinese, Korean, or other Asian-language fonts, check this feature to view additional text-related settings.

✳ Beep When Done—If checked, the computer's alert sound is played whenever a progress bar indicator-related task is completed.

✳ Dynamic Color Sliders—Enables you to dynamically change the foreground or background colors from the Color palette window. Click and drag each color slider to define the color you want to use with a drawing tool, stroke, or fill layer.

✳ Save Palette Locations—Preserves the last locations of the palette windows when you exit or quit Photoshop.

✳ Show Font Names in English—Displays non-English font names, such as some Asian fonts, in English.

✳ Use Shift Key for Tool Switch—Enables you to press the Shift key, combined with a letter key on the keyboard, to cycle through a tool in the toolbox.

✳ Reset All Warning Dialogs—Reverts dialog warnings to their default configuration. Some warning dialogs can be configured to never appear if a check box is selected the first time you see it. Pressing this button allows all those warning dialogs to appear.

✳ Reset All Tools—Reverts the tool options (which I call the options toolbar, located just below the menu bar) to Photoshop's default configuration.

To access these preferences, do the following:

1. Open the Edit menu, choose Preferences, and select General.

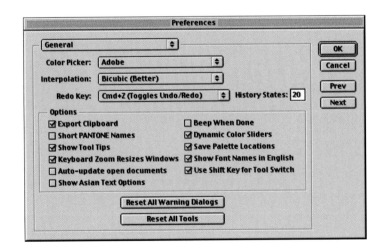

2. Examine the default settings, changing any you desire by selecting them from the pop-up windows or checking the check boxes. (I usually do not change any of the default settings.) Most of the general preferences affect the user interface, such as whether ToolTips appear in the toolbox and where or how windows appear in the workspace.

Bicubic interpolation provides the best image quality if an image is resized. This is probably one setting you won't want to change.

 If you've changed the location or ordering of any of the floating windows (also called floating palettes), select Reset Palette Locations from the Window menu to restore the floating windows to their default locations on the right side of the workspace.

3. To change the number of times you can undo tasks, type a lower or higher number into the History States text box.

4. Click on OK to accept your changes and close the General Preferences screen.

CHANGING PREFERENCES FOR SAVING FILES

Many of the things that Photoshop does when you start the application, open an image, or save a file can be adjusted by accessing Photoshop's Saving Files Preferences settings. Most of the default settings should work great for most people, but if changing a little feature here or there can make you more productive, keep reading.

Photoshop is initially set up to automatically save a preview image of a file when you choose the Save command. It also automatically changes the file name extension of any file you save. You can adjust these settings in the Saving Files Preferences window. Here's how:

1. Choose Preferences from the Edit menu, and then select Saving Files. Alternatively, you can press Ctrl/Command + K to open the Preferences window. Then press Ctrl/Command + 2 to view the Saving Files Preferences information.

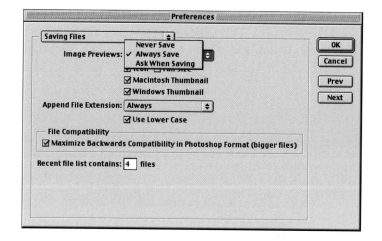

2. Click on the Image Previews pop-up menu to choose whether you want to save a thumbnail image of the picture whenever you execute the Save command.

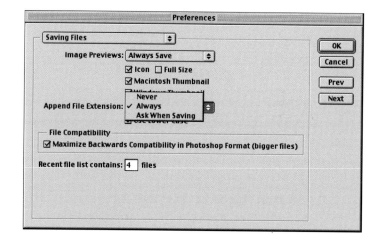

3. Click on the Append File Extension pop-up menu to view the options for this preference.

4. To activate any of the various features in the box, check their corresponding check box.

5. Type a number in the Recent File List Contains text box to set the number of previously opened files that appear when you choose the Open Recent menu command from the File menu.

SELECTING DISPLAY AND CURSOR PREFERENCES

Photoshop stores an image's color information in 8-bit grayscale channels if an image is set to RGB, CMYK, Lab, or multi-channel color modes. Alpha channels are used for creating and storing masks. Each alpha channel is an 8-bit grayscale image. Choose the Display and Cursor preferences command to adjust how alpha channels are displayed in the Channels window. You can also change the cursors for the toolbox tools in the Display & Cursors Preferences window.

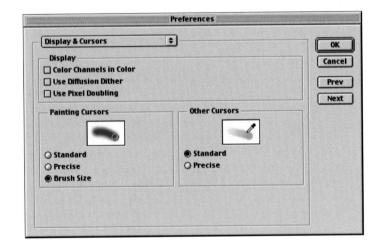

1. Open the Edit menu, choose Preferences, and select Display & Cursors.
2. You have a few display settings available to you:
   ❋ **Color Channels in Color.** Each color channel in the Channels palette appears in red, green, or blue (if an image is in RGB mode) instead of as a grayscale image if this option is enabled.
   ❋ **Use Diffusion Dither.** Enable this option to soften hard edges of color in the image window.
   ❋ **Use Pixel Doubling.** If this check box is checked, provides faster previews with the Move tool. Pixels in the image are temporarily doubled, halving the resolution of the image.

 For more information about channels, see Chapter 9, "Customizing Images with Masks," or Chapter 10, "Making Images Stand Out with Channels."

 Don't confuse display preferences with color-management features. Display preferences only change the way the image appears in the document or palette windows. These options have no effect on the pixels in the image file. Choose Color Settings from the Edit menu to view the color-management settings for Photoshop.

3. Click on the Standard, Precise, or Brush Size radio buttons in the Painting Cursors area. The cursor you select appears in the Painting Cursors preview box.
4. Select on either the Standard or Precise radio button in the Other Cursors area. The cursor you select appears in the Other Cursors preview box.
5. Click on OK to accept your changes and close the General Preferences screen.

ADJUSTING TRANSPARENCY AND GAMUT PREFERENCES

In the Transparency & Gamut Preferences screen, you can adjust Photoshop's transparency grid. The transparency grid represents the transparent areas of a layer in the image. Wherever you see the transparency grid in an image, Photoshop is telling you there's no image data in that part of the image. See Chapter 11, "Experimenting with Layers," to find out more about layers and transparency.

Additionally, in the Gamut Warning area, you can specify what color appears when an image contains a color that is not printable. A *gamut*, or color space, defines the range of printable colors for any particular image. The range of colors you can see is much larger than the RGB gamut, or any other color model. To avoid creating images that are not printable, configure Photoshop to display a gamut warning to help you identify the colors that are not defined by the gamut.

The transparency grid appears in the document window if all or part of an image is defined to be transparent. The default grid consists of white and gray squares. To configure these settings, do the following:

1. Open the Edit menu, choose Preferences, and select Transparency & Gamut.

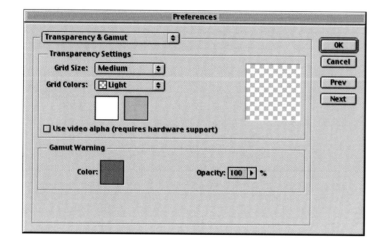

2. View the Grid Size options for the transparency grid in the pop-up menu. Medium is the default setting; choose Large or Small to increase or decrease the size of the squares in the grid. Preview the grid in the thumbnail located to the right of the pop-up menu. Choose None to make transparent areas appear white in the document window.

3. Click on the Grid Colors pop-up menu to choose a different combination of grid colors for the transparency grid. Alternatively, click on either one of the color picker squares to select the color of your choice from the color picker window. Click on OK to save the newly select color.

4. Click on the color square in the Gamut Warning area to pick a gamut warning color. A Color Picker window appears. Click on a color to select it. Click on OK to save the color change. The gamut warning color will replace any out-of-gamut colors when the image is previewed. Check the Color Settings window to make sure the color-management settings match the gamut warning settings.

5. Type a number into the Opacity text field. A lower value reveals more of the underlying image below the gamut warning color.

6. Click on OK to save your changes and exit the screen.

 Press Ctrl/Command+K to open the Preferences window. Press Ctrl/Command + numbers one through eight to access each of the Preferences panels.

SETTING UNITS AND RULERS PREFERENCES

The Units & Rulers Preferences screen enables you to specify default ruler settings. Rulers appear in every document window; you use them to align the artwork you create or edit in Photoshop. Additionally, this window enables you to set preferences for column size and point/pica size. These settings affect the way Photoshop works with actions so that it relies more on proportional size and location information than on specific pixels or other measurement information. See the section on the Actions palette in Chapter 4, "Using Photoshop 6 Tools."

1. Open the Edit menu, choose Preferences, and select Units & Rulers.

2. Click on the Rulers pop-up menu to view a list of available units for the window ruler. Select the one you want to use. To view your ruler changes, open an image document, and then choose Show Rulers from the View menu.

3. Click on the Width or Gutter pop-up menus to set the column size to inches, points, picas, or centimeters. Type a number in the Width or Gutter text edit boxes to change these settings. To create a document containing columns, choose New from the File menu. Then click on the Width pop-up menu and choose Columns.

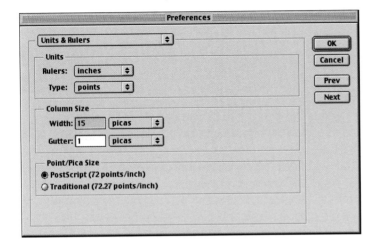

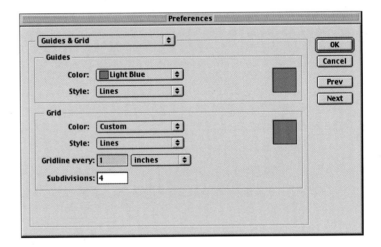

1. Open the Edit menu, choose Preferences, and select Guides & Grid.
2. Click on the Color pop-up menu in either the Guides or Grid area to view your color options; select a color to change it. Choose Custom to pick any color you like from the Color Picker window. Click on OK to save the newly selected color and return to the Preferences window.

4. Choose PostScript to set the Point/Pica size for the document to 72 points per inch if you are printing to a PostScript device. You probably don't need to select this option, but if you do choose Traditional, the Point/Pica Size is set to 72.27 points per inch.
5. Click on OK to save your changes and exit the screen.

CUSTOMIZING GUIDES AND GRID PREFERENCES

Guides and grids are visual tools that can be applied to the image window. You can move, remove, or lock a guide or grid to help design your image document. Guides and grids cannot be printed. Use the Guides & Grids Preferences settings to add or change the color of guide or grid lines. For example, you might want to create a guide with different colors than the image you are creating or editing.

To view the grid, choose Show Grid from the View menu. The grid lines are drawn over the image window. Choose New Guide from the View menu. Click on the View menu and choose Show Guide to view the guide in the window. The Guide line, which extends from the top of the image window to the bottom, appears on the left edge of the image. You might need to enlarge the image window to see it.

3. Change the style of guides or grids from the corresponding pop-up menu. Guides can appear as lines or dashed lines. Grids can be displayed as lines, dashed lines, or dots.
4. Set the distance between gridlines by typing a number in the Gridline Every box. Specify the unit of measurement in the accompanying pop-up menu.
5. Adjust the number of subdivisions for the grid by typing a larger or smaller number in the Subdivisions text box.
6. Click on OK to save your changes and exit the screen.

CONFIGURING PLUG-INS AND SCRATCH DISK PREFERENCES

It might be hard to believe that with 45MB of memory allocated to Photoshop, it also needs hard disk space to run its special brand of virtual memory so that you can open, edit, and save an image document. Most image data from any open image file is stored on the hard disk in Photoshop's scratch disk. As you open, edit, save, and close image files in Photoshop, the scratch disk loads, moves, and deletes data from one to four scratch disks. You can also configure Photoshop to recognize plug-in files that are not located in Photoshop's Plug-ins folder.

Photoshop's scratch disk settings work with Windows or Mac OS virtual memory settings. Adobe recommends setting the Mac OS virtual memory setting to 1MB more than the amount of physical memory installed in your computer. I turn virtual memory off on my Mac, but leave it on with my Windows PC when I use Photoshop.

To alter the scratch-disk settings, as well as enable additional plug-ins for your system, use the Plug-Ins & Scratch Disks Preferences window and review the following list of items:

1. Open the Edit menu, choose Preferences, and select Plug-Ins & Scratch Disks.

2. Click on a pop-up menu to assign a hard disk as a scratch disk. Assign the hard disk with the most free space available as the first scratch disk. The amount of scratch disk space affects the number and size of files you can work on in Photoshop.

3. Check the Additional Plug-ins Folder check box to enable additional plug-ins folders. These plug-ins appear in the Filter menu. There are many software publishers of Photoshop plug-in packages. Some of these publishers include Alien Skin, Altamira Group, Andromeda Software, Auto F/X, Chromagraphics, Xaos Tools, MagicMask, Scantastic, and 3D Dizzy. Some of the more popular plug-in packages are Total Xaos, Eye Candy, and Xenofex. To find out more about Photoshop plug-ins, visit **http://www.adobe.com/store/plugins/photoshop/main.html**.

4. Click on OK to save your changes and exit the screen.

 On a Windows PC, Photoshop uses a hard disk volume as its primary paging disk, in addition to a primary scratch disk. However, the paging disk is usually the startup disk. Choose a volume that is not the startup disk as the primary scratch disk in the Preferences window. If the same volume is used for both features, Photoshop's performance may be noticeably slower.

CHANGING IMAGE CACHE PREFERENCES

Image caches are used to speed up your access to all the application code and image data spread across your hard disk and the 45MB of memory allocated to Photoshop. A *cache* is a small amount of disk space set aside to store images that have been previously loaded into memory. Photoshop uses the cache settings to determine how much memory and disk space to allocate when you open a file. The higher the number, the more memory and disk space is set aside for each file. When you reload a cached image, Photoshop uses the image data stored in memory and on your hard drive to make the contents of the window redraw more quickly to your screen. To alter your cache settings, do the following:

1. Open the Edit menu, choose Preferences, and select Image Cache.

2. Type a number into the Cache Levels text box to set the number of cache levels for Photoshop. Enter 4 or 5 if you plan to work with image files that are up to 50MB.

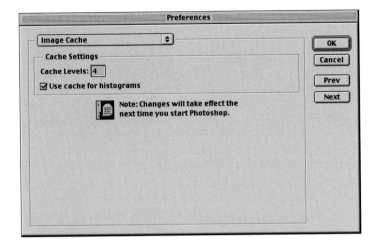

3. By default, the Use Cache for Histograms option is checked. Photoshop uses histograms to provide a snapshot of the tonal range of a picture, and illustrate how pixels are distributed across an image, graphing the number of pixels at each level of color intensity. A higher black bar in a histogram indicates there are more pixels in that particular color intensity level. Open an image and choose Histogram from the Image menu. When the Use Cache for Histograms option is checked, Photoshop displays a histogram based on a representative sampling of pixels in an image, instead of sampling all the pixels in an image.

4. Click on OK to save your changes.

5. If you're using Photoshop on a Windows PC, you can adjust the memory usage setting from the Image Cache Preferences window. Click on the drop-down menu and drag the slider to select the amount of memory you want Photoshop to use the next time you start it up. Click OK in the Preferences window to save your changes.

PART 2

PHOTOSHOP 6 BASICS

THE PHOTOSHOP WORKSPACE CONSISTS OF A MENU BAR, TOOLBOX, FLOATING PALETTE WINDOWS, IMAGE WINDOW, AND THE OPTIONS TOOLBAR. EACH WINDOW IN THE WORKSPACE CAN BE CLOSED OR HIDDEN BY CHOOSING THE CORRESPONDING COMMAND FROM THE WINDOW MENU, OR BY CLICKING THE CLOSE BOX OF A WINDOW. CLICK AND DRAG THE TITLE BAR OF A WINDOW OR TOOLBAR TO MOVE IT TO A NEW LOCATION IN THE WORKSPACE. PRESS THE F KEY TWICE TO HIDE THE DESKTOP AND MENU BAR. CLICK ON THE WINDOW MENU AND CHOOSE RESET PALETTE LOCATIONS TO RETURN THE PALETTES TO THEIR DEFAULT LOCATIONS IN THE WORKSPACE. THE PHOTOSHOP WORKSPACE CAN BE INTIMIDATING. HOWEVER, AS YOU LEARN TO INTERACT WITH THE WORKSPACE AND YOUR IMAGES, YOU'LL EVENTUALLY CUSTOMIZE A MORE EFFICIENT, COMFORTABLE WORKSPACE. THIS PART OF THE BOOK FAMILIARIZES YOU WITH THE PHOTOSHOP WORKSPACE, AND SHOWS YOU HOW TO DO SOME BASIC TASKS, SUCH AS CORRECTING AN IMAGE, APPLYING AN EFFECT, OR CREATING A MASK.

USING PHOTOSHOP 6 TOOLS

THIS CHAPTER GIVES YOU A QUICK TOUR OF THE TOOLS AND WINDOWS IN
PHOTOSHOP 6 THAT YOU WILL MOST LIKELY USE TO OPEN, EDIT, AND
CREATE WEB-READY DIGITAL PICTURES. SEVERAL WINDOWS ARE OPEN WHEN
YOU FIRST START PHOTOSHOP. THE TOOLBOX OPENS ON THE LEFT AND
FOUR FLOATING PALETTE WINDOWS OPEN ON THE RIGHT SIDE OF THE
WORKSPACE. IF YOU CLICK ON A TOOL, EDITABLE OPTIONS FOR THAT TOOL
APPEAR IN THE OPTIONS BAR AT THE TOP OF THE WORKSPACE.

ANATOMY OF THE TOOLBOX

Photoshop 6 is packed with 50 selection and drawing tools—22 of which are visible in the toolbox window. Each tool has a corresponding letter that you can press to switch the active tool in the image window. Although you can use all these tools to work with digital pictures, this book focuses on those you'll use most frequently to create and edit digital pictures with Photoshop 6 and ImageReady. The toolbox resides on the left side of the Photoshop workspace. The top-most toolbar, which Adobe calls the options bar, displays a number of options that change depending on which tools and palettes are selected.

SELECTION TOOLS

You use the selection tools to select a specific area, a range of colors, or an image that has been pasted into a Photoshop window. You'll find 14 selection tools in the toolbox. Seven are visible, and the other seven are hidden (click on a tool with an arrow in the lower-right corner to view hidden tools in the toolbox, as shown in the following figure). On a Windows PC, you need to right-click on these tools to reveal the additional tools.

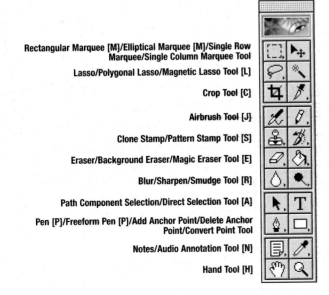

Rectangular Marquee [M]/Elliptical Marquee [M]/Single Row Marquee/Single Column Marquee Tool

Lasso/Polygonal Lasso/Magnetic Lasso Tool [L]

Crop Tool [C]

Airbrush Tool [J]

Clone Stamp/Pattern Stamp Tool [S]

Eraser/Background Eraser/Magic Eraser Tool [E]

Blur/Sharpen/Smudge Tool [R]

Path Component Selection/Direct Selection Tool [A]

Pen [P]/Freeform Pen [P]/Add Anchor Point/Delete Anchor Point/Convert Point Tool

Notes/Audio Annotation Tool [N]

Hand Tool [H]

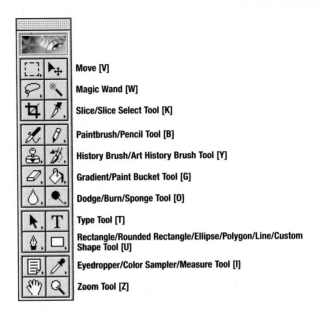

Move [V]

Magic Wand [W]

Slice/Slice Select Tool [K]

Paintbrush/Pencil Tool [B]

History Brush/Art History Brush Tool [Y]

Gradient/Paint Bucket Tool [G]

Dodge/Burn/Sponge Tool [O]

Type Tool [T]

Rectangle/Rounded Rectangle/Ellipse/Polygon/Line/Custom Shape Tool [U]

Eyedropper/Color Sampler/Measure Tool [I]

Zoom Tool [Z]

You'll find the following tools indispensable as you use Photoshop 6:

* **Move tool.** Use this to select and move any object or image in the window.

* **Marquee tools.** Use these to select a rectangular, ellipse, single row, or single column of information in the window.

* **Magic Wand tool.** Enables you to click on a color to select a common range of colors in an image. For example, select a particular shade of blue in a blue sky using the Magic Wand instead of trying to use one of the other selection tools, like the rectangle or lasso.

* **Crop tool.** Trim the edges off a picture with this tool. Alternatively, use the Image Size window to resize the entire image.

* **Slice tools.** Use these tools to cut or break up a large image into multiple, smaller files called *slices*. Slicing an image enables it to load more quickly when viewed by a Web browser.

* **Hand tool.** Move the content in the window with the Hand tool.

* **Magnify tool.** Zoom into or away from the window with the Magnify tool.

Most 1-, 2-, and 3-megapixel cameras create large images. Photoshop automatically opens these files at a smaller scale, such as at 50%, so you can view the entire image without having to scroll around the window.

IMAGE-EDITING TOOLS

Whether you are touching up a photo or creating a photo-realistic image, Photoshop provides a full range of image editing tools for editing both bitmap and vector graphics. Photos are bitmap or pixel-based graphics. Bitmap graphics don't scale well. For example, if you try to resize an 8×10 pixel image to 400×400 pixels, chances are you probably won't recognize the original, small image. Vector graphics on the other hand are calculated using software algorithms, designed to retain image quality as the image grows or shrinks in size. Use the shape tools to create vector graphics, such as buttons and line art to use with your photos and Web pages.

* **Eyedropper tools.** Choose from a Color Sampler, Measure, or the traditional Eyedropper tool to select colors for image editing. Select the Eyedropper tool. Then click on a color in the window. The Eyedropper replaces the foreground color in the color well. Holding down the Option key while selecting a color replaces the background color in the color well.

* **Stamp tools.** Clone part of an image with the Clone Stamp tool, or use the Pattern Stamp tool to add a pattern to an image.

* **Mask tools.** Use a selection tool to select part of an image. Apply the Quick Mask tool to the image. The selected area remains editable, while the unselected area cannot be edited. Mask tools let you customize specific areas of an image without the risk of accidentally changing the rest of the image.

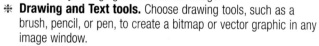
* **Drawing and Text tools.** Choose drawing tools, such as a brush, pencil, or pen, to create a bitmap or vector graphic in any image window.

* **Color Selection tools.** Change or switch the foreground and background colors from the toolbox using these tools.

NAVIGATING THE PALETTE WINDOWS

By default, Photoshop opens four floating palette windows to the right of the document window. Each window can contain one or all possible palettes. Each palette contains unique information about the image in the window. Some palettes enable you to modify the image, too.

Each window can be opened from the Window menu, or closed by clicking on the Close box. Each tab in a palette window can be clicked and dragged and separated from its original window. On the right side of the window, you'll find 12 floating palettes. As shown in the following figure, these palettes include the following:

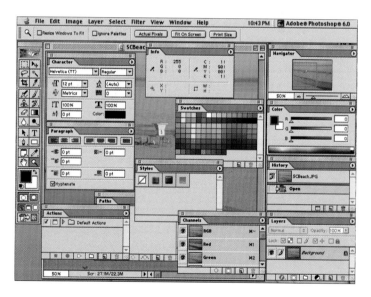

* The Navigator palette enables you to adjust the magnification level or scroll an image instead of manually resizing the image window.
* The Info palette displays the RGB and CMYK color values wherever you place the cursor in the image window. Also shows current x and y coordinates of the cursor.

✳ The Color palette displays the current foreground and background colors. Type in a new value for each color, or click and drag the sliders to change a color. Alternatively, click in the color bar at the bottom of the window to pick a new foreground or background color.

✳ The Swatches palette enables you to choose a new foreground or background color, or save or load a set of colors to the Swatches window.

✳ The Styles palette displays layer styles—predefined or custom groupings of layer effects. Click on a style to apply it to a layer in the image window.

✳ The History palette shows each edited state of the image for the current work session. Click on a state to revert a document to a previous edit. The History palette is cleared when you quit or exit Photoshop.

✳ The Actions palette enables you to record, play, or edit tasks and save or load action files. For example, if you create the action that applies a filter effect to an image, you can apply that action to other images using the Batch command in the File, Automate menu.

✳ The Layers palette shows a list of all layers and layer sets of an image. Layers appear in the order they are organized in the image window. For example, the background layer is always at the bottom of the list. You can create, hide, display, copy, merge, view, and delete layers from this palette.

✳ The Channels palette displays a list of color channels for each layer of an image. Create, hide, display, copy, and delete channels, including alpha channels, in this palette.

✳ The Paths palette shows a list of the saved vector graphics in an image. Create or delete a path, or choose selected, fill, stroke paths from this palette.

✳ The Character palette shows the current font, font size, and style if you've typed some text into the image window. Select text in the image window and use the Character palette to edit these font settings. You can adjust kerning, vertical and horizontal scale, baseline shift, and the color of the font here.

✳ The Paragraph palette displays the current alignment, justification, and hyphenation settings for any text selected in the image window. Adjust these settings of the selected text here.

 You can also create double-pane windows by clicking and dragging a palette to the top or bottom edge of another palette. Release the mouse, and watch the palette grow to fit two viewable palettes in the one window.

VIEWING A PICTURE WITH THE NAVIGATOR PALETTE

You can find out exactly what part of the window you're eyeballing by using the Navigator palette. A colored rectangle highlights the palette viewed area, and the scale of the image appears in the lower-left corner of the palette. You can pan and zoom the image by clicking and dragging the triangle-shaped slider control located at the bottom of the palette window. The following figure shows changes in the Navigator palette and image window after using the slider control to zoom into an image.

 Change the color of the rectangle by choosing Palette Options from the pop-up menu in the Navigator palette. This menu is selected by clicking the small triangle in the upper-right corner of the Navigator panel.

VIEWING COLOR SETTINGS WITH THE INFO PALETTE

If you need to know the exact combination of colors in your image, or if you're simply curious about color values, they're easy to find in the Info palette. Place the cursor anywhere in the image and the Info palette will show a breakdown of the current color information. Color values and cursor coordinates are updated instantly.

1. Open an image.
2. Move the cursor over a colored area in the image.
3. Red, green, and blue values are shown on the left side of the Info palette as you move the cursor around in the image window. Cyan (C), magenta (M), yellow (Y), and black (K) values appear on the right.

4. The x and y coordinates of the cursor appear in the lower-left corner of the Info palette.

 An exclamation point will appear beside a color value that is out-of-gamut, or beyond the scope of the pre-defined colors for a document's color space.

HANDLING COLOR WITH THE COLOR, SWATCHES, AND STYLES PALETTE

You can use the Color palette to select the foreground and background color. To choose a new color, click on one you like in the color ramp located at the bottom of the palette. Click and drag the slider control to view the tonal range of the selected color. Add or experiment with colors using the Swatches palette, which enables you to save or load swatches from other image-editing sessions.

The Styles palette enables you to save, edit, and load layer styles. Each style is a set of one or more layer effects that can be applied to any layer in a Photoshop or ImageReady document. For more information about layer effects, see "Adding Effects to a Layer" in Chapter 11, "Experimenting with Layers."

 When editing pictures, you'll probably rely more on the colors used within a particular document instead of creating new colors from the Color palette.

The easiest way to switch to a color in an image is to use the Eyedropper tool to click on the color you want to use, as described next:

1. Open an image file. Click on the Eyedropper tool in the toolbox.

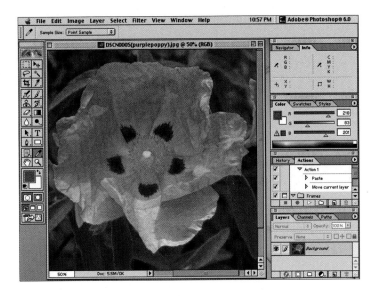

2. Click on a color in the Color palette.

3. Select the Paint Bucket tool from the toolbox.

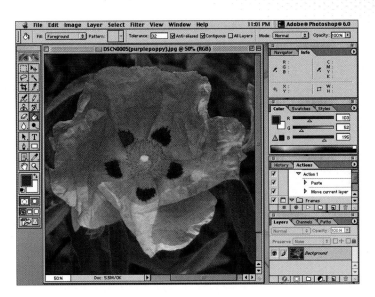

4. Click on the area in the window where you want to apply the color with the Paint Bucket tool. The new color replaces the range of colors where you clicked. In this example, I've used a selection tool to select one of the red circles in the flower, turning it blue using the Paint Bucket tool.

EDITING TEXT WITH THE CHARACTER PALETTE

You can add a date and timestamp, or add a narrative to digital pictures using the Text tool in the toolbox. Text is added directly to the image as a separate layer. You can also view text settings and modify text with the Character palette. As long as text remains in its original layer, you can edit it. If you choose Flatten Image from the Image menu, or merge the text layer with other layers, you will no longer be able to modify that text. To add text, do the following:

1. Open an image into the Photoshop workspace.
2. Click on the Text tool in the toolbox. Place the cursor where you want the text to appear in the image.
3. Type some text into the image.
4. Click on the Layers palette. The text appears as a separate layer there.
5. Ctrl/Command+click the text layer to select the text in the window.

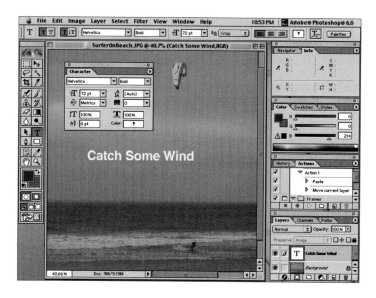

6. Select Show Character from the Window menu. Choose different settings in the Character palette to change the font, font size, and other text characteristics.

Fonts that appear in Adobe Photoshop are installed with your operating system. To access additional fonts in Photoshop, you must install additional fonts.

ORGANIZING TEXT WITH THE PARAGRAPH PALETTE

Using the Paragraph palette, you can change text alignment—options are left-alignment, center-alignment, and right-alignment. You can also enable hyphenation, and set additional format options such as indenting the first line, indenting the left or right margins, or adding a space before or after a paragraph. This palette doesn't appear among the ones on the right-hand side of the page; you'll learn how to access it next. To organize your text, do the following:

1. Using the image you edited in the previous example, click the layer containing the text you want to alter.

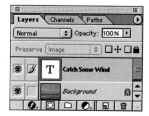

2. Click on the Type tool, and the click and drag to select the text in the image window.
3. Click on the Window menu and select Show Paragraph.

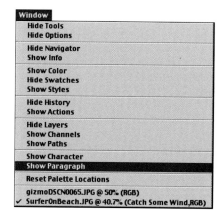

4. Select left-, center-, or right-alignment for the selected text.

5. Click on the pop-up menu for the Paragraph palette to reset the paragraph to its original setting or customize justification or hyphenation settings for the selected text.

REPLAYING EVENTS WITH THE HISTORY PALETTE

There are so many tools, effects, and filters in Photoshop 6, sometimes the best way to create an image is to experiment. Sometimes, however, experiments go awry. If this happens to you, you can use the History palette in Photoshop 6 to go back to a previous state of the document. To do so, simply click on an item in the History palette's History list to view a previous incarnation of the window.

AUTOMATING TASKS WITH THE ACTIONS PALETTE

You can add Web behaviors, filters, and effects from the Actions palette to automate tasks you do in Photoshop 6. Create your own actions by recording them using the built-in controls in the Actions palette. To use this palette, first open an image, and then do the following:

1. Open the Actions palette (click on the Actions tab).

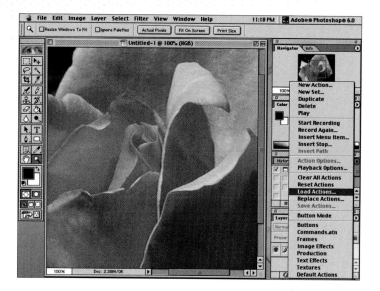

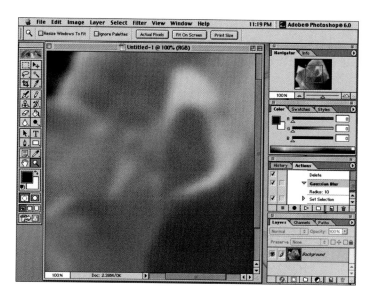

2. Choose Load Actions from the Action palette's pop-up menu. This pop-up menu is activated for each tab by the triangle in the upper-right corner of the panel.
3. Click on the collapsible triangle to the left of a folder or action.
4. View the list of actions in the Actions palette.
5. Choose an action you want to perform on the selected image.

6. Click on the Play button to perform the action selected in the palette. For example, in the figure above, I chose Gaussian Blur from the Actions list, and the effect was applied to the image.

To record an action, do the following:

1. Click on the Record button (the circle icon) at the bottom of the Actions palette.
2. Perform one or more tasks on the window.
3. Click on the Stop button to save the action, which will appear at the bottom of the Actions palette.

ARRANGING IMAGES WITH THE LAYERS PALETTE

When you first open an image in Photoshop, a background layer is created. Photoshop creates a new layer for any images you add. You can also copy any part of the background image into a new layer. Each layer contains its own channel information. For example, if a document is in RGB color mode, each layer can have unique settings for each red, green, or blue channel. Create, delete, edit, and organize layers with the Layers palette. To use this palette, first open an image, and then do the following:

1. Click on the New Layer icon in the Layers palette.
2. A new, empty layer appears in the Layers palette.
3. Select the background layer and drag it over the New layer icon.

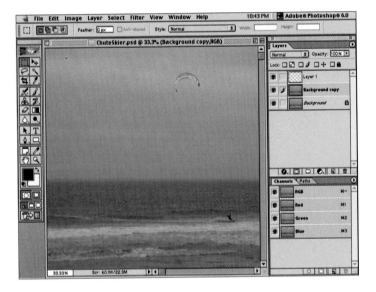

4. A copy of the image from the background layer is created in a new layer.

For more information about working with Layers, see Chapter 8, "Combining Images with Layers."

CREATING MASKS WITH THE CHANNELS PALETTE

Channels display the color information for an image. For example, you'll find red, green, and blue channels in this palette if an image is in RGB mode. Here you can hide, display, or create channels and channel masks for an image. For more information about masks and channels, see Chapters 9, "Customizing Images with Masks," and 11, "Experimenting with Layers."

To use this palette, first open an image, and then do the following:

1. Click on the Channels tab to view the list of channels in the Channels palette.

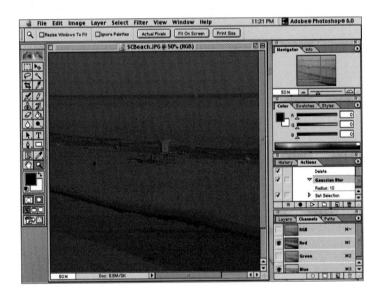

2. De-select the eye icon to turn one or two channels off.
3. Choose a selection tool from the toolbox. Click and drag the tool and select an area of the image in the image window.

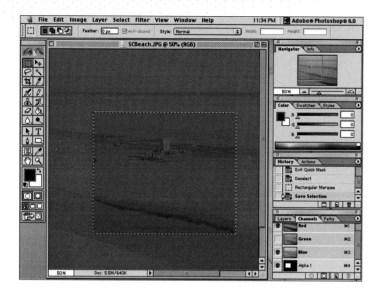

4. Click on the Save Selection as Channel icon (the icon showing a gray square with a white circle in the middle) in the Channels palette.
5. An alpha channel named Alpha 1 appears in the Channels palette. An alpha channel is an 8-bit grayscale channel that can be used to store a mask.
6. Click on the alpha channel in the Channels window to view the mask in the window. A mask enables you to edit, isolate, or protect certain parts of an image. For example, you can edit any part of the image within the white color of the mask. But you cannot edit any part of the image within the black color.

WORKING WITH THE PATHS PALETTE

The Paths palette contains a list of any line art, including fill or stroke paths, in an image. Use a pen or a shape tool to create a path in an image. A thumbnail of each path appears next to the name of each path. Create, delete, show, hide, or select a path from the Paths palette. The following steps show you how to add paths to an image.

1. Choose a pen or shape tool from the toolbox.
2. Draw an object or path in the window.

3. View the path in the Paths palette.
4. Click on the New Path icon (the small rectangle icon) to create a new path layer.
5. Select the new path. Then pick a shape tool from the toolbox. Click and drag the tool in the image window to create a path or object.

INSTALLING PLUG-INS

Adobe creates its own plug-ins for Photoshop, but shares
this technology with other developers so that you can add
more plug-ins to extend the kinds of effects and images
you can create. Most plug-ins appear in the Filters menu,
enabling you to apply an effect, like sharpen or blur, to an
image. Plug-ins can also appear in the Import and Export
menus to perform tasks such as downloading images from
a digital camera or controlling a scanner. More than 100
plug-ins are installed with Photoshop 6. To find out how to
install a plug-in, see Chapter 2, "Getting Started: Installing
Photoshop 6 and Obtaining Digital Images." For more
information about how to use a plug-in, see chapter 6,
"Enhancing Images with Filters and Effects."

CHAPTER 5

CORRECTING IMAGES

YOU MIGHT HAVE THOUGHT THAT A CERTAIN PICTURE LOOKED GREAT WHEN
YOU TOOK IT, BUT ONCE YOU GOT IT ONTO YOUR COMPUTER AND STARED
AT IT NEXT TO ANOTHER PICTURE, OR TRIED TO COMBINE PARTS OF ONE
PICTURE WITH ANOTHER, YOU REALIZED YOU NEEDED TO DO SOME
TWEAKING. PHOTOSHOP 6 IS A GREAT TOOL FOR MAKING SMALL CHANGES
TO AN ENTIRE PICTURE, OR TO A FEW PIXELS IN A PICTURE.

CORRECTING COLORS

An image can be too dark or too bright across the entire picture, or only in sections of the picture. You can use Photoshop 6 to manually or automatically adjust the tonal range of colors in a picture, or to correct a picture that's too blue. This section focuses on how to manually change colors in a picture. However, you can access Auto Levels and Auto Contrast commands by selecting the Image menu and choosing Adjust.

CHANNEL MIXING THE BIG PICTURE

Depending on how you plan to use a picture—as a stand-alone showpiece, or combined with other images—you might need to make changes that affect the entire document. Use the built-in filters and tools in Photoshop, like the channel mixer, to correct colors and make a good picture look better. The following steps show you how to change an image using the Channel Mixer command.

The Channel Mixer command enables you to combine a percentage of color from one channel to create part of another channel. You can use the channel mixer to adjust colors in a picture, swap or duplicate channels, or create a black and white, sepia, or other-color-tinted image from a color image. Many of the effects created with the channel mixer can also be created using the Image, Calculations command. However, you may find the channel mixer is easier to use.

1. Open an image in Photoshop.
2. Select Adjust from the Image menu, and then choose Channel Mixer.

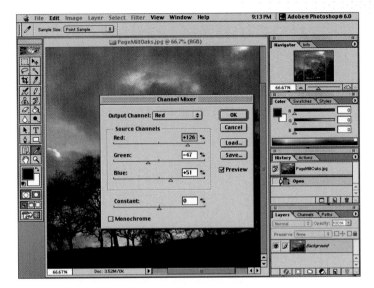

3. Notice in the Channel Mixer dialog box that there are three output channels for the image: red, green, and blue.
4. Click on a slider and drag it to the left to lower the color value across the picture. Values range between –200% and +200% selected in the text box or using the slider controls.
5. The Constant slider at the bottom of the window adjusts the opacity of the output channel. Negative values act as a black channel and positive values act as a white channel. Experiment using the Constant slider before and after making changes to each color channel.
6. Click on the Monochrome check box. Adjust the slider controls to adjust the amount of contrast in the grayscale image. You can use this option with each color channel to create a hand-tinted final image. Click on the OK button to save your changes.

 Choose New Adjustment Layer from the Layers pop-up menu, and then select Channel Mixer, or any other submenu item. Photoshop creates a special layer for the effect. Click on the eye icon in the Layers panel to turn the effect on and off.

REPLACING SPECIFIC COLORS

Make a blue sky gray, or green grass greener, by using a combination of selection tools and adjustment layers. Correcting or replacing colors can be a tedious, if not frustrating, task. Sometimes it can be difficult to select or adjust a range of colors without ruining the original quality of a picture. The following steps show you how to experiment with replacing and changing colors using the Magic Wand selection tool:

1. Choose the Magic Wand tool from the toolbox.
2. Click on a small area of color in the window.
3. Photoshop surrounds the set of pixels with a dotted line, also known as a *marquee*.

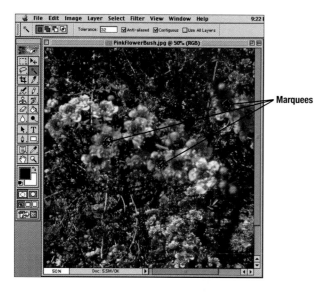

Marquees

4. Click on Image from the menu, and then choose Hue/Saturation from the New Adjustment Layer submenu in the Layer menu so you can easily edit, add, or remove this effect. Alternatively, choose Hue/Saturation from the Image/Adjust menus if you prefer to use the History panel to undo any changes.

5. In the Hue/Saturation dialog box, click on a slide and drag it to the left or right to decrease or increase the hue or saturation of the selected area in the window.
6. To edit the Hue/Saturation adjustment layer, select its layer in the Layers panel. Then choose Layer Content Options from the Layer menu. The Layer Content Options menu command opens the corresponding window for the selected adjustment layer.
7. The Hue/Saturation window appears. Make any changes you like. Click on OK to save these changes to the Adjustment layer.
8. Preview your changes in the window. Click on OK in the Hue/Saturation window to save your changes.

 Swap adjustment layers by choosing Change Layer Content from the Layer menu. First select an adjustment layer from the Layers palette. Then choose the Change Layer Content menu command from the Layer menu, and choose the adjustment layer you want to use.

BALANCING COLORS

If you have a scanned picture or one taken under low-light conditions, the resulting image might have a subtle, unnatural brown, yellow, or green hue. Depending on the quality of the scanned or digital image and the colors in the image, the color change might be more obvious. You might want to correct the image by removing the color imbalance.

To see a color imbalance, you need to set your monitor to display millions of colors (also referred to as 24-bit color). If your monitor is set to display 256 colors, the color imbalance won't be as noticeable. To change the color depth of your monitor from Windows 2000, choose True Color (24-bit) from the Settings tab of the Display Properties control panel window. On a Mac, open the Monitors control panel and click on Millions.

To correct a color imbalance, do the following:

1. Choose Color Balance from the Image, Adjust menus. Alternatively, choose Color Balance from the Layer, New Adjustment Layer menus.
2. Choose a label color from the color pop-up menu in the New Layer window. Type a name for the adjustment layer. Click on OK to create the new layer.

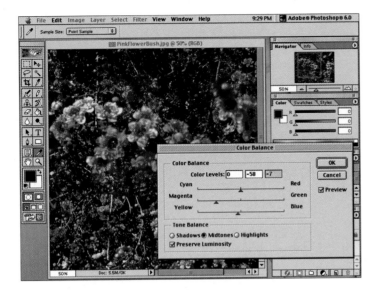

3. Adjust the Color Balance settings by moving the triangles along the scale as needed.

4. Select either the Shadows, Midtones, or Highlights radio button to set the tonal balance affected by the color changes. Preview your changes in the image window. Click OK to save your changes.

Use the layers to adjust the color levels of the picture. If you want to save the picture with a particular color correction, choose Flatten Image from the Layer menu. Give the file a unique name. You might want to keep a copy of the original picture with the layer settings in case you want to revisit color balancing.

ADJUSTING TONAL LEVELS

You can adjust the tonal range of dark and light colors to correct a photograph's contrast. For example, if a photo is comparatively lighter or darker than your other photos, you can correct all or part of the image using the Levels tools.

DEFINING TONAL RANGE

The tonal range of an image is made up of different levels of white and black values. Adjusting the limits of the white, or highlight, of an image, as well as the black, or shadow, of an image involves redistributing the midtone pixels of that image. Photoshop displays the tonal range using a histogram. Higher or taller bars in the histogram indicate more pixels in a particular black or white level of the image. View a histogram to find out how the pixels are distributed in a picture.

To view the histogram of an image, choose the Image, Histogram command. Choose a channel from the Channel drop-down menu. Then pass the cursor over any part of the histogram to view a particular tonal range level. Levels are represented by lower numbers on the left side of the histogram and higher numbers on the right side of the histogram. The Histogram window also displays the mean, standard deviation, median, and pixel count of the selected image.

To adjust the tonal range, first open an image, and then do the following steps:

1. Find out exactly what part of the image you're eyeballing with the Navigator panel.

2. Choose Levels from the Image, Adjust menus. Alternatively, choose Levels from the Layer, New Adjustment Layer menus. Name the adjustment layer, and then click OK.

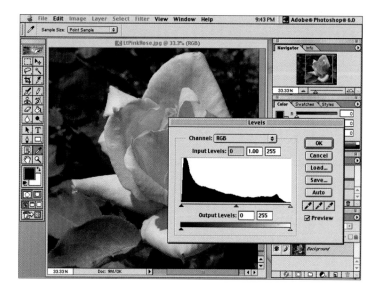

3. View the histogram for the image in the Levels window. Move the left slider to the right to reduce the tonal range of dark colors. Check the Preview check box and preview your changes in the image window.

4. Move the right slider to the left to reduce the tonal range of the light colors.

5. Drag the middle triangle to adjust the midtone levels for the picture.

6. View the intensity of light and dark colors in the histogram. Click OK to save your changes.

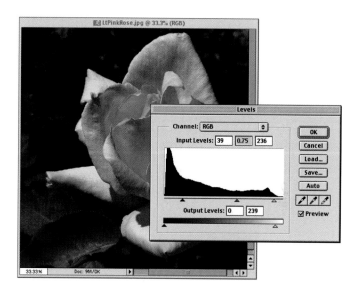

 Move the sliders inward if there are no extreme dark or light values in the histogram in the Levels window. White space, which appears as a flat line in the histogram in the Levels window, can increase an image file's size even though you can't see any difference.

CHANGING CONTRAST AND BRIGHTNESS

The brightness and contrast controls in Photoshop work similarly to those on a computer monitor or television. Brightness levels can increase or decrease the amount of light, or white colors, in an image. Contrast affects both white and black, or highlights and shadows, in an image. Adjust brightness and contrast settings independently—or in tandem—to intensify or soften the colors in a picture. Here's how:

1. Click on Image from the menu, choose Adjust, and then choose Brightness/Contrast. Alternatively, choose Brightness/Contrast from the Layer, New Adjustment Layer menus.
2. Click and drag the Brightness triangle to the Brightness/Contrast dialog box. This will adjust the brightness levels of the photo.

3. Click and drag the Contrast triangle to increase or decrease the amount of light and dark contrast in the photo.
4. Preview your changes. Click on OK to save them, or on Cancel if you do not want to save your changes.

 Another way to adjust the light in a photo is to use the Dodge tool in the toolbox (it lives with the Sponge and Burn tools). Modify the tool by changing its brush, range, and exposure settings in the option bar located at the top of the workspace. Click and drag the tool in the window to make a small area in the photo lighter.

EMBELLISHING IMAGES

It's not uncommon to see a picture that looks truer than life on a Web site or in a magazine. I'm not talking about people with perfect proportions, or even Laura Croft proportions (she's a 3D character in a game, for those who aren't gamers). I'm referring to photos that morph the head of one person onto the body of another and into a picture of outer space. Sure, this technique has been used in photographs as well as on television and in the movies, but let's find out how to create these effects in Photoshop. Such techniques can still be used to entertain and annoy your friends and relatives.

USING THE CLONE STAMP TOOL

The Clone Stamp tool resembles a rubber stamp icon in the toolbox. It is probably the most magical tool in Photoshop. You can use it to capture part of an image and apply it to any other part of the same document. To use this tool, do the following:

1. Select the Clone Stamp tool from the toolbox.
2. Hold down the Option key on the Mac (or Alt key for Windows users) while dragging the tool over the area of the picture you want to use as the master image.

3. Release the mouse button and Alt/Option key.
4. Click and drag the mouse in a different location in the image.

5. The captured image is drawn in the new location. Photoshop displays the original location of the master image as you apply its clone to the image. The master image remains unchanged, while its clone is applied to any new location.

> Use the Clone Stamp tool to make all the faces in a crowd identical, or to remove (or add) dust, spots, or glitches from a photo.

> If you're not sure whether cloning part of an image is the right thing to do, save a copy of the original image, or create an adjustment layer, before applying the Clone Stamp tool.

REPLACING COLORS IN AN IMAGE

If you have a photo with a faded blue sky, or if the clouds just wouldn't go away when you were taking pictures on the beach, you can use Photoshop to correct or replace areas of color in a picture. The following steps show you how to use the Magic Wand tool combined with the Levels and Replace Color menu commands to replace the colors in an image.

1. Open the image you want to edit, and then select the Magic Wand tool from the toolbox.
2. Click on the color area you want to edit. All instances of that color in the image are selected.

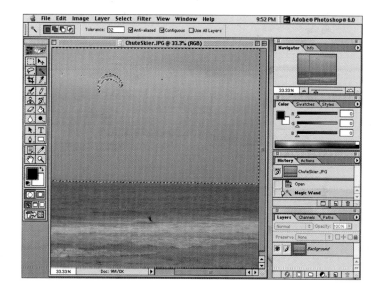

3. Choose Levels from the Image, Adjust menus.

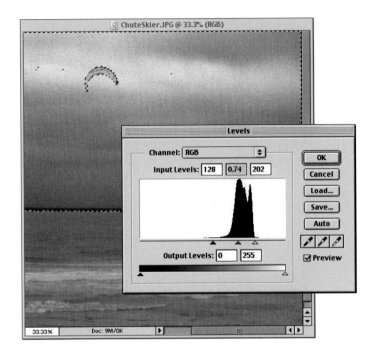

4. Adjust the levels of the selected area by dragging the left, middle, or right triangles. Then click on OK.

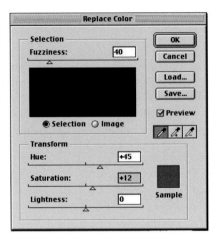

5. Choose Replace Color from the Image, Adjust menus.

6. Click on the black square in the middle of the Replace Color window. Click and drag the Hue, Saturation, and Lightness sliders to change the sample color.

7. Click on the plus or minus Eyedropper tool to add or subtract a color from the selection.

8. Click on OK to save your changes, or click on the Save button to store the settings in a file on your hard drive.

 One of the last things to do to correct an image is to use the Unsharp Mask filter located in the Filter menu, under the Sharpen submenu. This filter adjusts the contrast of the edge detail in a picture, creating the illusion of a clearer, focused image.

CROPPING AN IMAGE

The Crop tool resembles a rectangular frame with a thin diagonal line running across it. My dad, an architect, used a similar tool on his drawing board to frame part of an image. Photoshop's Crop tool works similarly to imaging crop tools in the real world. If you want to quickly remove fringe elements in a photo, use the Crop tool. Here's how:

1. Open the image you want to edit, and then choose the Crop tool (C) from the toolbox.

2. Click and drag the tool over the area you want to crop.
3. Click on any of the borders of the cropped area to enlarge or shrink the cropped region of the picture. Click and drag any corner handle to resize the cropped area.

4. Click on the Commit button (check mark button) in the option bar to complete the crop. To exit the crop tool without saving any changes, click on the Cancel button in the option bar (X button).

 When cropping an image, try to apply the same composition rules to the cropped image as you would when taking a picture with a camera. First consider balance. Decide whether you want the shadows, light, shapes, or lines of the image to be symmetrical or informal design. Second, consider the rule of thirds. Place the main subject and any subordinate elements in the picture near one-third point intersections in the picture, breaking a picture up into nine equally shaped areas.

ROTATING AN IMAGE

You can use the Rotate Canvas commands, located in the Image menu, to change a picture's rotation by 180° or 90° clockwise or counter-clockwise. To rotate an image, open one, and then click on the Image menu. Then choose Rotate Canvas and choose either 180°, 90° CW (clockwise), 90° CCW (counter-clockwise), Arbitrary, Flip Horizontally, or Flip Vertically. Photoshop will change the orientation of the image in the window.

Use the Rotate Canvas commands to turn a picture upside down or to create a mirror image effect. You can also combine the Arbitrary Rotate Canvas command with the Measure tool (which is located with the Eyedropper and Color sampler tools) to straighten the vertical alignment or flatten the horizontal alignment of any picture.

STRAIGHTENING AN IMAGE

No matter how careful I am, I always take a crooked picture. Fortunately, I can straighten my photo using the Measure tool in Photoshop 6. Here's how:

1. Open the image you want to edit, and then choose the Measure tool from the toolbox.

2. Draw a vertical line between two vertical points on the image. Because the image is crooked, your vertical line should be slightly slanted as well.

3. Choose Rotate Canvas, Arbitrary from the Image menu.

4. Photoshop 6 places a value in the Rotate window. Click on OK. The value represents the angle difference between the y axis and the vertical line you drew in step 2.

5. View the straightened image.

If you draw a straight line (versus a crooked one) with the Measure tool, Photoshop will not input a value into the Rotate Arbitrary window. The Measure tool compares the difference between the line drawn to the true horizontal or vertical axis of the image.

After straightening an image, use the Crop tool to remove any white space along the border of the image. To find out how to use the Crop tool, see the section "Cropping an Image" in this chapter.

CORRECTING THE HORIZONTAL AXIS

Alternatively, you can correct the horizontal axis of a picture using the Measure tool. Here's how:

 1. Open the image you want to edit, and then choose the Measure tool from the toolbox.

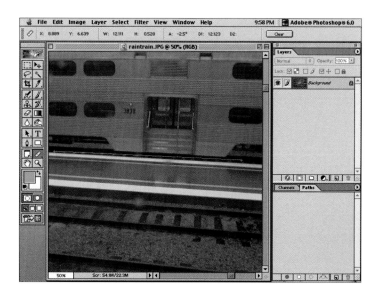

2. Draw a (slightly slanted) horizontal line between two horizontal points of the image. For example, follow the slanted horizontal line in the image.

3. Choose Rotate Canvas, Arbitrary from the Image menu.

4. Photoshop 6 places a value in the Rotate window. Click on OK. The value represents the angle difference between the x axis and the horizontal line you drew in step 2.

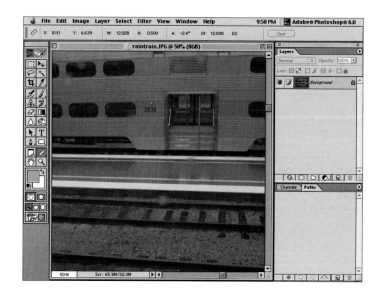

5. View the straightened image.

CHAPTER 6

ENHANCING IMAGES WITH FILTERS AND EFFECTS

PHOTOSHOP ENABLES YOU TO CLEAN UP, CORRECT, STYLIZE, OR DESTROY A PICTURE BY APPLYING FILTERS AND EFFECTS. MOST FILTERS AND EFFECTS ARE PLUG-IN FILES THAT ARE INSTALLED WITH PHOTOSHOP. PHOTOGRAPHER'S FILTERS, USED TO CORRECT DIFFERENT TYPES OF LIGHTING CONDITIONS, WERE THE INSPIRATION FOR NAMING PHOTOSHOP'S FILTERS. HOWEVER, PHOTOSHOP FILTERS GO BEYOND TRADITIONAL PHOTOGRAPHY FILTERS AND CAN BE USED TO CORRECT COLOR, DECONSTRUCT IMAGES, OR ADD A VARIETY OF STROKE-BASED AND OTHER KINDS OF SPECIAL EFFECTS TO AN IMAGE.

WHAT ARE PLUG-INS?

The folks at Adobe created the plug-in design in Photoshop to enable developers to create their own custom plug-ins. Today, many graphics applications, including Web browsers, follow the plug-in model as an easy way to add new features to an application. To install one, simply designate a plug-in folder for Photoshop from the Preferences window, or place a plug-in file in the Photoshop Plug-Ins folder prior to starting Photoshop. Click on the Filter menu to access the plug-in.

FILTERS

Although it's easy to categorize all filters as effects, or vice versa, I categorize filters as plug-ins that affect the quality of a photographic image, such as sharpening, blurring, or color correcting an image. Effects, on the other hand, change a picture by adding a style, stroke, or distinctive visual element, like fur or metal, to an image. The following sections explain two different categories of filters.

CORRECTIVE FILTERS

You can apply sharpen or blur filters directly from the Filter menu or tweak levels, contrast, and colors from the Image, Adjust menus.

You can also create new adjustment layers to add filters one by one to an image. Choose Auto Levels or Auto Contrast from the Adjust submenu in the Image menu if you want Photoshop to take its best shot at correcting image levels or contrast. Otherwise, choose the Levels, Curves, Color Balance, Brightness/Contrast, Hue/Saturation, or Desaturate commands from the Image, Adjust or Layer, New Adjustment Layer menus to adjust the way your picture looks.

DESTRUCTIVE FILTERS

Some of the filters in Photoshop, such as the filters in the Pixelate submenu, break up an image, as opposed to making an image clearer. In some cases, for example, if you have a screen shot of a password, or your home phone number, you can use a filter on a specific area of an image to blur or decompose the pixels so the image details are no longer recognizable.

If you're making changes across an entire image, you probably won't be using corrective and destructive filters together. However, to fix a few pixels here or there, it's possible to sharpen part of an image, and destroy another part.

EFFECTS

Adobe includes a group of stroke, stylize, texture, and distort effects with Photoshop. You can purchase additional plug-ins from a wide range of Photoshop plug-in developers such as Xaos Tools (**www.xaostools.com**), Alien Skin Software (**www.alienskin.com**), Extensis (**www.extensis.com**), and Andromeda (**www.andromeda.com**). Visit **www.adobe.com/photoshop** to find a complete list of Photoshop third-party plug-ins.

All effects can be applied directly to an image layer. A subset of effects can be applied as a Layer Style from the Layer menu. Each Layer Style appears as a separate layer effect in the Layers panel. Layer effects are also called live effects because this type of effect doesn't directly affect the pixels in the image. Click on the eye icon to hide or show a layer effect in the image window. The stylize and distort effects are highlighted in the following sections.

STYLIZE

Choose Stylize from the Filter menu to choose from among Diffuse, Emboss, Extrude, Find Edges, Glowing Edges, Solarize, Tiles, Trace Contour, and Wind effects. Depending on the content of your picture, these effects might look great or might not make any noticeable change. The Find Edges effect is shown here.

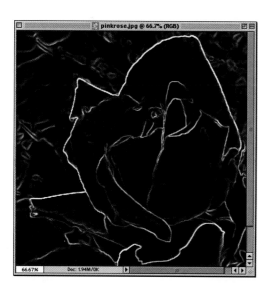

DISTORT

As with the other effects, the names of the distort effects won't give you an exact idea of what they can do to an image. Even so, you'll probably have the most fun with these filters. Choose from Diffuse Glow, Displace, Glass, Ocean Ripple, Pinch, Polar Coordinates, Ripple, Shear, Spherize, Twist, Wave, and ZigZag. Each effect has a corresponding panel, enabling you to customize the effect for a picture. The Diffuse Glow effect is shown here.

 A filter cannot be applied to an image in Bitmap, indexed-color mode, or to 16-bit images. For the examples in this book, change the color mode to RGB by selecting RGB Color from the Image, Mode menus.

APPLYING EFFECTS AND FILTERS

Apply an effect to a single image, or experiment with multiple effects by moving an image to a layer or layer set, then turning off all layers except one to view and compare effects. To create an experimental layer for viewing effects, copy and paste an image to a new layer and apply individual or combinations of effects to the image layer. To view a particular effect, click on the eye icon box to show a particular effect layer, then hide all the other layers. You can also turn effects on or off by selecting entries in the History panel.

BLUR FILTERS

When you're taking pictures, image clarity and focus are critical for capturing a clear, crisp picture. You can use blur effects, however, to create a soft focus, emphasize another part of the picture, or to de-emphasize a specific part of a picture—for example, a face, or if you're working with a screen capture, a password, or login name. To blur the entire image (I've chosen to apply a radial blur), do the following:

1. Open an image file. Open the Filter menu, choose Blur, and select Radial Blur.
2. View the settings for this effect in the Radial Blur window. I chose the default settings for this effect.
3. Click on OK. Photoshop applies the effect to the image.

4. View the new image.

To blur a portion of the image (I've chosen to apply a motion blur), do the following:

1. Use the lasso or rectangular selection tool to select a particular area of an image.
2. Open the Filter menu, choose Blur, and select Motion Blur.
3. Click and drag the slider control to adjust the distance between pixels.
4. Type a number into the Angle text box if you want to create a motion blur at a specific angle.
5. Click on OK. View the effect in the image window.

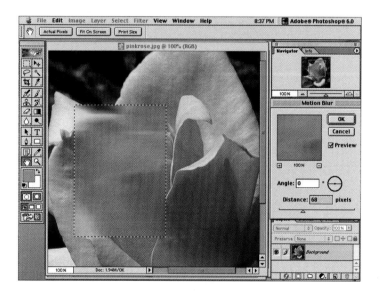

 Blur effect menu commands can blur a selected area or an entire image. To blur a small area of an image, choose the Blur tool from the toolbox. Press Shift+R to cycle through the tools that share toolbox space with the Blur tool or right-click to select one of them from a menu. Click and drag this tool over the image to blur specific pixels. You might need to use the Zoom tool prior to selecting the Blur tool to get a closer look at the pixels you want to blur.

 Once a filter or effect is selected from the Filter menu, it appears as the top-most menu item in the Filter menu. Press Ctrl/Command+F to re-apply the last filter applied to an image from the Filter menu.

SHARPEN FILTERS

Depending on the type of digital camera used to create a source image, you might want to try to improve the clarity of an image with Photoshop's sharpen effects. Don't set your expectations too high, though; the sharpen filter can't increase the amount of pixelation or hard edges in digital pictures. The resulting image may not appear to be any clearer than its original.

If you see large, coarse, or squarish-looking pixels in an image, you're looking at pixelation. Applying the sharpen filter to this type of image will not make it any clearer. You may want to try applying the Unsharp mask with different settings to see if this filter helps decrease the pixelation.

A sharpen filter increases the contrast between neighboring pixels. If the image lacks the pixel information to increase the contrast or clarity of all or part of an image, the sharpen filter won't change the original image. You probably won't notice any difference after applying a sharpen effect to a blurry picture. The following steps show you how to apply sharpen effects to the image window.

1. Open an image file. Open the Filter menu, choose Sharpen, and select Sharpen.

2. If you do not see any change in the image, select the Zoom tool (Z) and increase the image to 200 or 300 percent. The original image is shown on the bottom and the image after applying the sharpen effect is shown at the top.

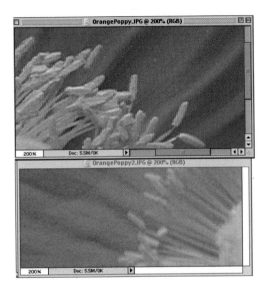

3. Press Ctrl/Command+Z to undo the effect. Alternatively, select Undo from the Edit menu.
4. Choose Sharpen More from the Sharpen submenu. The effect should appear in the History panel.

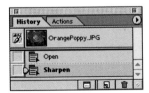

5. View the updated image.
6. Choose Unsharp Mask from the Sharpen submenu.
7. Click and drag each slider, or type in a new value to adjust the Amount, Radius, and Threshold settings in the Unsharp Mask window. Amount enables you to assign a value between 1 and 500 to determine how sharp to make the image. Choose a number between 1 and 250 pixels

to define the radius of how sharp the edges should be made. Select a number between 0 and 255 for the Threshold setting to tell Photoshop how it should recognize edges in the image. Preview the changes in the Unsharp Mask window.
8. Click on OK to apply the filter to the image window.

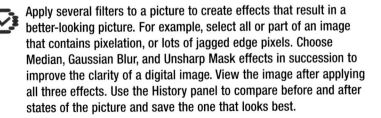

Applying sharpening effects across an entire picture can over-emphasize edges and alter parts of the picture that were fine before the sharpen effect was applied. Compare the image before and after applying several doses of the sharpen effect. Click on a previous state in the History palette to undo any accidental abuse of the sharpen effects.

Apply several filters to a picture to create effects that result in a better-looking picture. For example, select all or part of an image that contains pixelation, or lots of jagged edge pixels. Choose Median, Gaussian Blur, and Unsharp Mask effects in succession to improve the clarity of a digital image. View the image after applying all three effects. Use the History panel to compare before and after states of the picture and save the one that looks best.

Adobe provides the Sharpen effects in menu and tool forms. Use the menu commands to apply the effect across an entire picture, or to a selected area of the picture. If you only need to edit a comparatively small area of pixels, press Shift+R to cycle through and select the Sharpen tool in the toolbox. Click and drag this tool over the image to sharpen specific pixels. You might need to use the Zoom tool to benefit from this tool.

TEXTURE EFFECTS

Experiment with non-traditional photographic effects by adding a texture effect. Choose from Texturizer, Stained Glass, Patchwork, Mosaic Tiles, Grain, or Craquelure in the Filter menu's Texture submenu. To apply such an effect, do the following:

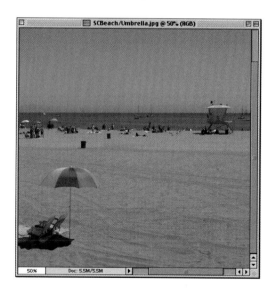

1. Open an image file. Open the Filter menu, select Texture, and choose Craquelure.
2. Click and drag the sliders to adjust the Craquelure settings.
3. Click on OK, and then view the changes in the document window.

ARTISTIC AND SKETCH EFFECTS

Some effects, such as Artistic and Sketch effects, combine the foreground and background colors with settings in the effect window. To apply such an effect, do the following:

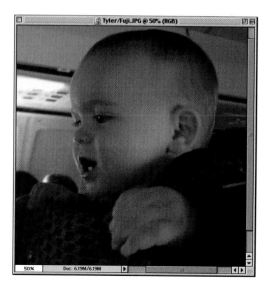

1. Open an image file. Open the Filter menu, choose Artistic, and select Smudge Stick.
2. Adjust any of the smudge settings in the effect window.
3. Click on OK, and then view the effect on the image.

 You can view your picture beyond the bounds of the document window. Change the document view of the front-most image by pressing the F key, or by choosing a view mode from the toolbox. Pressing the F key once will grow the image to fill the screen below the menu and toolbars. Pressing F a second time hides the menu bar. The third time brings you back to the document window view.

TINT AND FADE EFFECTS

There are a few ways to adjust the color tint of a picture. One way is to add a layer, and then use the paint bucket to apply a solid color to it, and then adjust the opacity in the Layers palette. See Chapter 11, "Experimenting with Layers," to find out more about adding a tint using layers. This example shows you how to add a tint with the Neon Glow and Fade effects. Try these steps:

1. Open an image file. Open the Filter menu, choose Artistic, and select Neon Glow.
2. Click and drag the sliders to set the glow size, glow setting, and glow color. Then click on OK to save the changes.
3. Choose Fade Neon Glow from the Edit menu.

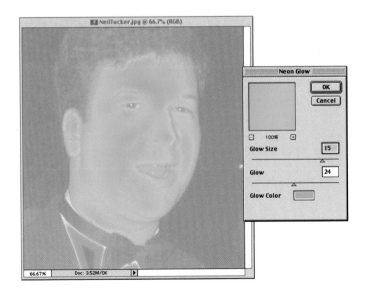

4. Click and drag the slider to set the opacity.

5. Click on OK. View the Fade effect in the document window.

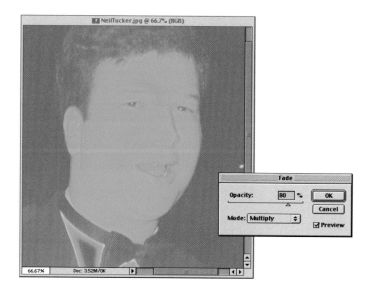

HALFTONE EFFECTS

Halftone effects can serve two purposes: they create a neat looking effect, and they reduce the number of colors used in an image. If you don't want to pay for full-color printing costs, or you simply want to keep images on your Web site as small as possible, consider using halftone effects on your images. The following steps show you how to apply two kinds of halftone filters to a picture.

1. Open an image file. Open the Filter menu, choose Pixelate, and select Color Halftone.

2. Type a radius size to define how many pixels are used to create the halftone dots. Type a new value between 1 and 256 into any of the channel text boxes to adjust the screen angle of the halftone dots.

3. Click on OK to save the changes. Wait for Photoshop to render the effect.

4. View the color halftone effect in the document window.

5. Alternatively, open the Filter menu, choose Sketch, and select Halftone.
6. Choose a pattern type for the halftone, and adjust any settings by clicking and dragging the slider controls.
7. View the halftone image in the document window.

 Halftone effects reorganize the pixels in an image into spot-shaped cells, or halftone cells. A halftone image doesn't contain the clarity of a traditional photograph image, but can give a simple image a distinct look.

COMBINING EFFECTS

Combining effects can be tricky. You can use layers to view how one effect will look, but because each effect is based on the current picture, it's not easy to determine which effect to add when, and with what settings, in order to create a particular look from a group of effects.

There are a couple of ways you can experiment with effects without ruining the original picture. Obviously, you can create a copy of the original, and add and undo effects until your picture evolves into something you want to save. Memory permitting, you can add as many effects as you like. If you never choose the Save command, you can always close the image without saving the changes.

If you have plenty of hard disk space, you can add layers with different sets of effects to an image. Then save the file as a Photoshop file. Keep in mind that a 1MB JPEG image can easily grow beyond 20MB if it's saved as a Photoshop file.

APPLYING STROKE EFFECTS

Although Photoshop has a set of stroke-related features for drawing on an image, this section focuses on stroke effects, which can add brush strokes to a digital photo. Stroke effects can be found in a couple of Filter submenus: Brush Strokes and Sketch. The Sketch effect uses the colors in the color well to create a particular effect, whereas the Brush Strokes effect works solely with the image's pixels.

BRUSH STROKE EFFECTS

When you choose a Brush Stroke effect, a preview window appears, enabling you to adjust the settings for that effect and preview your changes in the effect window. Use the Hand tool to move the preview image around to see how the effect applies to different areas of the image. The following steps show you how to apply the Crosshatch and Sprayed Strokes effects to an image.

1. Open an image file. Open the Filter menu, select Brush Strokes, and choose Crosshatch.

 If you don't like a particular effect or combination of effects, simply click on a previous effect in the History panel. The document window will revert to the effect settings chosen in the History panel.

SKETCH EFFECTS

Select a foreground color in the toolbox, and then select a sketch effect to apply the effect based on the selected color. The following steps show you how to apply the Bas Relief effect to an image.

1. Open an image in Photoshop.

2. Open the Filter menu, choose Sketch, and select Bas Relief.

2. Click and drag the Slider control to adjust the stroke settings for this effect.

3. Open the Filter menu, choose Brush Strokes, and select Sprayed Strokes. Adjust the settings, and then click on OK.

4. View the effects in the window.

3. View the effect in the document window.

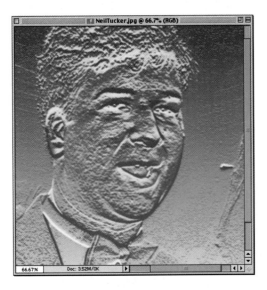

STYLIZE EFFECTS

Most of the stylize effects work with edge patterns in an image to create a special effect. Naturally, it's not always obvious what a stylize effect can do. However, if you adjust the contrast or levels of an image prior to applying edge-related effects, you can force some effects to stand out a little more. The following steps show you how to apply the extrude effect to an image.

1. Open an image file.

2. Open the Filter menu, choose Stylize, and select Extrude.

3. Adjust the Type, Size, and Depth settings. Click on OK, and view the effect in the document window.

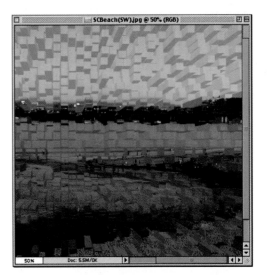

ADDING 3D EFFECTS

Convert part of an image into a three-dimensional object by applying the 3D Effect Render filter to a picture. This effect opens a 3D Transform and includes a toolbox in addition to a preview window and tool options. Choose a square, sphere, or cylinder 3D tool from the toolbox. Click and drag in the miniaturized grayscale preview image to create the 3D object. Use a selection tool to place the 3D object in the 3D Transform window. Edit the 3D shape with the Direct Selection tool. Do the following steps to create a 3D effect in a picture:

1. Open an image file. Open the Filter menu, choose Render, and select 3D Transform.

2. Choose a 3D tool, like the sphere, from the toolbox in the 3D Transform window. Click and drag the sphere in the image window. Place it over the part of the image on which you want to apply the 3D effect.
3. Click on the Trackball tool (second row from the bottom) to rotate the 3D image in the sphere.

4. If you move the sphere with the Pan Camera tool, you'll notice the image from the original document has been copied to the sphere. The sphere can cover the original image, or appear as a separate image in the document window.
5. Click on OK and view the 3D effect in the document window.

 Combine the 3D effects with other pictures. Use layers, masks and channels to create your own image compositions.

LIQUIFYING IMAGES

Use the Liquify tool to create interesting effects, or to reconstruct, freeze, or thaw part of an image being previewed. Freeze and thaw tools work similarly to masks. Frozen pixels, which are usually marked by a special color such as red, cannot be edited, whereas thawed pixels can. Unlike the other effects, which are located in the Filter menu, the Liquify tool is located in the Image menu.

The following steps provide a brief tour of the effects in the Liquify command:

1. Open an image file. Open the Image menu and choose Liquify.

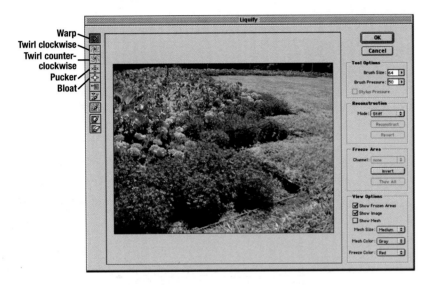

2. Click on the Warp tool, located at the top of the toolbox. Drag it over the image and watch the pixels distort in the direction of the cursor as you move it.

3. Choose one of the two Twirl tools from the toolbox. Click and hold down over an area of the image; watch the tool twirl the pixels.

4. Choose the Pucker and Bloat tools to expand selected pixels.

5. Change the brush size and pressure, and other settings. Experiment with the other tools in the Liquify window. Click on OK to save your changes.

 Press Ctrl/Command+Shift+X to open the Liquify window.

CREATING OBJECTS
AND GRADIENTS

CUSTOMIZE AN IMAGE BY CREATING OR SELECTING AN IMAGE OBJECT IN
THE IMAGE WINDOW. AN OBJECT, OR IMAGE OR GRAPHIC OBJECT, CAN BE A
BITMAPPED IMAGE OR A VECTOR GRAPHIC. BECAUSE YOU'RE EDITING
DIGITAL PICTURES, THIS CHAPTER FOCUSES ON HOW TO WORK WITH
BITMAP GRAPHICS USING THE SELECTION AND DRAWING TOOLS. YOU CAN
CREATE VECTOR OR BITMAP GRAPHICS IN PHOTOSHOP 6 USING THE SHAPE
AND DRAWING TOOLS IN THE TOOLBOX. USE THESE TOOLS TO CREATE
CUSTOM GRAPHICS AND MASKS, ENHANCE A SPECIFIC COLOR, OR APPLY A
GRADIENT TO PART OF A PHOTO. (A GRADIENT IS A TYPE OF COLOR
CHANGE WHERE ONE COLOR BLENDS INTO ANOTHER WITHIN A PARTICULAR
AREA, SUCH AS WITHIN AN IMAGE OBJECT.) YOU CAN COMBINE VECTOR
GRAPHICS WITH BITMAP GRAPHICS TO CREATE GREAT-LOOKING PICTURES.

 See Chapters 9, "Customizing Images with Masks," and 12, "Creating Custom Masks," for more information about masks.

DRAWING WITH PHOTOSHOP TOOLS

Even if you're not an artist, you can use Photoshop's drawing tools to follow the lines in a photo to create a custom shape. The Pen tool enables you to create a line that can match any photographable shape. You can draw directly on a layer, then copy and paste the image to a new layer or to a different image window. You can also use the Shape, Pencil, Paintbrush and Paint Bucket tools to add or edit graphics.

You'll find a great group of selection tools, plus a powerful set of bitmap editing tools, such as the Smudge tool, in the toolbox. Access or edit foreground and background colors from the toolbox, or from the Color or Swatches palettes. At the bottom of the toolbox is a button that takes you directly to ImageReady, which contains even more tools organized similarly to those in Photoshop.

CREATING OBJECT PATHS

Don't be thrown off by such an ambiguous name. Object paths, also referred to as paths, or path objects, are lines made up of points. You can use the Shape or Pen tools to create and edit paths. However, only shapes are created as vector graphics—resolution-independent graphics that preserve detail and clarity if scaled to a larger or smaller size.

Paths created with the Pen tool or shapes created with a Shape tool appear in the Paths palette. Click on a layer in the Layers palette, then view any paths stored in that layer in the Paths palette. Add, remove, and group vector graphics to help create effects localized to specific objects in a picture. The following steps show you how to create a path object with the Pen tool.

1. Select the Pen tool from the toolbox.
2. The first click in the image window creates the first point of the path. If you click and drag the first point, you can set how much the line will curve when the point is created. Click a second time to create the second point in the path. If you click and drag the second point, you can set the curve of the line to that point. Press the Delete key to remove the previously created point. Click on the first point to close the path, or click on the Move tool (V) to de-select the Pen tool. Create a line that completely surrounds an object in the image window by clicking along the borders of the object. This creates a connect-the-dots effect. Keep going until your end point crosses your starting point.
3. Be sure to click on the starting point to close the path object.

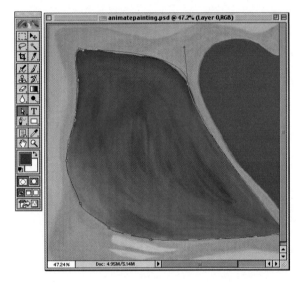

4. Use the Paint Bucket tool to fill the path object. Select path object, then click on the Paint Bucket tool in the toolbox. Click inside the path object to fill it with the foreground color.

7. Choose Copy from the Edit menu. Select a different layer, or create a new layer in the Layers palette. Then choose Paste from the Edit menu. The path object should appear in the new layer.

8. Use adjustment layers to blend in colors, gradients, or effects to the path object. Select a layer containing an object path. Click on the Layer, New Adjustment Layer menus, and choose Color Balance or Brightness/Contrast. Click and drag the pop-up slider control for the Opacity setting to adjust transparency levels for the adjustment layer and the object path layer. Be sure the adjustment layer is placed above the object path layer in the Layers palette.

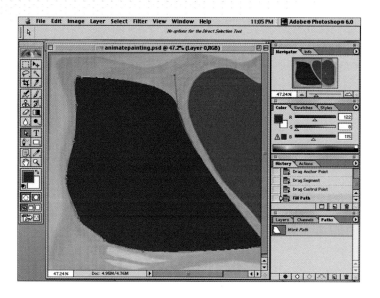

5. Create a second path object. Choose a different color to fill the path object.
6. Click on the Paths tab to view the Paths palette.

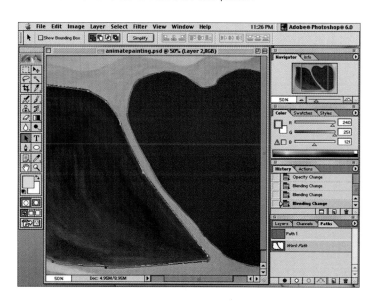

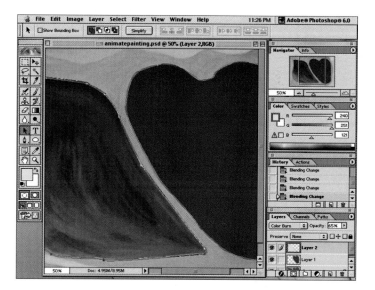

 Press P to select the Pen tool in the toolbox. Press Shift+P to cycle between the Pen and Freeform Pen tool.

 You can use the Add Anchor Point or Delete Anchor Point tools to add or remove points to a vector graphic. You can also select a path and apply commands, like the Transform command (Ctrl/Command+T).

EDITING GRAPHICS WITH BITMAP TOOLS

Images are bitmaps, which is a fancy name for a group of pixels. Bitmap tools, such as the Nudge and Smudge tools, let you create or edit pixels. Other tools, like the Levels command, enable you to adjust the tonal range of pixels across an image object. If you zoom into a digital photograph, you'll notice a huge matrix of pixels. With thousands or millions of colors to choose from, it's pretty tough to just go in and tweak a pixel with the Pencil tool. Because bitmap images can be so complex, tools like the Clone Stamp, Nudge, Smudge, and Blur tools are invaluable image-editing tools. See Chapter 5, "Correcting Images," to find out how to use the Clone Stamp tool.

LEVELS TOOL

The Levels tool is available as an adjustment layer (which is probably the best way to use this kind of tool), as well as from the Image, Adjust menus. Alternatively, press Ctrl/Command+L to open the Levels window. If an object or gradient doesn't quite match the tonal range of the rest of the picture, try applying a levels adjustment layer to the object or gradient layer to see whether this combination results in any improvement. The Levels tool enables you to adjust the highlight and shadow (white and black) levels that represent the tonal range of a picture. The following steps show you how to adjust the tonal range levels of a selected bitmap image object.

1. Choose a selection tool (I've chosen the Magic Wand [W]), and select a particular area to edit in the image window.
2. Open the Levels window using one of the methods described previously.
3. Move the left slider to adjust the darker levels in the picture. Move the right slider to adjust the lighter tones, and move the middle slider to adjust the mid-range tones.

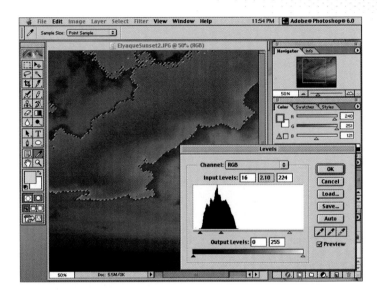

4. Click on the Set Black, White, or Gray point buttons to customize the levels in the picture.
5. Select a specific channel from the pop-up menu to view the levels for a red, green, or blue channel. In RGB mode, Photoshop stores any image color information in red, green, and blue channels. Click on a red, green, or blue channel to see whether the Level adjustments had any effect on any single channel. See Chapter 10, "Making Images Stand Out with Channels," to find out more about how channels work.

SMUDGE TOOL

Make fine-tuned adjustments to an object or gradient using the Nudge, Smudge, and Zoom tools. Smear pixels around in an image with the Smudge tool. If you need to make more exact edits, use the Zoom tool to zoom into the pixels. Then zoom back out (hold down the Alt/Option key and click on the image with the Zoom tool) to see whether you created a desirable effect. The following steps show you how to use the Smudge tool.

1. Click on the Smudge tool (it's the hand with a pointed finger icon) in the toolbox, or press Shift+R to cycle through the Sharpen and Blur tools to get to the Smudge tool.
2. Click and drag the mouse in the image window.

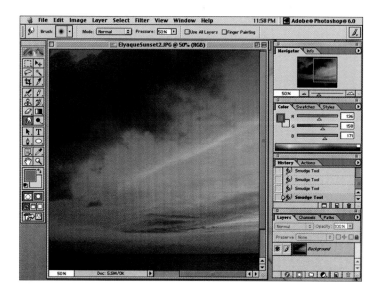

3. Undo a smudge by selecting an earlier instance of the Smudge tool in the History palette. Or open the Edit menu and choose the Undo command.

WORKING WITH FOREGROUND AND BACKGROUND COLORS

The foreground and background colors are stored in the toolbox as well as the Color palette. Use the Eyedropper tool to view a specific color of an object in an image. Or edit the foreground or background colors by clicking on their corresponding color square in the toolbox. You can choose from thousands or millions of colors to work with. This range of selectable colors is limited, however, to the amount of dedicated video or graphics memory installed in your computer, and to the Mac OS or Windows resolution setting in the Monitors control panel.

CHOOSING A COLOR

Changing or selecting a color is a fairly simple task. First click on the foreground or background color square in the toolbox or in the color palette to open the Color Picker window. Then click on a general color in the vertical color bar (I'm referring to the Adobe Color Picker here), and click on a color in the left side of the color picker window. Click on OK and the foreground or background color changes.

Photoshop uses color-management settings to define the range of colors that make up the RGB color mode, or any of its other color modes, such as CMYK. The biggest problem color management helps solve is that it provides a consistent definition of how a color should look on a monitor, camera, video tape, printer, or other image-related computer peripheral. Without color management, a yellow in Photoshop might appear as an orange or green color on a different computer or printer.

Color management is a complex subject, and although it's definitely a topic worth reading about, I'm recommending you leave the color-management settings as the Photoshop defaults. Unless the colors in an RGB image are wrong, don't change the color-management settings. Choose ColorSync Workflow (on a Mac) or Web Graphics Default.

When choosing a color, the most important window is the Color Picker. On a Mac you can choose from Apple or Adobe's color picker. Both offer a spectrum of colors. However, the Photoshop color picker displays a wider range of colors than Apple's color picker window. Press Ctrl/Command+K to open the Preferences window. Choose a Color Picker from the General section of the Preferences window.

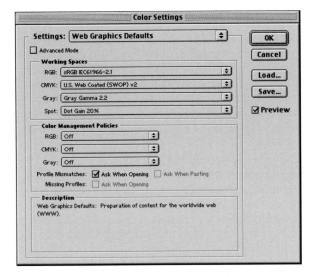

You can mix color settings and create a color spontaneously by clicking and dragging the sliders in the Color palette of the Color Picker window.

You can also select and edit colors using the Swatches palette. The Swatches palette enables you to create, edit, group, or delete a custom set of colors, which can be saved to a file and used with other image files. Click on the foreground or background color in the Color palette or from the color well in the toolbox to select a color from the color picker. The color picker displays the same ranges of colors no matter which mode the image file is set to.

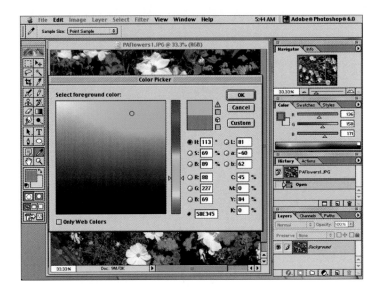

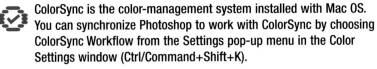 Choose sRGB IEC61966-2.1 from the RGB drop-down menu in the Working Spaces section of the Color Settings window. If you save an image file with this color setting, most colors will translate correctly if the image file is opened with another graphics application, such as Macromedia's Fireworks.

ColorSync is the color-management system installed with Mac OS. You can synchronize Photoshop to work with ColorSync by choosing ColorSync Workflow from the Settings pop-up menu in the Color Settings window (Ctrl/Command+Shift+K).

On a Windows PC, ColorSync is not available. However, you can choose a color-management system from the Settings drop-down menu in the Color Settings window.

CHANGING COLORS WITH THE SWATCHES PALETTE

Save color palettes from other Photoshop files, or simply change the foreground or background color by clicking on a color in the Swatches palette. Click on the document icon to add a new foreground color to the Swatches palette. The following steps show you how to change the foreground color using the Swatches palette.

1. Open an image file and then select the Swatches palette.

2. Click on the Eyedropper tool in the toolbox. Select an area of color in the image window.
3. Click on a different color in the Swatches palette. The foreground color changes in the color well. Click on the pop-up menu and choose Save Swatches to save the set of colors as a swatch to your hard drive. Type a name for the swatch and then click on Save. Then, if you ever have to work on a similar image, you can reload the swatches file and save time putting that custom set of colors back together.

4. Select the Paint Bucket tool and click in the selected area.
5. Select the History palette to view the color palette changes.
6. Click on any item in the History palette to revert the image window to that state.

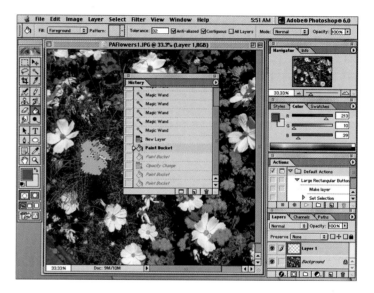

 You can copy and paste a specific area of a picture and save it to its own layer. Then edit specific colors before moving it back to the original image.

DEFINING A GRADIENT

You can fade in or out of one color to another by creating, defining, and applying a gradient to an image. A *gradient* is a gradual blending of two or more colors. The gradient colors are defined by the Gradient tool, located in the toolbox. A gradient is defined by the foreground and background colors.

There are five kinds of gradients in Photoshop: Linear, Radial, Angular, Reflected, and Diamond. Each type of gradient represents a unique pattern that can be applied to the image. Each icon shape in the options bar reflects its corresponding gradient shape and pattern. The linear gradient creates a layered blend of colors whereas the radial and angle gradients blend the colors in a circular pattern. As you might expect, the diamond gradient blends its colors in the shape of a diamond. Two or more linear gradients are blended outward in the reflected gradient.

Choose from any of the pre-installed gradients or create your own in the Gradient Editor window. Gradients can be used to blend images together in a picture, or enhance an image.

SELECTING AN OBJECT

A gradient can be applied across an entire image, or to a selected area of an image or object. Choose from the Magic Wand, Lasso, or Shape selection tools to customize a specific part of an image with a gradient. To apply a gradient to a particular range of colors, select the Magic Wand tool. Click on a color in the image window to select a range of colors. Then select the Gradient tool, and the gradient you want to apply to the selected object in the image window. Click and drag the cursor in the image window to apply the gradient to the object.

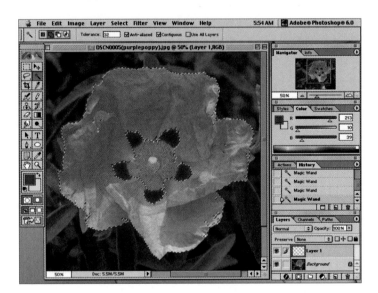

 Press M to select the Rectangular Marquee tool from the toolbox. Press Shift+M to cycle between the Rectangular, Elliptical, Single Row, and Single Column marquee tools.

 Press W to select the Magic Wand tool from the toolbox.

CHOOSING COLORS

The selected gradient appears on the left side of the options bar if the gradient tool is selected in the toolbox. Click on the gradient to open the Gradient Editor window and view the currently selected colors. Most gradients are defined by the foreground and background colors in the color well. Click on the foreground and background colors, and make any changes to them prior to applying a gradient to the image. Each of the five types of gradients also appears in the toolbar. Select the type of gradient prior to creating the gradient in the image window. You can adjust dither, transparency, opacity, and mode settings after the gradient has been applied to the image if the gradient is created as a New Fill Layer gradient.

Choose Layer, and then select New Fill Layer. Choose Gradient to add a gradient layer to the Layers palette. Modify the gradient layer by selecting it first, and then choose Change Layer Content from the Layer menu. Click on the Edit Gradient area of the options bar to open the Gradient Editor. Then adjust gradient colors by clicking on a color square, and choosing a color from the Color Picker window. For more information about editing the gradient, see the next section.

 The best way to experiment with gradients is to add a fill layer, and adjust then the gradient colors in the layer. When you've finalized the gradient settings, merge or flatten the layers together.

EDITING THE GRADIENT

There are two ways to apply a gradient to an image. Both use the Gradient tool in the toolbox. If you create a gradient as a New Fill Layer, you can edit it anytime you like. The more permanent way to alter an image with a gradient is to apply the gradient directly to a layer. You can undo the gradient, or click on a previous state in the History palette, as long as you don't exit or quit Photoshop. I recommend adding a gradient as a New Fill Layer.

To edit a gradient, first select the Gradient tool from the toolbox. Click in the Edit Gradient area, located on the left end of the options bar, to open the Gradient Editor window. Click on a gradient to view the colors for that gradient. Click in the color square below the gradient color bar to edit a gradient color. Type a name for the gradient in the Name text box. Click on the New button to create a new gradient.

CHANGING GRADIENT COLORS

Once you've created a gradient, you can edit and add colors to the gradient from the Gradient Editor window. Load one of several groups of gradient settings by choosing the Load button. Alternatively, click on the Save button and create your own set of gradients.

GRADIENT EDITOR WINDOW

You can customize gradient colors, as well as load or save new gradients from the Gradient Editor window. Here's how:

1. Open an image file. Click on the Gradient tool in the toolbox. Click on the gradient in the tool options bar to open the Gradient Editor window.

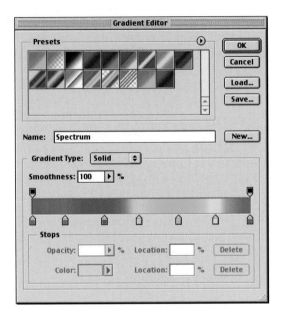

2. Select the drop-down menu to view the gradient menu commands, which also appear in the tool options bar.

3. Each color in the gradient appears in a slider control below the color bar in the Gradient Editor window. For example, the Gradient Editor window in the previous figure shows seven color squares, each representing a color in the selected gradient. Click and drag each color square to define where the color appears in the gradient. Double-click on the color square to view and edit the gradient color.

4. Adjust the gradient settings in the Gradient Editor window. Click on OK to save your changes. Then follow the steps in the next section to learn how to apply the gradient.

APPLYING A GRADIENT

You might have noticed that the angle and length of the stroke you draw in the image window affects the way Photoshop creates a gradient. The type of gradient selected in the Gradient options bar affects the gradient pattern you create in the image window. Also, the number of colors in a gradient contribute to how the gradient is applied to the angle and stroke you create.

The first click you make in the image window defines the center of the gradient. The angle of the stroke, or line that appears when you drag the cursor, defines the angle of the radius of gradient. The length of that line determines the radius size of the shape, or type of radius chosen in the option toolbar. The diamond gradient works a little differently than the other types of gradients. The line drawn defines a corner location and shape of the diamond gradient. To apply a gradient to an image, do the following steps:

1. Open an image and use a selection tool from the toolbox to select the area to which you want to apply the gradient. In this example, I used the Magic Wand selection tool.

2. To apply a gradient, select the Gradient tool from the toolbox. Choose the type of gradient from the options bar. The highlighted shape icon indicates what the gradient pattern will look like in the image.

3. Click and drag the Gradient tool in the image window. Click and drag the line in the direction you want the gradient to be drawn. Release the mouse and then wait for Photoshop to create the gradient.

4. View the gradient in the image window.

Press G to select the Gradient tool in the toolbox. Press Shift+G to cycle between the Gradient and Paint Bucket tools.

CUSTOMIZING A GRADIENT

Gradients can add soothing colors to an image, or bring a photographic composition together by sharing a common color across dissimilar objects. Use the History palette to view different gradients applied to the image window, or to revert to an earlier version of the image if you don't like a gradient. Once you've created a gradient, give it a custom name, so you can identify it from the default gradient settings.

DIRECTING A GRADIENT

Customize a gradient by creating a gradient that falls in a particular direction coinciding with a pattern in the photographic image. Here's how:

1. Open an image file and select a particular area of the image to which you want to apply the gradient.
2. Select the Gradient tool from the toolbox.
3. Click and drag the Gradient tool in the image window.
4. Choose an opacity setting around 50%. View the gradient applied to the image.
5. If the colors in the gradient don't complement the picture, go to the History palette and re-apply the gradient. Click and drag the mouse in the opposite direction, or choose a different type of gradient.

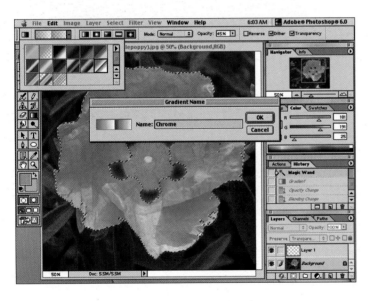

CHANGING A GRADIENT'S NAME

Create gradients for a particular image, or for certain types of images, such as a studio portrait. The following steps show you how to change the name of a gradient.

1. Click on the pop-up menu arrow in the Gradient toolbar.
2. Double-click on a gradient to view its name.
3. Alternatively, choose Rename Gradient from the pop-up menu located in the gradient pop-up window.
4. A thumbnail image of the gradient appears next to the Name text box. Type a name for the gradient. Click on OK to save your changes and return to the Gradient pop-up window.

CHAPTER 8

COMBINING IMAGES WITH LAYERS

LAYERS ARE A MAGICAL PART OF PHOTOSHOP. LAYERS ENABLE YOU TO
MAKE CHANGES TO AN IMAGE WITHOUT AFFECTING OTHER IMAGE DATA.
LAYERS ARE LIKE TRANSPARENT SHEETS OF PAPER THAT CAN BE USED TO
STORE IMAGES. ALL LAYERS SHARE THE SAME RESOLUTION, CHANNELS,
AND IMAGE MODE (SUCH AS RGB IMAGE MODE). YOU CAN MOVE, ADD,
DELETE, AND DRAW ON A LAYER WITHOUT AFFECTING THE IMAGE CONTENT
IN OTHER LAYERS IN AN IMAGE FILE.

Any image file you open in Photoshop is created in a background layer. As layers are added to the image file, you can turn any layer on or off from the Layers palette, but all active layers (marked as visible in the Layers palette) are always viewable in the image window. Image objects that are copied or pasted from another image window or application are created in a new layer. As you complete an image in Photoshop, you can merge selected layers or flatten all layers into one.

You view, edit, and delete layers from the Layers palette; many of the commands located in the Layers palette can also be found in the Layers menu. This chapter covers layer basics. See Chapter 11, "Experimenting with Layers," for more advanced layer topics.

 To use layers, you must save a file as a Photoshop document.

WORKING WITH THE LAYERS PALETTE

Any layers created for an image file can be viewed, hidden, copied, merged, locked, edited, or deleted from the Layers palette. When you add a layer to an image file, it appears as the top-most layer in the palette window. However, you can click and drag layers to reorganize them in the Layers palette. With Photoshop 6, you can create *layer sets* to group specific layer settings with a selected set of layers.

THE BACKGROUND LAYER

The background layer is sort of sacred in Photoshop, but don't take my word for it. Try to find layer properties or apply a blending mode for the background layer, and you'll find that these settings are disabled in the Layers palette. You must double-click on the background layer to adjust mode and opacity settings.

The background layer is always the bottom-most layer. Its stacking order cannot be changed. However, you can copy and paste the image to another layer or image window. You can make a copy of the background layer, or copy the background to a new layer, in the Layers palette.

To add a new layer to the background layer, do the following:

1. Open an image in Photoshop.
2. Notice that the image appears in the Background layer of the Layers palette.

3. Click on the Create a New Layer icon (located beside the Trash icon) in the Layers palette.

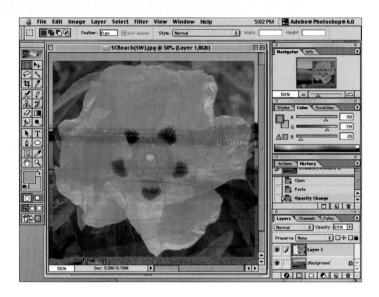

4. A new layer is created in the Layers palette.

Although Photoshop will technically let you create up to 8,000 layers, the number of layers you can create is limited to the amount of physical memory installed in your computer as well as the amount of free disk space on your hard drive.

If you have a Mac, you might need to increase the amount of memory allocated to Photoshop if you plan to work with image files that contain many layers. To do this, select the Photoshop and ImageReady icons and then choose Get Info from the File menu in Finder. Quit the Photoshop application. Choose Memory from the pop-up menu. Type a larger number into the Preferred Size text box. Double-click on the Photoshop application to start it.

Windows users can adjust this setting in the Edit, Preferences, Memory & Image Cache window. Go to Chapter 3, "Viewing Picture Information and Setting Preferences," for more information about how to adjust the memory settings for Photoshop on a Windows PC.

ICONS AND BUTTONS

Every palette window in Photoshop has a common set of icons and buttons similar to the ones you'll find in the Layers palette. For example, there's a right arrow button in the upper-right corner of every palette window. If you click on this button, you'll see a pop-up menu containing commands for that palette. Most palettes also have an icon of a document to create a new item in the palette windows trashcan for deleting items, and a couple of custom icons. The following steps show you how to use the icons and buttons in the Layers palette.

1. Open an image file. Click on the Layer, New Adjustment Layer menus and select Levels. The icon is a half-black, half-white circle. Solid Color and Gradient fill layer options appear at the top of the pop-up menu. The remaining menu commands create adjustment layers in the Layers palette.
2. A new layer is automatically created in the Layers palette, and the Levels window appears.

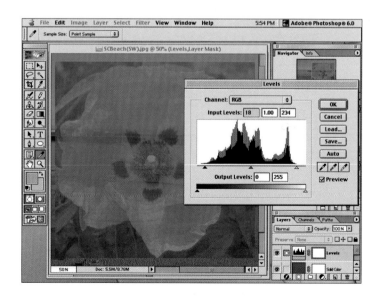

3. Adjust the levels for the image, and then click on OK. To find out more about how to adjust the controls in the Levels window, go to "Adjusting Tonal Levels" in Chapter 5, "Correcting Images."

4. Click on the folder icon at the bottom of the Layers palette to create a new layer set. Click and drag any layers into the layer set folder in the Layers palette.

5. Click on the eye icon next to a layer to toggle that layer on or off.

6. Click on the check box next to the eye icon. A link icon appears, linking the selected layer with the layer below it.

7. If a layer contains a channel or mask, a dark square with a white circle appears in the right check box.

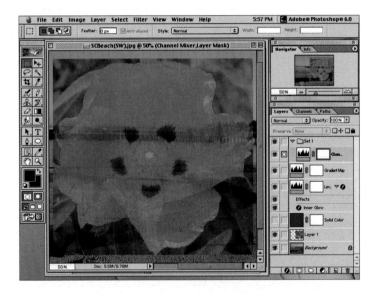

Right-click or Ctrl-click in any layer to view a contextual pop-up menu for the selected layer.

Lock transparent, image, position, or all pixels in a layer by selecting one of the corresponding Lock check boxes located at the top of the Layers palette.

LAYERS AND LAYER SETS

All the functions handled by icons and buttons accessible from the Layers palette are also available in the Layer menu. Choose from 6 ways to create a new layer, 3 types of fill layers, or 11 kinds of adjustment layers. Grayed-out items in the Layer menu indicate that the option is not available for the currently selected layer. The following sections explain the visual elements of a layer and layer set.

WHAT'S IN A LAYER?

Considering all the kinds of layers you can work with in Photoshop, it's surprising, and a little relieving, to find that most layers contain similar characteristics. You can create, edit, or delete a layer by choosing one of the many commands in the Layer menu. Each layer in the Layers palette has its own layer properties. Layer Properties enable you to give each layer a name and color. You can also assign a blending mode, opacity setting or lock transparency, image, position, or all layer properties for the selected layer.

Blending modes consist of a base color (from the selected layer), blend color (from the layer below it), and the result color (the blended result appears in the image window). Blending modes only affect the layer directly below the selected layer. If there's no image below the selected layer, changing blending modes won't produce any visible change to the selected layer. Choose from Normal, Dissolve, Multiply, Screen, Overlay, Soft Light, Hard Light, Color Dodge, Color Burn, Darken, Lighten, Difference, Exclusion, Hue, Saturation, Color, or Luminosity blending modes.

The following list contains a brief description of each blending mode. You will find some or all of these blending modes in other command windows, such as the Apply Image or Calculations windows. You can also apply a blending mode to a tool by choosing the mode menu from the options bar for the selected tool.

❋ **Normal.** This is the default mode of a layer.

❋ **Dissolve.** Randomly replaces blend colors with base colors to create result colors.

❋ **Multiply.** Multiplies the base color with the blend color, usually resulting in a darker color.

❋ **Screen.** Multiplies the inverse of the blend and base colors, usually resulting in a lighter color.

❋ **Overlay.** Screens and mixes the base and blend colors and multiplies them to show the lightness or darkness of the original color.

❋ **Soft Light.** Depending on the blend color (dodges or burns depending on whether the blend color is lighter or darker than 50%gray), will lighten or darken resulting colors.

❋ **Hard Light.** Depending on the blend color (screens or multiplies depending on whether the blend color is lighter or darker than 50%gray), will lighten or darken resulting colors.

❋ **Color Dodge.** Brightens the base color to reflect the blend color. No change occurs if you try to blend with black.

❋ **Color Burn.** Darkens the base color to reflect the blend color. No change occurs if you try to blend with white.

❋ **Darken.** Selects the base or blend color (the darker of the two colors) as the result color.

❋ **Lighten.** Selects the base or blend color (the lighter of the two colors) as the result color.

❋ **Difference.** Subtracts either the base from the blend color or vice versa, depending on which has the higher brightness value. Blending with white inverts the base colors. No change occurs if you blend with black.

❋ **Exclusion.** Creates result colors similar to difference mode, but with lower contrast.

❋ **Hue.** Combines the luminance and saturation of the base color with the hue of the blend color.

❋ **Saturation.** Combines the luminance and hue of the base color with the saturation of the blend color.

❋ **Color.** Uses the luminance of the base color and the hue and saturation of the blend color to create the result color.

❋ **Luminosity.** Combines the hue and saturation of the base color with the luminance of the blend color creating an inverse of the Color blending mode.

Choose Layer Styles from the Layer menu to customize a layer's blending options with the layer below it or add a layer effect. Combine two or more layers by choosing one of the Merge commands from the Layer menu. The following steps provide a brief overview of the layer settings in the Layers palette, as well as the Layer menu commands.

1. Open an image file. Select a layer in the Layers palette. The blending mode and opacity setting appears at the top of the Layers palette. Click on a layer to view its blending mode and opacity settings.

2. Click on the pop-up menu to view the opacity setting, or drag the slider to select a new setting. The lower the opacity level, the more transparent the selected layer becomes. Choose the lock settings by clicking on a check box. Lock the transparency, image, or position by clicking on one of the first three check boxes, or click on the right-most check box to lock all layer properties.

3. Choose Save from the File menu. Choose Photoshop as the file format. Select the Layers check box to save all the layer information with the file.

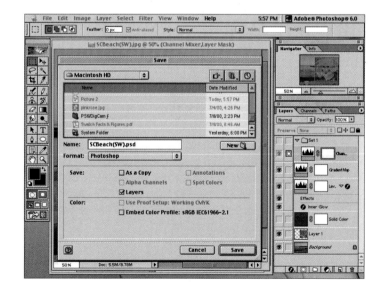

4. Access the New Fill Layer or New Adjustment Layer commands from the Layer menu. These commands create editable layers in the Layers palette.

5. There are two kinds of layers: regular layers and adjustment layers. Both types have layer style settings, which you can view by clicking on the F button in the Layers palette, or by opening the Layer menu, choosing Layer Style, and selecting one of the options.

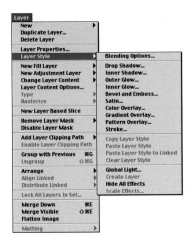

6. Select a layer and choose Group with Previous from the Layer menu to organize layers within the Layers palette. Alternatively, create a layer set, or click on the middle column to link layers together.

 Access the Layer Style and Fill or Adjustment Layer commands from the icons at the bottom of the Layers palette. The Layer Style icon contains an italicized *F* in the middle of a black circle. The Fill or Adjustment Layer icon is a circle with the top half filled with black and the bottom half with white. Click and hold down either icon to view its pop-up menu commands.

 Double-click on a layer in the Layers palette to view the Layer Style window. You can set styles, opacity, and blending modes from this window.

LAYER MASKS

Adjustment and regular layers can contain layer masks in the Layers palette. Layer masks can hide or show specific pixels in a layer or layer set. If a layer contains a layer mask, a layer mask icon will appear beside the eye icon of that layer in the Layers palette.

You can apply effects to the layer mask without affecting the pixels in that layer. Apply the mask by clicking between the thumbnail and mask icons in a layer (a Link icon appears). Click on the mask layer, and then click on the Trash icon to remove a layer mask.

To create a layer mask, select all or part of an image in a layer. Then click on the Add a Mask icon (gray rectangle with a white circle in the middle) in the Layers palette to create a layer mask in the selected layer. Layer masks can be saved along with any layers in the Photoshop file format. For more information about layer masks, see Chapter 11, "Experimenting with Layers."

LAYER MATTES

If a layer contains a masked image, use the Matte commands in the Layer menu to define how the edges of the image are combined with the image from another layer. The term *matte* reminds me of all the cool-looking matte paintings George Lucas used to create the *Star Wars* movies. Matte paintings showed futuristic cities, with space ships or live action scenes blue-screened into them. Photoshop mattes have many characteristics similar to a mask.

Choose between Defringe, Remove Black Matte, and Remove White Matte when moving or pasting one image into another. Photoshop anti-aliases the edges of the image, blending it into the rest of the image. For more information on how to use the Matte command, see Chapter 12, "Creating Custom Masks."

WHAT'S IN A LAYER SET?

A layer set is a folder exclusive to the Layers palette that can be used to store layers. Click and drag any layer except the background layer into a layer set to add that layer to it. Because a layer set is not an image, you can't apply any effects or edit this kind of layer. However, you can adjust a layer set's opacity level, blending mode, and whether the red, green, or blue channels appear in the image window. Choose Layer Set Properties to change the name of a layer set, assign a color label to it, or to determine the color channels you want to use. Like regular layers, layers stored in a layer set are ordered so that the bottom layer in the set is affected by any layers above it. The following steps show you how to create a layer set.

1. Open an image file. Click on the folder icon in the Layers palette, or open the Layer menu, choose New, and select Layer Set.
2. A folder icon appears in the Layers palette. Click on the triangle to collapse or expand the contents of the layer set folder.
3. Click and drag a layer to the folder icon to add it to the set. Drag an item away from the folder to remove it from a set.

A Photoshop file storing layers and channels can easily occupy 20MB of hard drive space. On a PC, right-click on the My Computer icon to find out how much disk space is available. On a Mac, view the amount of available space in a Finder window.

USING ADJUSTMENT AND FILL LAYERS

Create layers to experiment with color correction and effects for a single image, or with multiple images you want to merge into one picture. Adjustment layers enable you to toggle specific level, color, and filter settings in a particular layer. Create a solid color or gradient fill layer to enhance the colors in a picture.

CORRECTING COLORS

Adjustment layers enable you to place adjustable levels, curves, color balance, brightness/contrast, hue/saturation, selective color, channel mixer, gradient map, invert, threshold, and posterize settings within separate layers. Make small adjustments to a tint or hue of a picture by adding a fill layer to an image. Try different level settings, or turn on different combinations of adjustment layers to tweak a picture until it looks just right.

ADJUSTMENT LAYERS

Add an adjustment layer to an image to actively edit color and level settings for that image. Click on the eye icon to turn any adjustment layer on or off. If you decide you don't want to use the adjustment layer, delete it by dragging it to the Trash icon in the Layers palette. The following steps show you how to add an adjustment layer to an image layer.

1. Open an image file containing one or more layers. Select a new adjustment layer from the new Adjustment Layer menu in the Layer menu.
2. Click on OK to create the new layer.

3. View the adjustment layer settings. Check the Preview check box to view any changes you make in the image window.

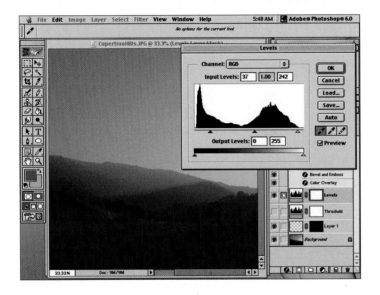

4. When you're ready to save your changes, click on OK.

COLOR LAYERS

Enhance photos by adding semi-transparent layers of colors. Make a blue sky bluer, or a sunset rosier, by adding a fill layer to an image. For a similar effect, add a color gradient layer to add color more dynamically across an image. The following steps show you how to add a gradient fill layer.

1. Open an image file. Open the Layer menu, choose New Fill Layer, and select Gradient.
2. Click on OK to create the new layer.

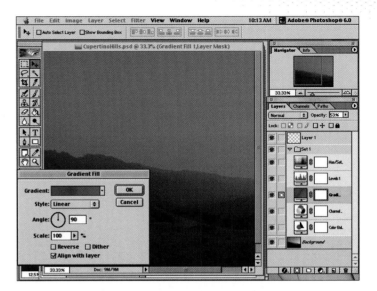

3. Click on the gradient colors to view the settings for the gradient, or choose a new gradient.
4. Click on OK in the Gradient Editor window.
5. Click on OK in the Gradient Fill window.
6. Adjust the opacity in the Layers palette by clicking and dragging the slider control.

 Gradient and fill layers work best if you have a picture with a neutral background like a white wall or blue sky. Add several fill layers to find the best combination of colors for the image you're working with.

ADJUSTING LEVELS

Set the highlight and shadow settings for an image by adjusting the sliders in the Levels window. The Levels window displays a histogram of the image or image selection. Adjust the dark, light, and mid-range points for the image using an adjustment layer. The following steps show you how to use the Levels and Variations commands to adjust the colors in an image.

Edit levels or other adjustment layer settings by selecting the adjustment layer, and then choosing Change Layer Content from the Layer menu.

1. Open an image file. Choose Levels from the New Adjustment Layer menu.
2. Move the left and right sliders to the edges of the histogram. Hold down the Alt/Option key while dragging the sliders to enter the threshold mode. View the darkest or lightest parts of an image while dragging the dark or light slider controls.

3. Open the Image menu, select Adjust, and choose Variations.
4. Choose a radio button: Shadows, Midtones, Highlights, or Saturation. Then click on one or more of the thumbnail images to change the colors of the image, using the Current Pick thumbnail image to view the results of your selections.

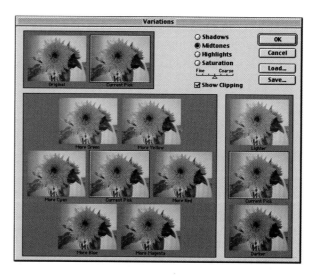

5. Lighten or darken an image by clicking on the Lighter or Darker image on the right side of the window.
6. Select Brightness/Contrast from the New Adjustment Layer menu, or from the pop-up menu in the Layers palette.
7. Click and drag the Brightness or Contrast settings and preview the changes in the image window. Click on OK to save the changes.

MERGING LAYERS

Photoshop gives you the flexibility of combining all layers or layer sets into one single layer, or selectively combining two or more layers or a layer set into one layer. Although I don't cover this in my book, you can also merge layers in a linked group, or into a clipping group. As you complete a layer or layer set, you can merge the partial image together into one layer, or flatten the image into the background layer.

FLATTENING ALL LAYERS

Because most image formats don't preserve layers created by Photoshop, there will come a time when you want to save a JPEG image, and Photoshop won't let you save it until you flatten all the layers. The Flatten Layers command merges all layers into the background layer. Use the Flatten Layer command to finalize all layer edits and remove any layers from the image file. If you plan to continue working on an image, your best bet is to save it as a Photoshop file before performing the following steps.

 If a layer is hidden, its changes won't appear in the final background layer.

1. Open an image file containing one or more layers. Open the Layer menu and choose Flatten Image. Whether you have one layer or 800, the Flatten Image command will combine all layers into the background image.

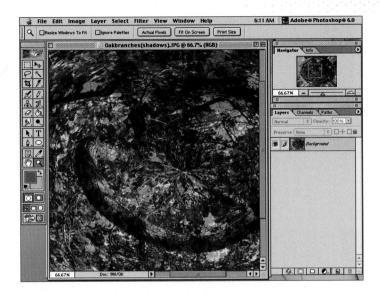

2. Notice that there is now only one layer, the background layer, in the Layers palette.

 Make a mistake? Press Ctrl/Command+Z to undo the Flatten Layers command. Alternatively, choose a previous state in the History panel.

MERGING SELECTED LAYERS

You might have already discovered you can select only one layer at a time in the Layers palette. How then, is it possible to merge two or more layers together without flattening the whole image? One way is to use the Merge Down command in the Layers menu. It merges the selected layer with the layer below it in the Layers palette. To merge two layers, select the layer above the one you want to merge it with, and then choose the Layer, Merge Down menu command.

A better way to finalize layers of a picture is to use layer sets, or group layers together as parts of an image are completed. Select the layer set (which, by the way, must contain at least one layer) in the Layers palette, and then choose Merge Layer Set from the Layer menu. The layer set icon is replaced by a layer icon in the Layers palette.

The most precise way to merge layers is to use the eye icon in the Layers palette and the Merge Visible menu command in the Layer menu. Here's how:

1. Open an image file containing one or more layers. Click on the eye icon and make a layer viewable if you want to merge it with another layer. Hide any layers you don't want to merge.

2. Choose Merge Visible from the Layer menu.

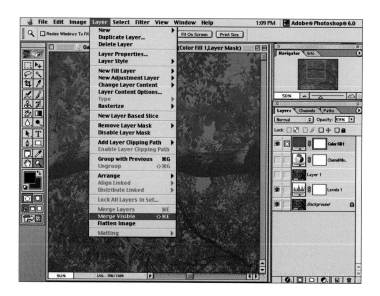

3. The selected layers are merged with the background layer, but the hidden layers remain in the Layers palette.

4. Select an existing layer, or add new layers and continue to work on the image.

 Merge a layer with the viewable layer directly below it by choosing Merge Down (which becomes Merge Layers if you select a layer) from the Layer menu.

CHAPTER 9

CUSTOMIZING IMAGES WITH MASKS

A BASIC MASK IN PHOTOSHOP FUNCTIONS SIMILARLY TO A CUTOUT MASK IN THE REAL WORLD. THE CUT OUT AREAS CAN BE ISOLATED AND EDITED IN THE LAYER BELOW THE MASK, BUT ANY AREA COVERED BY THE MASK IS PROTECTED FROM BEING EDITED. A SIMPLE MASK IS CREATED WHENEVER YOU USE A SELECTION TOOL. THE AREA SELECTED CAN BE EDITED, BUT AREAS OUTSIDE THE SELECTION ARE PROTECTED AND CANNOT BE EDITED. THIS CHAPTER CONTAINS SEVERAL SETS OF STEPS THAT SHOW YOU HOW TO CREATE A MASK IN ONE IMAGE WINDOW, THEN MOVE IT TO A SECOND IMAGE WINDOW.

DEFINING A MASK

There are several kinds of masks you can create in Photoshop. The fastest way to create a mask is with the Quick Mask tool. However, alpha channel and layer masks provide the most flexibility. Layer masks are masks created in a specific layer. Channel masks, including alpha channel masks, are the most permanent and dynamic kinds of masks you can create. Each image can have up to 24 alpha channels.

An alpha channel, which contains 8 bits, or 256 shades of gray, defines the transparency information of an RGB image. An RGB image is a 32-bit image made up of red, green, and blue channels, or 24 bits of color information. In Photoshop an alpha channel is used to store a channel mask.

Like alpha channels, each layer can have its own 8-bit mask, called a *layer mask*. All masks are bitmap graphics, except for a Layer Clipping. A Layer Clipping is a sharp-edged vector graphic mask that can be applied to an image layer. You must use a Shape tool from the toolbox to create a Layer Clipping. To find out how to create a layer clipping, see Chapter 11, "Experimenting with Layers."

To create an alpha channel or layer mask, use a selection tool to define the mask. The layer is visible in the white area of the mask, and hidden behind any black areas of the mask. When you first create a layer mask, it is linked to the image in the selected layer. Click on that link icon to turn the layer mask on or off in the layer.

SELECTING A CHANNEL

When you create an image mask, you can use a particular channel to help isolate the image you want to use to create a mask. You then use a selection tool to select the mask before switching back to full-color mode. Having selected the part of the image you want to use as the mask, you can drag it to another image window and create a whole new picture, or remove it from the existing picture. The following steps show you how to duplicate a channel in the Channels palette as the first step toward creating a channel-based mask.

1. Open an image and select the Channels palette.

2. Press Ctrl/Command+1, +2, or +3 to view the red, green, or blue channel for the image.

3. Select the channel that best isolates the part of the image you want to work with.

4. Click and drag the channel to the Create New Channel icon (which looks like a document icon) at the bottom of the Channels palette.

5. A copy of the channel is created in the Channels palette. The next set of steps show you how to use a selection tool to define the mask in the image window.

 If an image looks more or less the same across all channels, you might want to create a copy of the image in its own layer and adjust the levels so that the edges of the area you want to edit stand out a little more. Then pick a channel you want to use to create the mask.

 To view the mask against the RGB image, select the mask using the Magic Wand tool. Press Command/Ctrl+~ to switch from the alpha channel view to the RGB channel view. The alpha channel only contains the transparency information of the image. To move the colors for the image, you also need to select the red, green, and blue information.

PREPARING A CHANNEL MASK

After you've created a copy of a channel, you can use filters, effects, and drawing tools to turn it into a channel mask. Before a mask can be created, the edges of the mask must be clearly visible. Follow these steps:

1. Open the Filter menu, choose Other, and select the High Pass filter.
2. Adjust the radius of the pixels to see whether the edges of the image mask are any easier to see.

3. Choose Levels from the Image menu and move the sliders to the edges of the alpha channel's histogram edges.

4. Now the edges of the mask are defined. You can use the Eraser and Drawing tools to create more detailed mask edges and complete the mask.

 An alternative to using masks to merge two images is to prepare the images, and then use layers to merge them. See Chapter 11, "Experimenting with Layers," to find out more about how to work with blending options.

MODIFYING A MASK

If the edges of the image you want to turn into a mask are clearly defined, use one of the selection tools, such as the Magic Wand or Lasso, to define a mask. Once a mask is created, you can edit it anytime you like. Ctrl/Command + click to quickly select a mask along with its channel in the Channels palette. Then press ~ to view the masked area in the image window. Edit the mask by selecting and applying a drawing tool to the image window.

You need to save a file as a Photoshop file to preserve layers, channels, and masks so you can edit any of these elements later. If you flatten and save an image in something other than Photoshop format, any layers, masks, or channels are permanently lost.

SELECTING THE MASK

Selecting part of an image that you want to convert to a mask can be one of the most challenging things you do in Photoshop. The Lasso tool enables you to define a freeform selection area. Wherever you drag the mouse in the image window, the Lasso tool defines it as part of the selection area. This kind of selection tool can be helpful if you want to select a uniquely shaped image. The following steps show you how to define a mask using the Lasso tool.

 1. Pick a selection tool from the toolbox. In this example, I've chosen the Lasso tool.

2. Click and drag the selection tool in the image window to select the masked or unmasked area.

3. Choose Save from the File menu.

4. Type a name for the picture, and choose a file format that supports saving layers and channels, such as the Photoshop file format. Check the Layers and Alpha Channels check boxes. Click on the Save button to save the file.

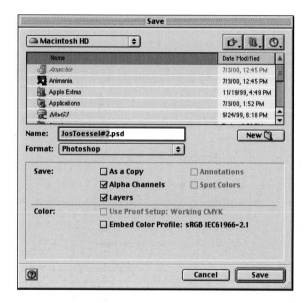

5. Use the Levels and Brightness/Contrast commands in the Image menu to darken the masked area. Use the selection tool to delete any parts of the image you don't want to include in the mask. Normally you'd want the masked area to be white, which represents the editable area of a mask. Since the area I want to mask primarily consists of dark colors, I'll use the commands in the Image menu to darken the mask to black. Then apply the Invert command in the following section.

 Use the Paint Bucket or the Erase tool to change image pixels to a solid black or white color.

 If the image has clear edges, you can try using the Magnetic Lasso tool to have it automatically select the edges of an image. Click once on the edge of the image you want to select, and then move the cursor slowly around the image. The Magnetic Lasso tool wraps its line around the image. Double-click on the starting point of the selection to close the lasso.

INVERTING A MASK

Masks usually hide areas covered in black, and display areas covered in white. However, sometimes it is easier to create a mask using the inverse colors. For example, if the image you want to mask contains extreme light and dark areas, it might be easier to select the areas around it and use a tool such as the Levels command to fade the background to white or black. Select the all-black or all-white background. Then use the Invert command to swap black pixels with white pixels. You can also use the Invert command to protect the pixels in the masked area, as shown in the following steps.

1. Open an image file that contains a channel mask. Click on the mask in the Channels palette and drag it over the document icon located at the bottom of the Channels palette. This first step is optional, you can edit the channel directly if you like. However, I've chosen to work on a copy of the channel mask to show the original and inverted masks side by side in the Channels palette.

 2. Select the Magic Wand tool and click inside the black area of the image to select the masked area in the image window.

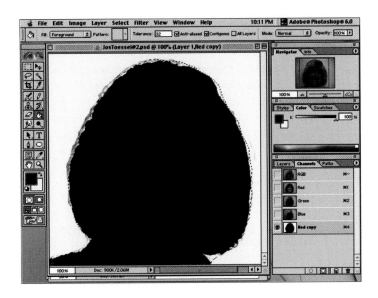

3. Choose Invert from the Image, Adjust menus.
4. View the masked image.

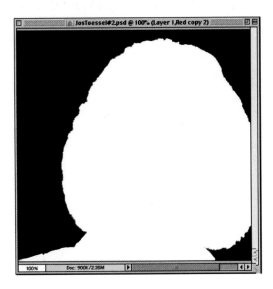

5. Press Command/Ctrl+~ to view the selected area with the full-color image in the image window.

APPLYING THE MASK

Now that you've created a mask, you can move the full-color masked image to a new image window. Here's how:

1. Using the image from the previous task, Ctrl/Command+click on the channel mask in the Channels palette to select the mask and its channel. If you click on the channel containing the mask, you can select the mask by using the Magic Wand tool to select the white area of the mask. Press Command/Ctrl+~ to view the full-color masked image.

2. Holding the Ctrl/Command key, click and drag the full-color image to a second image window.

3. The masked image appears in the second image window.

CREATING A QUICK MASK

Creating a layer or channel mask can take quite a bit of time. The fastest way to create a mask is to use one of the selection tools combined with the Quick Mask button, which is conveniently located in the toolbox. It's the button containing an icon of a gray rectangle with a white circle in its center. The Standard Mode button is located next to it. Use these buttons to hide or show a quick masked image.

DEFINING THE MASK

A quick mask is created in the same way as any other mask. First you must pick a selection tool. Then you have to select part of the image you want to turn into a mask. Here's how:

1. Choose a selection tool and use it to select the part of the image you want to mask. In this example, I chose the Lasso tool.

2. Click on the Channels palette and select a channel that highlights the image's edges. You can use the channels to see if the selected area correctly matches the mask you want to create.

3. Click on the Quick Mask button. Its icon is a white circle surrounded by a gray rectangle.

4. A pink hue covers the unmasked area of the image, and a Quick Mask layer appears in the Channels palette.

 Consider resizing your image so that it scales to the image it is being moved to. You can also resize it along with the rest of the image, after the mask is created. For more information about how to change a file's size, see the section "Viewing a File's Size," in Chapter 3, "Viewing Picture Information and Setting Preferences."

EDITING THE MASK

Once the mask is created, use white or black to edit the mask or unmasked parts of the image. You can use the Paint Bucket, Erase, or drawing tools to create a clearer mask edge. The following steps show you how to use the Paintbrush tool to edit a quick mask.

1. Make sure that the image is in Quick Mask mode (the Quick Mask button should be selected in the toolbox).

2. Click on the Pen, Paintbrush, or Pencil tool to choose the tool you want to use to edit the mask. In this example, I chose the Paintbrush tool.

3. Click on the arrow icon in the color well to toggle the foreground color. Use white to define the masked area. Click on the Zoom tool (Z) to magnify the edges of the mask. Use black to define the unmasked area.

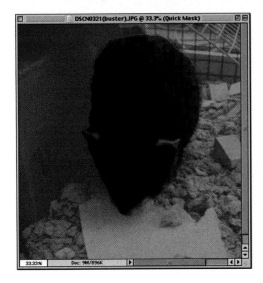

4. Hide the other channels by clicking on the eye icon in the Channels palette.

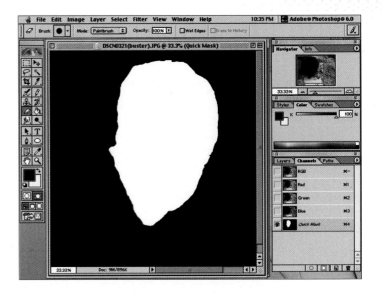

5. View the mask in the image window.

 Although all images are edited in RGB mode, you might find that one picture is clearer than the one it is moving to. If you plan to combine images with a mask, check the resolution and dimensions of the image file before combining the images.

MOVING THE MASK

Cleaning up a mask can be a tedious process, especially when you have a lot of rough edges in the original image. Once the mask is completed, you can move the masked image to another image file. Moving a mask to another image is relatively straightforward and simple. It's basically a drag-and-drop process.

1. Select the masked image in Quick Mask mode. I used the Magic Wand tool to select the image in Quick Mask mode, and then switched to full-color mode by pressing Ctrl/Command+~.

2. Hold down the Ctrl/Command key and drag the masked image to the second image window.

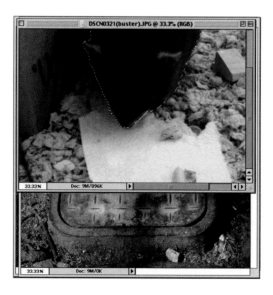

3. If the image is fairly large, you might need to wait for Photoshop to process the masked image before it appears in the second image window.
4. View the masked image in the new image window.

5. Select the Layers palette. The masked image is added to a new layer in the second image window.

WORKING WITH THE FINAL IMAGE

Continue to edit the mask after moving it to another image window. The following steps show you how to work with the masked image after it has been moved to another image window. First you adjust the mask in the image window, and then create a channel mask.

1. Ctrl/Command+click on the layer containing the full-color masked image in the Layers palette. This key combination selects the masked image in the window.

2. Click on the Select menu and choose Feather. This tool helps break up the edges of the mask so that it blends with the other image layers. Type the number of pixels you want to feather along the edge of the image. Then click on OK.

3. Select the Move tool (press V). Click and drag the masked image and place it in the window.

4. Once the image is placed where you want it, you can create a mask in the Channels palette. With the masked image selected in the image window, click on the Channels tab. Then click on the Add a Channel icon (the document icon). A new alpha channel appears in the Channels palette. Save the file as a Photoshop file if you want to preserve layer, mask, and channel settings for future editing opportunities.

CHAPTER 10

MAKING IMAGES STAND
OUT WITH CHANNELS

PHOTOSHOP CREATES COLOR INFORMATION CHANNELS WHEN IT OPENS AN
IMAGE FILE. FOR EXAMPLE, YOU CAN WORK WITH A PICTURE'S COLOR
INFORMATION IN RGB (RED, GREEN, AND BLUE) OR CMYK (CYAN, MAGENTA,
YELLOW, AND BLACK) IMAGE MODES, PLUS VIEW A COMPOSITE (COMBINED
RGB OR CMYK) CHANNEL PHOTOSHOP CREATES TO SHOW ALL CHANNELS.
BECAUSE PHOTOSHOP OPENS DIGITAL PICTURES IN RGB FORMAT, THIS
BOOK FOCUSES ON RGB RATHER THAN CMYK, EVEN THOUGH BOTH TYPES
OF CHANNELS WORK SIMILARLY. CMYK IMAGE MODE IS MOST COMMONLY
USED FOR PRINTING COLOR IMAGES. SOME PRINTERS AUTOMATICALLY
CONVERT RGB COLOR INFORMATION IN AN IMAGE FILE TO CMYK
INFORMATION. OTHER PRINTERS REQUIRE YOU TO CREATE YOUR OWN CMYK
IMAGE FILE IN ORDER TO PRINT. AN IMAGE FILE IN RGB COLOR MODE
CONTAINS 32 BITS OF INFORMATION, A RED, GREEN, AND BLUE CHANNEL,
AND AN 8-BIT CHANNEL (AN ALPHA CHANNEL) CONTAINING
TRANSPARENCY INFORMATION. PHOTOSHOP OPENS AN IMAGE IN THE
BACKGROUND LAYER. EACH LAYER IN PHOTOSHOP CONTAINS ITS OWN SET
OF RGB CHANNEL INFORMATION. THE CHANNELS PALETTE OF AN RGB
IMAGE DISPLAYS A RED, GREEN, AND BLUE CHANNEL, PLUS AN RGB
CHANNEL. THE RGB CHANNEL IS NOT A REAL CHANNEL LIKE THE RED,
GREEN, OR BLUE CHANNELS. PHOTOSHOP CREATES THE RGB CHANNEL TO
ENABLE YOU TO SEE THE RED, GREEN, AND BLUE CHANNELS COMBINED.

The red channel tends to show warmer, red colors. Red colors appear as white if the red channel is the only visible channel in the image window. The green channel usually highlights the elements that make a picture sharp. The blue layer tends to capture junk elements of an image, such as graininess or scratches.

Each time a layer is added to an image, another set of RGB channels is added to the image file, thus increasing its file size. Even though one set of RGB channels appears in the Channels palette, each layer can have its own color settings. For example, you can have a grayscale image layer in the same image file that also contains a full color image. Channels can be used to create masks and to manipulate selected areas of an image to created sophisticated, great-looking, high-resolution images. This chapter contains a series of steps that show you how to work with channels to create channel masks.

WORKING WITH CHANNELS

You can create several kinds of channels in Photoshop. Red, green, and blue channels are automatically created by Photoshop when you open an image in RGB mode. An alpha channel contains 8 bits of grayscale information that can be stored as a separate channel to create a mask. A mask can be used to isolate or protect a selected area of an image. You can use spot color channels to add plates to an image if you plan to print that image with spot color inks. Each channel in an RGB image contains roughly one-third of the color data for an image.

You copy a channel by selecting it and then dragging and dropping it over the Create a New Channel button (document icon) at the bottom of the Channels palette. When you copy a channel in an RGB file, the image's file size will grow by one third. If you plan to save images with editable channel information, be prepared to have plenty of hard disk space to store these larger files. The current file size is the number on the right in the lower-left corner of the image window. The original image size appears beside the current file size.

Channels are only saved when you select Photoshop, DCS 2.0, PICT, TIFF, or Raw as the image's file format.

NAVIGATING THE CHANNELS PALETTE

You manage channels with the Channels palette. Create, split, or merge channels by choosing pop-up menu commands or by clicking on a button in the toolbar at the bottom of the palette. View a thumbnail image of each channel mask as you work. The following steps provide a brief tour of the features in the Channels palette. Here, you learn how to use keyboard shortcuts to view each channel in the image window, and create an alpha channel.

1. Open an image file. View a channel in the image window by pressing the channel's Ctrl/Command+key equivalent, which appears to the right of each channel in the Channels palette. For example, press Ctrl/Command+1 to view the red channel, Ctrl/Command+2 to view the green channel, Ctrl/Command+3 to view the blue channel, and Ctrl/Command+~ to view all three channels in the image window.

2. Use a Marquee or Magic Wand selection tool to select the part of an image you want to turn into a mask. In this example, I've chosen the Rectangular Marquee selection tool.

3. Click on the Save Selection as Channel button (gray rectangle icon with a white circle in the middle) to create an alpha channel mask in the Channels palette.

4. View the mask in the Channels palette.

5. Click on the arrow button to view a list of menu commands.
6. Choose Palette Options from the pop-up menu to determine the size of the thumbnail image that appears in the Channels palette window.

In this book, I use the terms alpha channel, alpha channel mask, channel mask, and mask synonymously. If I'm not referring to a channel mask, I'll use a specific term, such as layer mask.

CHOOSING A CHANNEL

Each channel color has unique characteristics. For example, the red channel tends to store the broadest range of contrast values, whereas the green channel tends to store more image detail information. Each channel's contents also depend on the contents of the picture. Therefore, the blue channel might hold a bunch of noise and jitter in one picture, but store more image-related data in a picture of a blue sky or screen. If you're using a channel to define a mask, view each channel separately in the image window. Then pick the channel that most clearly distinguishes the edges of the object to create a mask. The following steps show you how to hide and show channels from the Channels palette.

1. Open an image file. Hide the red channel in the Channels palette by clicking on the eye icon. (You can show or hide multiple channels by dragging the cursor through the eye icon column in the Channels palette.) If the eye icon is not visible in the Channels palette, that channel is hidden.

2. View the green and blue channels in the image window.

3. Click on the eye icon for the green channel to hide it.
4. Notice the blue channel appears as a grayscale image.

 Click on a single channel in the Channels palette to view that channel's grayscale information in the image window.

DEFINING A CHANNEL

Select one or two channels to see how channels define the image you want to edit. By comparing two channels with a single channel, you can see which colors bring together different aspects and objects in a picture. The following steps show you how to compare the contrast between channel images. The channel with the highest contrast between the image you want to mask and the rest of the picture is the channel you use to create an alpha channel mask.

1. Open an image file. Select the red and blue channels in the Channels palette. Click in the column to the left of the red channel until you see the eye icon. Repeat this step for the blue channel.
2. View the combined channels in the image window.

3. Show the red and green channels.
4. Notice how the green channel seems brighter than the blue channel in this particular image. More detail is visible, too, although no particular object stands out with any given channel.

5. Select the channel you want to use to create a mask. Click and drag it over the Create New Channel button (the document icon) in the Channels palette.
6. A copy of the selected channel appears in the Channels palette.

 If you don't see the edges of the object you want to mask in the red, green, or blue channels, try using the Channel Mixer command to combine channels together. For more information on how to use the Channel Mixer command, see Chapter 13, "Experimenting with Channel Operations."

EDITING CHANNELS

If you find a channel that can be used to create a mask, duplicate it in the Channels palette. Apply effects or adjust the tonal range in the Duplicate channel to make the mask edges as white or black as possible. When you can identify the edges of the image you want to turn into a mask, you can turn the alpha channel into a channel mask. The following sections show you how to take the image in a channel and change it into an image mask.

CLEANING UP A CHANNEL

Channels aren't really dirty by nature. A mask is defined by black and white colors to determine which parts of an image are visible or hidden. When I use the phrase "cleaning up a channel," I'm referring to the process of defining the masked image in a channel. This can be accomplished by applying a combination of drawing tools, filter effects, and level adjustments to the duplicate channel created in the previous section. If you think you're spending too much time editing a channel, you might want to give that channel a break, or try using a different process to create that mask. Sometimes it can be faster to use the Magnetic Lasso tool combined with the Delete key to create a mask.

 The Paint Bucket, Eraser, and Paint Brush tools can be used to effectively clean up a mask. Alternatively, you can use any of the selection tools to remove larger chunks or odd-shaped pieces of an image.

The following steps show you how to use the Magic Wand tool to define the masked and unmasked areas of a channel.

1. Open an image file that contains a channel mask. Pick a selection tool from the toolbox, for example, the Magic Wand. Select the layer associated with the channel mask from the Layers palette. Use the selection tool to select the areas you do not want masked. Choose Adjust Levels from the Image menu to adjust the tonal range of the image. Use the Levels settings to change the selected areas that do not need to be in the mask to black or dark colors.
2. Press Ctrl/Command+~. This key combination brings the RGB channels into the image window. Compare the mask to the full-color image to see whether all the elements you want in the mask are in white. Press Ctrl/Command+~ to view the masked image in the image window.
3. Choose Filter, select Other, and choose High Pass to access the High Pass filter. Adjust the settings in the filter's window to increase the light and dark contrast in the channel. Click OK to apply the effect to the image window.

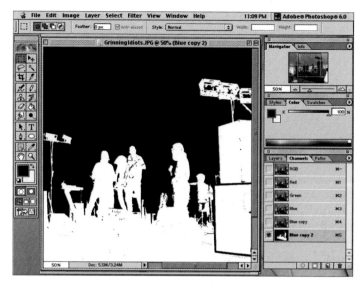

4. Choose the Magic Wand tool.
5. Click in the white area of the image to select the image mask. Click on the Save Selection as Channel button (the document icon) in the Channels palette to create a mask.

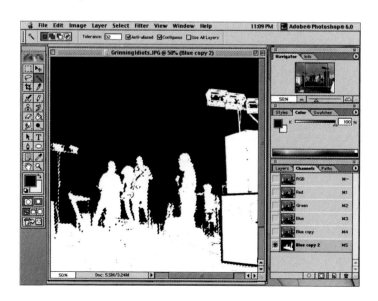

ADJUSTING COLORS ACROSS IMAGES

Although you can edit the masked image after moving it to a new image window, you can also apply any number of filters or color changes while the mask is selected, before moving it to another image window. When an image mask is created, the black and white mask is mapped to a full-color RGB image. The composite image of the black and white mask is the newly masked full-color image. You can use the Ctrl/Command+~ keys to toggle between these composite images. Because alpha channels consist of black, white, and 254 shades of gray, you can use a command such as Feather to smooth the edges of a mask, or matting to blend the mask into another image. Here's how:

1. Press Ctrl/Command+~ to view the masked area in the composite, or full-color layer.
2. Click on Select and choose the Feather command. Type a number to determine the range of pixels feathered on the masked image. Then click on OK.
3. Apply any filters or color changes directly to the image.

4. Ctrl/Command+click and drag the image to another image window.
5. Use the Move tool to position the mask in the new image window.
6. Ctrl/Command+click on the new layer to reselect the masked area. Click on the Channels palette tab and then click on the Add a Channel button to create a masked channel.
7. Click on the Layer menu, select Matting, and choose Defringe. The masked image edges should blend more smoothly into the background image.

CLAMPING OR CHOKING A CHANNEL

Masked images aren't always as easy to convert to straight black and white images. In some cases you might have a partially gray area of an image. On the other hand, part of an image might have a hard edge, or bright spot. Clamping and choking a channel is the process of applying the other 254 shades of gray in a channel in order to overcome the limitations of what black and white can do to define a mask.

CLAMPING AN IMAGE

Adjust the bright and dark areas of an image with the Curves window by applying a clamping technique. You can adjust white and dark areas of an image to pure white or black without affecting the midtones. The following steps show you how to use the Curves tool to clamp a masked image.

1. Open an image file that contains a masked image. Select a layer in the Layers palette. Open the Layer menu, choose New Adjustment Layer, and select Choose Curves.
2. Darker colors are represented by the bottom part of the Curve line, and light or highlight colors are represented at the top of the curve.
3. Move the upper or lower portion of the curve and preview changes in the image window.
4. When you've created the desired effect, click on OK. Select the channel or its layer and view the image mask in the image window.

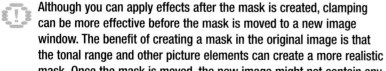

Although you can apply effects after the mask is created, clamping can be more effective before the mask is moved to a new image window. The benefit of creating a mask in the original image is that the tonal range and other picture elements can create a more realistic mask. Once the mask is moved, the new image might not contain any information to enable you to complete the missing information.

CHOKING AN IMAGE

Soften hard edges of a mask by applying a blur filter, such as a Gaussian blur. Alternatively, choking an image can also involve using filters to make a soft edge more defined. The following steps show you how to choke a channel mask.

1. Open an image file containing a channel mask. Click on the layer containing the channel mask in the Layers palette.
2. Choose an effect from the Filter menu. In this example, I've chosen Gaussian Blur. Click and drag the Hand icon in the preview window to view a specific area of the image.
3. Adjust the settings for the effect and then click on OK to apply the effect to the image window.

ADDING A CHANNEL

Combine channel masks from multiple image files to create a single, unique photographic composition. Photoshop lets you add as many channels as its memory permits. The following steps show you how to move a channel mask to another image window.

1. Open an image file that contains a channel mask. Use the Magic Wand or one of the Lasso tools to define an image mask.
2. Create a new alpha channel by clicking on the Save Selection as a Channel button (mask icon) in the Channels palette.
3. Use the Pen, or other drawing tool, combined with a black or white foreground color to add or remove pixels from the masked area. Select the channel in the Channels palette. Then pick a drawing tool, such as the Paintbrush tool (B). Click and drag the tool in the image window. A white foreground color extends the mask. A black foreground color defines the unmasked area of the image.

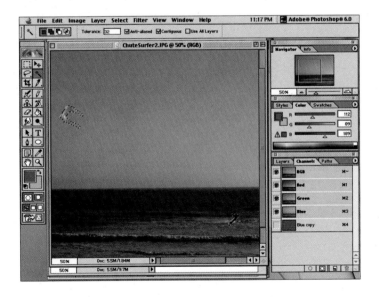

4. Press Ctrl/Command and click on the alpha channel to select the image mask in the image window. Then press Ctrl/Command+~ to show the RGB colors combined with the image mask in the image window. Ctrl/Command+click and drag the masked image into the target image window.

5. The channel is added as a new layer to the target image window.
6. Ctrl/Command+click on the image in the new layer to select the image mask. Then click on the Save Selection as a Channel icon in the Channels palette to create an alpha channel mask.
7. Click on the eye icon in the Layers palette to hide or show this image in the image window.

USING APPLY IMAGE COMMAND

Moving a channel involves a *source*, the image file where the channel was created, and a *target*, which is the image file where the channel is moved to. The process of working with source and target channels is called *channel operations*. Use the Apply Image command to pick a source and target channel with exactly the same pixel resolution to combine one or all channels of both images into one color image. The Calculations command, covered in Chapter 13, "Experimenting with Channel Operations," works similarly, but can only output a single grayscale channel, file, or selection. The Duplicate command is another channel operations command you can use in Photoshop. The following sections show you how to use the Apply Image command.

INVOKING THE APPLY IMAGE COMMAND

Open the target image files before choosing the Apply Image command. The source image must be the same size as the target image. For example, open two image files that are each 1,600×1,200 pixels. Use the Apply Image window to combine an entire image, or to combine specific channels of two images together. The following steps give you a brief tour of the Apply Image window settings.

1. Open a single image file or two or more image files that share the same dimensions. The selected image window will be the target image in the Apply Image window. In this example, I chose a single image file containing multiple layers.

2. Choose Apply Image from the Image menu.

3. Check the Preview check box to preview your changes in the image window. Choose the source image from the Source pop-up menu. If the source file is different from the target file, you will see two images appear in the image window.

4. Click on a channel from the Channel drop-down menu in the Apply Image window. Choosing red, green, or blue changes the source image to a grayscale image. Choose a blending option from the Blending drop-down menu for the target image. Choosing a blending option can add color if a single channel is selected and the source image is the same as the target image. See the following section for more details about how to apply blending modes.

5. Click on OK to save your changes and view the results in the image window.

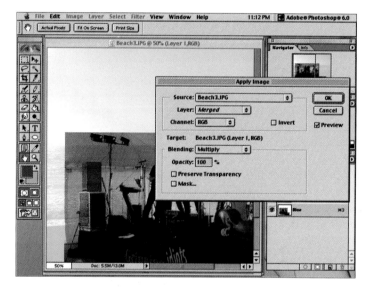

 Check the Mask check box to apply the source or target file as a mask in the image window. Select a channel from the Mask area of the Apply Image window to add an additional blend element to the picture. If the mask channel appears too light, check the Invert check box to invert the masked area.

 The Apply Image window can combine any two images, whether or not the source file has a mask.

BLENDING CHANNEL SETTINGS

You can also apply a blending mode across a single picture, two pictures, or across two layers in the Apply Image window. Many of the blending options in the Apply Image window are similar to blending options available in the Layers palette. The source image can combine all three channels or a single channel with the target image. The following steps show you how to use blending options to combine RGB channels with a mask in the same image.

1. Open a single image file or two or more image files that share the same dimensions. The front-most image window will be the target image in the Apply Image window. Open the Image menu and choose Apply Image. Select a source image from the Source drop-down menu.

2. Choose a blending mode from the Blending drop-down menu for the target. Check the Preview check box to preview your changes in the image window.

3. Type in a value below 100 in the Opacity text box if you want to make the source image somewhat transparent against the target image.

4. Select the Mask check box to apply a mask from another image file to the target image.

5. Choose a layer and channel from the Mask area of the Apply Image window to customize the mask. Preview your selections in the Image window. If you like what you see, click on OK to save your changes.

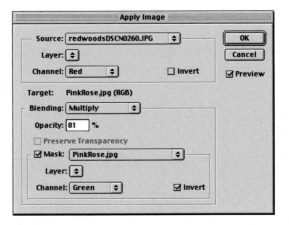

 If you choose Add or Subtract for a blending mode, two additional settings appear in the Apply Image window—Scale and Adjust. Type a value between 1 and 2 to adjust or experiment with the scale setting. Enter a number between –255 and 255 as the offset value. Preview your changes in the image window and click on OK if you want to save them.

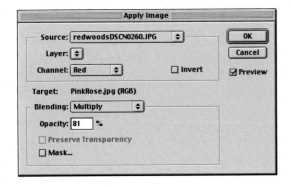

CREATING COMPLEX IMAGES

TAKING A GROUP PHOTO, OR COMPOSING A PICTURE WITH ALL THE RIGHT
ELEMENTS, CAN BE AS TOUGH AS HERDING CATS. SOMETIMES, THE PICTURE
YOU WANT TO TAKE ISN'T PHYSICALLY POSSIBLE. ALTHOUGH A PICTURE
CAN BE A GREAT COMPOSITION RIGHT OUT OF THE CAMERA, YOU CAN USE
PHOTOSHOP TO COMBINE ALL KINDS OF IMAGE ELEMENTS FROM DIFFERENT
PICTURES INTO ONE IMAGE FILE. YOU CAN ADD ONE OR DOZENS OF IMAGES
TO AN IMAGE WINDOW AS WELL AS CORRECT COLORS IN LAYER SETS OR
ACROSS LAYERS. YOU ALSO LEARN HOW TO COMBINE LAYERS, CHANNELS,
AND MASKS, AND APPLY FILTERS AND EFFECTS TO CREATE SOPHISTICATED
IMAGES AND ANIMATION.

CHAPTER 11

EXPERIMENTING
WITH LAYERS

BLEND LAYERS TOGETHER, COMBINE THEM INTO SETS, PUT THEM INTO
GROUPS, AND THEN MERGE SOME AND FLATTEN THEM ALL TO CREATE A
NEW, IMPROVED PICTURE. THERE ARE SO MANY THINGS YOU CAN DO WITH
IMAGES; THE BEST WAY TO PUT MULTI-LAYERED IMAGES TOGETHER IS TO
EXPERIMENT WITH A BUNCH OF DIFFERENT LAYER COMBINATIONS.

INTEGRATING LAYERS WITH BLENDING OPTIONS

Blend any two image layers together in Photoshop. There are three ways you can blend two layers together. Each layer in Photoshop can be modified with a Layer Style blending option. The Apply Image and Calculation commands contain even more dynamic blending options such as saving the resulting blended image as a channel or file. You can also apply blend modes to a Fill tool, a Stroke command, or a layer in the Layers palette. This section shows you how to apply layer style blending options to two image layers.

COMBINING COMPLEMENTARY IMAGES

Images have different balances of light and dark colors in addition to the range of millions of colors that make a picture what it is. When you combine two images, one with a lighter range of colors and a second image containing a darker range of colors, you can adjust blending option settings for each image or choose a layer from each image to make the two pictures appear as one. Each picture might need to undergo some preparation to make one lighter or darker in certain areas in order to make the blending of the two images more complementary. The following two sections of steps show you how to create two image layers before blending their images. The following steps show you how to add an image layer to an image file.

1. Open an image that contains a combination of darker and lighter tones.
2. If the image contains some streaks of light tones, use the Levels or Brightness and Contrast commands in the Image, Adjust menus to adjust the image to darker (or alternatively lighter) tones. To find out how to adjust the levels and brightness settings, see Chapter 5, "Correcting Images."

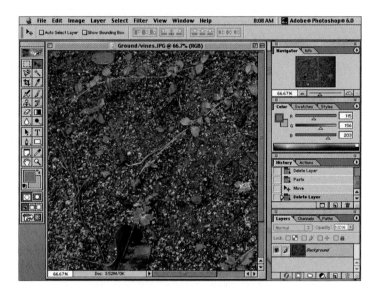

3. Open a second image that contains contrasting tones to the first image.
4. Choose a selection tool from the toolbox. In this example, I chose the Magnetic Lasso tool. Select an area of the second image, and copy and paste it into the first image. The copied image will appear in its own layer in the Layers palette of the first image. Use the Move tool (V) to position the copied image in the image window. Follow the steps in the next section to adjust the blending options between two image layers.

 If it's difficult to tell whether two images have complementary tonal qualities, try adding the second image into the first as a layer. Adjust the blending options between the two layers to see how well the images blend together. (More information about blending options is found in the following sections.) If the images don't blend together easily, try hiding the secondary image layer, and adjusting the tonal settings of the original image. Then toggle the eye icon from the secondary image on and see whether there is an improvement.

Here's a shortcut for duplicating image layers. Select an image layer in the Layers palette, then hold down the option key and click and drag the image to automatically create a copy of the image in a new layer.

APPLYING BLENDING OPTIONS

Double-click on a layer to see its Blending options and layer styles. If you have multiple layers in an image, you can adjust the opacity setting on one image layer so that the selected image blends with the image layer below it, producing a ghost effect. The lower the opacity number, the more the image blends with other layers. An opacity value of 100 means the image has no transparency.

The Blending Mode drop-down menu enables you to select a blending option that affects the image and the layer below it without changing any pixels. Advanced blending options offer another group of blending features such as selecting a particular channel to blend or knock out. Another way to blend layers is to adjust the slider settings in the Blend If area of the Layer Style window. Continuing from the previous set of steps, the following steps show you how to blend two image layers together using the Layer Style window.

1. Double-click on the newly added layer in the Layers palette. The Layer Style window opens.
2. Drag the dark or light (left or right) slider control toward the middle of the gradient bar. Notice the darker areas of the flower image disappear as the dark slider is moved to the right and vice versa for the light slider.

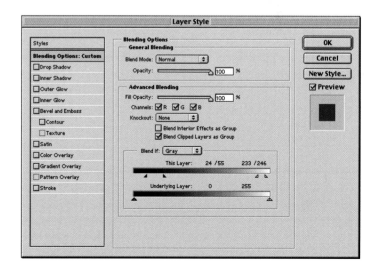

3. Hold down the Alt/Option key and drag the left or right side of the dark or light slider control (it's shaped like a triangle with a line down its middle). Photoshop blends colors in the area between the left and right sides of the slider control triangles.
4. Notice the darker shades from the image in the layer blend into the background image. Adjust the slider controls for the background image to blend dark or light areas of the background image with the selected image layer.

 To view different blend modes of a layer, select the layer. Press the Shift key combined with the plus or minus keys to change the selected blending mode for that layer in the Layers palette. Press the Ctrl/Command+Shift+an arrow key (up, down, left, or right key) to nudge an image in 10-pixel increments.

 To link two layers in the Layers palette, click on a layer you want to link. Then click on the box immediately to the left of another layer. A link icon should appear in the box, indicating that layer is linked to the previously selected layer in the Layers palette. Select a linked layer. Open the Layer, Align Linked menus, and then choose from align the top, bottom, left, or right edges, or horizontal or vertical centers to align the linked layers.

WORKING WITH LAYER SETS

Group one or several image layers, and any related effects, in a Layer Set folder. Quickly reorganize layered images and related effects by clicking and dragging Layer Set folders to a new layer position within the Layers palette window. Turn off sets of effects or layer adjustments with a click of the mouse. The series of steps in this section use layer sets and masks to create a grayscale and color image in one image window, and then move it all to a second image window.

LOCALIZING EFFECTS

Don't like the color of that shirt or dress? Want to use grayscale instead of color to emphasize a specific element in a picture? Layers are great for isolating effects in an image. Use layer sets to group an image with a set of filters or effects, or combined with a mask. In this example, I create one image mask of the person in the picture. Then create a second mask of the apron. I wanted the apron to stand out in the picture, so I added a channel mixer adjustment layer to the first mask to apply a grayscale setting. Then I added the apron mask to the first mask to create my final hybrid color and grayscale image mask. The following steps show you how to use a layer set to create a hybrid image.

1. First, create a backup of the original image. Open an image. Click and drag the background layer and drop it over the Create a New Layer button (document icon) in the Layers palette to create a copy of the background layer. Select the layer containing the copy of the background image. Use a selection tool to create an image mask in the image window. If you make a mistake, you can delete the copy layer and start over with the original image in the background layer.
2. Next, create an image mask from the selected image. Click and drag the selection tool around the area of the image you want to turn into a mask. Then click on the Save Selection as Channel button (mask button) in the Channels palette to create an alpha channel mask.
3. Click on the folder icon in the Layers palette to create a layer set. Click and drag the image layer containing the mask over the layer set folder icon. The layer containing the mask should be indented from the left compared to other layers in the Layers palette.

4. Ctrl/Command+click on the image mask in the Layers palette. This key combination selects the masked image along with its layer. Open the Layer menu, select New Adjustment Layer, and then choose Channel Mixer.

5. Check the Monochrome check box, and then click on OK. The masked image should now appear as a grayscale image. In this example. I've placed this image, along with any adjustment layers or effects for it, in the same layer set folder.

6. Create a second mask (in this example, it's the apron mask) from a subset of pixels from the first mask. Use the background layer and a selection tool to outline the image you want to mask. Then press the Save Selection as Channel button (mask icon) in the Channels palette. Place the second image mask in its own layer set folder. The following image shows the original picture in the image window. The layer set, entitled Colorized, appears in the Layers palette and contains the first mask, an adjustment layer, and the second mask (the apron mask). The copy of the background layer, along with any other layers that I deemed experimental, are located in the experiment folder in the Layers palette.

7. Because you want the apron to be in color, you can move it to the layer above the adjustment layer responsible for the grayscale effect. Click and drag the second masked image (the apron mask) to the top of the

layer set in the Layers palette window. Notice that all layers below the Channel Mixer adjustment layer in the layer set folder appear in grayscale.

8. Finally, use the Move tool (V) to select the second mask and place it over its grayscale counterpart in the first masked image. First click the layer of the second masked image to select its image layer in the Layers palette. The layer name appears in the title bar of the image window, too. Then choose the Move tool (press the letter V) from the toolbox to place the colored mask over the grayscale-masked image. View the contents of the layer set by de-selecting the eye icon for all other layers in the Layers palette. The following image shows the masked image created in the layer set folder. The checkerboard pattern indicates the transparent areas of the image where there is no image data.

 If you're not sure which layer an image belongs to, on a Mac, press the Control key and click on an image in the image window. A pop-up label appears over the image containing the name of the layer for that image. On a Windows PC, hold down the Ctrl key and right-click in the image window to see the pop-up label appear with the image's layer information.

ADDING SETS TO OTHER DOCUMENTS

Layers, including merged layers and background layers, cannot be moved from one Photoshop document (also called an image file) to another. However, you can copy and paste complete images to your heart's content. Any image pasted into an image window is created in its own new layer. Create a layer set to group all the adjustment and effect layers together for an image. Then flatten the layer set to move a partial image from one image file to another. After all the layer set is merged into a single layer, the Photoshop file size shrinks, although the numbers of pixels in the image are unchanged. The following steps show you how to merge layers and move a partial image to another image window.

1. First, merge the layers together in the first image. Make sure the eye icon is visible for the layers or layer sets you want to merge.

2. Click on a layer set in the Layers palette. Open the Layer menu and choose Merge Layer Set. The Merge Layer Set menu command only appears when a layer set is selected in the Layers palette. If a layer is selected, the menu command appears as Merge Layers, which will merge all layers together.

3. Notice that all the layers in the layer set disappear from the Layers palette.

4. Merging a layer set results in an overall smaller file size. For example, before the merge, the file in this example was 33MB. After the merge it changed to a 13MB file, similar to the size of an image containing two layers.

5. Next, select the contents of the merged layer set in the Layers palette. Ctrl/Command+click on the image layer. If you want to smooth the edges of this image, choose the Feather command from the Select menu. Then Ctrl/Command+click on the image to reselect it.

6. Now you can use the Copy and Paste commands to move the image from one image window to another. Click on the Edit menu and choose the Copy command, or press Ctrl/Command+C. Open the image file you want to move the image to. Click on the Edit menu and choose Paste.

7. The merged layer set image appears in a new image window.

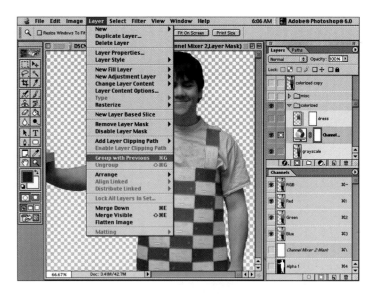

 There are several ways to retain image clarity, yet shrink the size of a file. One way is to convert an RGB image to indexed color, and then choose a GIF or JPEG file format. Use ImageReady to preview image quality and file size differences between GIF, JPEG, and PNG file formats before saving the final image.

GROUPING LAYERS IN A SET

A layer can be grouped with the layer below it. There are two ways to group layers. The most obvious is to choose the Group with Previous menu command in the Layer menu. The second method is to hold down the Alt/Option key and click on the line that separates two layers. The cursor changes to an icon made up of three circles. Click on the line between the layers to group them together. The following steps show you how to use the Group with Previous command to group two layers.

1. Open an image file that contains at least two layers. Click on the top layer in the Layers palette.
2. Choose Group with Previous from the Layer menu.

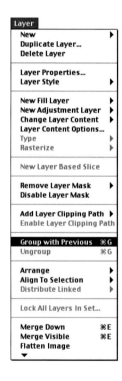

3. An arrow appears to the left of the selected layer, indicating that it is grouped with the layer below it. Any change made to the bottom layer affects the layer above it, too.

4. To ungroup the layer, select it, and then choose Ungroup from the Layer menu.

CREATING LIGHTING EFFECTS AND LAYER MASKS

The following sections show you how to create a layer mask and add layers to adjust the lighting of an image layer. To find out more about masks, see Chapter 9, "Customizing Images with Masks."

Lighting can make an image that's been added appear more or less realistic. Although it's difficult to edit the original light source in a picture, you can use the Lighting Effect filter to add an alternative light to an image, or to enhance the color of the light with a fill or gradient layer. The easiest way to experiment with light sources is to add a solid color or gradient fill layer to an image layer.

LIGHTING EFFECTS

Adjust the way an image is lit by adding a solid color fill layer, or a two- or three-color gradient layer. Apply a fill or gradient layer directly to a layer, or experiment by adding an adjustment layer that can be toggled on or off from the Layers palette. Pull image layers out of the lighting effect by dragging them to the top layers of the Layers palette, or drag them below a fill or gradient layer to see how they blend in with other fill layers. The following steps show you how to add a solid color and gradient fill layer to an image.

1. Open an image file containing image layers. Open the Layer menu, select New Fill Layer, and choose Solid Color. The color picker window appears.
2. By default, the foreground color appears in the color picker window. Click on a color in the vertical color bar. Then click on a more precise color in the left area of the color picker window. A circle appears around the selected color. The newly selected color appears to the right of the vertical color bar. Click on OK to save and select the color you've chosen.

3. The image window is filled with the color selected in the previous step. Now, you can blend the fill layer with the image layer. Select the fill layer, and then click and drag the opacity level slider control in the Layers palette to 50–70%. The fill layer color blends with the image layer or layers below it.
4. Hide the fill layer in the Layers palette by clicking on the fill layer's eye icon. To create a gradient fill layer, open the Layer menu, select New Fill Layer, and choose Gradient. Type a name for the gradient and then click on OK.
5. Click on the Gradient pop-up menu to select a gradient. Click on the gradient colors to open the Gradient Editor window. If you want to enhance the light in the picture, choose orange, yellow, or red colors. Make any changes to the gradient, then click OK. Click and drag the gradient tool in the image window to define the gradient. Release the mouse and then wait for Photoshop to create the gradient in the image window. To find out more about how to use the Gradient Editor window settings, see Chapter 7, "Creating Objects and Gradients."
6. Click and drag the slider control to the left to lower the gradient's opacity level. The gradient layer color blends with the image layers below it.
7. De-select the eye icon from the gradient fill layer in the Layers palette. Click on the eye icon for the solid fill layer. Compare the light effect from the fill layers by turning each fill layer on or off.

Add a more focused light source to a picture by choosing the Lighting effect from the Render submenu of the Filter menu.

 Create complex lighting effects by adding solid and gradient fill layers to a picture. Localize fill layers by creating a mask and alpha channel.

CREATING LAYER MASKS

Layer masks can be used to control a masked area within a layer or layer set. The position of the layer mask in the Layers palette affects how other fill or gradient layers interact with it. Layer clipping (vector) paths and layer (raster) masks are the two types of layer masks that can be created in Photoshop. Both appear in the Layers palette to the right of the thumbnail picture of an image layer. The following steps show you how to create layer masks.

1. Open an image file. Click on the Create a New Layer button (document icon). Copy and paste the background image into the new layer. To copy and paste the background image, first click on the background layer, select the image (press Ctrl/Command+A), then copy it (press Ctrl/Command+C). Click on the new layer and then press Ctrl/Command+V. The background image should appear in the new layer in the Layers palette. Hide the background image if you only want to view the new image layer in the image window.
2. Click on the new image layer. Use a selection tool to select part of the image in the image window. In this example, I chose the Rectangular Marquee tool (M).
3. Open the Layer menu, choose Add Layer Mask, and select Reveal Selection.

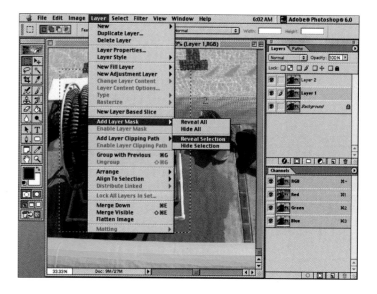

4. The layer mask appears in the Layers palette. Hide the background image to view the masked image in the image window. The areas surrounding the masked image become transparent (the gray and white checkboard in the image window).
5. Click on the background image layer. If it was hidden, it becomes visible again. Choose a selection tool and select a different part of the image window. Create a new layer (as you did in step 1) and copy and paste the image from the background layer to the new layer. Ctrl/Command+click on the image in the new layer. This key combination selects the partial image stored in the layer. Click on the Add a Mask button to create a second layer mask.

6. Select the Move tool (V) and drag the masked image to a new location in the image window.

7. Note how the mask appears with a link icon beside it in the Layers palette. As you move the masked image, the mask moves along with it. Click on the link icon to disable the mask from its image layer.

USING ADJUSTMENT LAYERS AND LAYER STYLES

Many of the commands found in the Image, Adjust menu are accessible as adjustment layers from the Layer menu. Adjustment layers let you experiment with an image without making any permanent changes to the original image. You can adjust levels, curves, color balance, brightness and contrast, hue/saturation, and gradient map. Invert, posterize, and view the threshold image as an adjustment layer, too.

Although most effects from the Filter menu are not available as layer styles, it is possible to apply a small set of effects to a layer without changing any of the original pixels. You can add a drop shadow, inner shadow, outer glow, inner glow, bevel and emboss, satin, color or gradient overlay, and stroke or global light effect to an image layer. These effects can be turned on or off with the eye icon in the Layers palette. Combine multiple effects with adjustment layers to create the image you like best. The following sections show you how to add effects to image layers and preserve layers when you save an image file.

WORKING WITH LEVELS AND LAYERS

Depending on how you want to compose a picture, you might want a specific image mask to blend in with another layer, the background, or another global image. Add adjustment layers to preview and experiment with different level, curve, color, and other image settings. Name each adjustment layer to indicate how it affects a particular image, or how well it works with the rest of the picture. The following steps show you how to apply a lighting effect to an image layer and apply an adjustment layer to experiment with tonal ranges in the image window.

1. Open an image file containing image layers. Select an image layer in the Layers palette.

2. Open the Filter menu, choose Render, and select Lighting Effects.

3. Click and drag the circle on the left side of the Lighting Effects window to adjust the direction of the light. Click and drag the sides of the circle to adjust the areas where the light will shine on the image below it. Then click on OK to save any changes. View the effect in the image window.

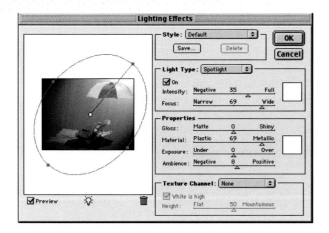

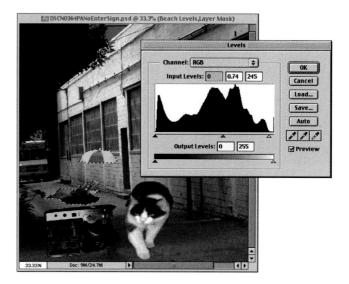

4. Open the Layer menu, choose New Adjustment Layer, and select Levels.

5. Click and drag the dark slider toward the middle to set the tonal range for dark colors in the picture. If you see histogram information that extends to or beyond the left side of the Levels window, you probably don't need to adjust the slider.

6. Click and drag the middle slider to adjust the midtone ranges of the image. Moving the slider to the left will brighten the image, and moving it to the right will darken it.

7. Click and drag the white slider to adjust light tonal ranges in the image. Move the white slider to the edge of the histogram (if the histogram doesn't extend beyond the right side of the window).

8. Preview the level changes in the image window. Click on OK to save your changes, or Cancel if you do not want to save the changes. To adjust the levels, select the levels adjustment layer, and then open the Layer menu and choose Change Layer Content. Adjust the settings as you did in steps 5 through 7 to change the levels of the image layers below it.

If you have plenty of memory and hard drive space, make a backup of any image layers you want to experiment with. Ctrl/Command+click on an image to select it. Then press Ctrl/Command+J to make a copy of a layer. Be sure to hide the copy so that you view accurate renderings of any adjustment layers. It might be helpful to store copies of layers in a layer set that is always hidden.

To add pixels to an existing layer selection, Ctrl/Command+Shift and click on a layer or layer mask thumbnail in the Layers palette. To subtract pixels, press Ctrl/Command+Alt/Option and click on a layer or layer mask thumbnail. To load an intersection of pixels plus an existing selection, Ctrl/Command+Alt/Option+Shift+click on a layer or layer mask thumbnail in the Layers palette.

ADDING EFFECTS TO A LAYER

Add as many layer effects as you like to an image. Create a layer set to group effects with a particular image layer. Each effect appears in the Layers palette with an *f* beside the thumbnail image of a layer. Turn one or more effects on or off and re-organize them in the Layers palette. This allows you to find the best combination of effects for an image. The following steps show you how to add a layer effect to a masked image.

1. Open an image file. Choose an image file containing a layer with an image mask. Ctrl/Command+click on a layer to select the masked image along with its layer.
2. Choose Layer Styles from the Layer menu, and then select Bevel and Emboss.
3. Select a style from the pop-up menu, and then adjust the depth and size of the effect's structure.
4. Change the angle by clicking and dragging the asterisk in the Angle graphic. Click in the Highlight Mode or Shadow Mode color wells to pick shading colors.
5. Click on OK and view the effect on the selected image layer.

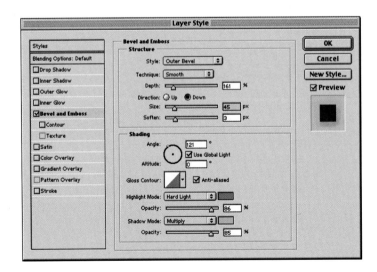

6. Click on the eye icon on the background layer in the Layers palette.

7. The background image disappears, revealing any fill layers, layer sets, or other layer objects.

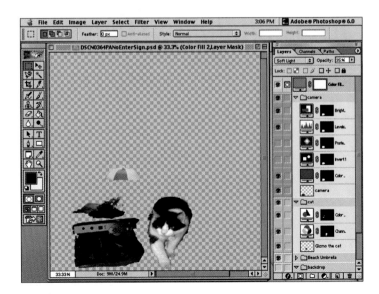

✅ Create a copy of the background image in order to apply a layer style to it. De-select the eye icon to hide the background layer while applying layer effects to the copy of the background image layer.

✅ Choose Hide All Effects from the Layer Style submenu under the Layer menu to de-select all effects for a particular layer or layer set.

PRESERVING LAYER INFORMATION

Experimenting with layers takes time, memory, and hard disk space. On the rare occasion that you complete a layering experiment in one sitting, flatten the image and save the file optimized for the Web. If you plan on returning to the image for future experimentation, it's best to sacrifice disk space, and maybe even make a backup to a Zip disk or second hard drive and save the image and all its layers as a huge Photoshop file. Here's how:

1. Open an image file and add several kinds of layers to it. Choose Save As from the File menu. Type a name for the image being saved.
2. Select Photoshop from the Format pop-up menu.

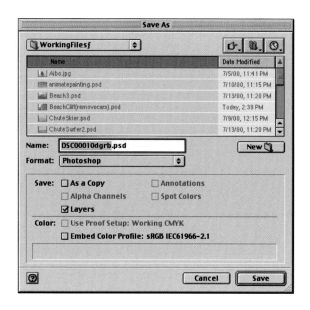

3. Check the Layers check box to preserve any layers created in that image file.
4. Choose Open from the File menu. Navigate through the files and folders and open a Photoshop file.
5. If the image is part of a layer or layers, view any layer by selecting the Layers palette from the Window menu.

 The Photoshop file format can preserve all the new layer features created with Photoshop 6.0. If you choose JPEG, GIF, or another file format, layers are flattened prior to being saved as a file, and all layer information is removed from the file.

ADJUSTING COLOR WITH LAYERS

Combine several fill and gradient layers to experiment with different colors for masked images in a picture. A picture might have fine colors. However, as you add other images, or put it side by side next to other images, its color might seem too light or too bright. Add adjustment fill and gradient layers combined with layer masks and clipping groups to preserve the original image, and enhance it using a wide range and combination of colors.

COMBINING FILL LAYERS

Create a variety of lighting and color effects by arranging and rearranging solid and gradient fill layers. Apply fill and gradient layers to a single mask to adjust its colors, or to the entire picture to create colorful effects. If you like a specific combination of fill and image layers, you can merge them together. Here's how:

1. Open an image file that contains image layers. Select an image layer in the Layers palette. Then add a few solid and gradient fill layers to the background image.

2. Ctrl/Command+click and drag a masked image from another image file into the one where the fill layers were added in step 1. Notice the fill layers do not affect the new image because the new image is on the top-most layer of the Layers palette and the image window, and all the fill and gradient layers are below it.

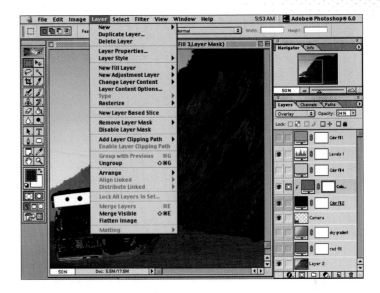

4. The selected layers are combined into the background layer of the image file.

3. Open the Layer menu and choose Merge Visible to combine the fill and gradient layers that have the eye icon selected.

CREATING A LAYER
CLIPPING GROUP

Layer clipping groups (not to be confused with layer clipping paths) enable you to do two things: control two levels of transparency in an image and create an 8-bit mask affecting multiple layers. A layer clipping allows you to create a mask on top of an image. The following steps show you how to create a layer clipping.

1. Open an image file. Create a quick mask or an alpha channel mask. Select the mask and copy and paste it to a second image window.
2. Place the mask in the layer below a layer containing the main image. You may need to move the background image to a new layer to complete this step.
3. Select the layer above the image mask layer. Click on the box to the left of the masked image layer. The link icon should appear in the box. Choose Group Linked from the Layer menu.

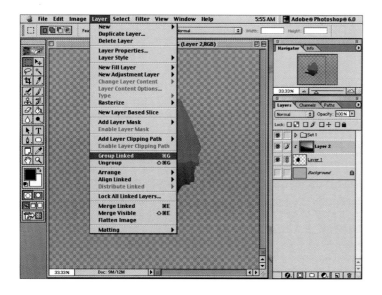

4. The image above the mask appears within the shape of the masked area below it.

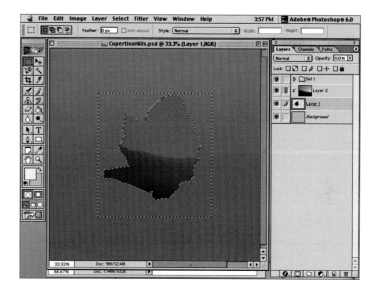

 Group any two layers together by holding down the Alt/Option key, and clicking on the line between two layers in the Layers palette.

ADJUSTING COLORS ACROSS
LAYERS

Move any adjustment layers to the top of the Layers palette if you want specific fill or gradient layers to affect all other layers, including the background layer. Create adjustment layers to adjust levels and channel mix colors, or create solid color or gradient fill layers that apply to the entire picture.

Place all the adjustment fill and gradient layers in a layer set. Turn them all off by de-selecting the eye icon, or view individual adjustment or fill layers by turning one off and another on. The following steps show you how to change the color of an image by changing the order of layers in the Layers palette.

1. Open an image and add one or two objects.

2. Add adjustment, gradient, or fill layers to the image file.

3. Click and drag a fill layer and move it below an image layer. The fill color does not affect the image layers above it.

4. Click and drag a fill layer and move it above other image objects. The fill layer color is applied to the layers below it.

5. Move fill layers and image objects layers to different positions in the Layers palette. The appearance of the image in the image window will change depending on the order of the fill and image layers in the Layers palette.

CHAPTER 12

CREATING CUSTOM MASKS

MASKING PART OF AN IMAGE IS SIMILAR TO SELECTING TEXT IN A
DOCUMENT. A MASK ENABLES YOU TO SELECT A SPECIFIC SET OF PIXELS IN
AN IMAGE, WHILE PROTECTING ALL THE OTHER PIXELS FROM BEING
EDITED. PHOTOSHOP ENABLES YOU TO SELECT THE LAYER OR CHANNEL
CONTAINING A MASK AND APPLY EFFECTS AND LAYERS TO A MASKED
IMAGE. MASKS CAN ALSO BE USED AS MATTES. A MATTE CAN HELP BLEND
THE FRINGES OF A MASKED IMAGE WITH THE MASK'S BACKGROUND IMAGE.

WORKING WITH CHANNEL MASKS

There are several ways to create a mask in Photoshop. Layer masks are created by clicking the Add a Mask button in the Layers palette, whereas alpha channel masks and quick masks are created by clicking the Save Selection as a Channel button in the Channels palette or by clicking the Quick Mask button in the toolbox. A *mask* is a one-bit image where white is the editable area, and black is the uneditable, or protected area of a picture.

The fastest way to create a mask is with the Quick Mask tool, covered in Chapter 9. A Quick Mask is a temporary mask if you compare it with all the things you can do with an alpha channel mask. The whole point of creating a mask is to isolate areas you want to edit and protect. Quick masks let you quickly create and edit a mask from the image window.

If you plan to create a complex image or want to experiment with applying color or filter effects, use an alpha channel mask. An alpha channel is made up of 8 bits of data, or 256 shades of gray. Therefore an alpha channel mask gives you the flexibility of using 254 additional shades of gray to define an alpha channel mask.

A layer mask is similar to an alpha channel mask, except the mask is applied directly to a particular layer. Apply filters, effects, or color adjustments that only affect the pixels in that layer mask. Merge layers to make the mask permanent, hide or show it to see how it looks with other image layers, or remove the layer mask if you don't like it. This section focuses on creating channel masks. Layer masks are explained in Chapter 11. For more information about quick masks, see Chapter 9.

USING CHANNELS TO CREATE A MASK

The key to creating a mask is to find an image with clear, distinct edges that stand out from the background image. Sometimes you can use a red, green, or blue channel to help isolate the edges of an image. If you combine an effect, like the High Pass filter, with a channel, you may be able to bring out the edges of that image, then use a selection tool, such as the Lasso tool to define the mask.

Use the eye icon to find a channel you want to use to create your mask. Then create a copy of that channel in the Channels panel. After you copy the channel, you can apply filters, adjust levels, and add effects to any single channel in Photoshop to make it easier to find the edges of the image you want to use to create a mask.

To copy a channel, select it and drag it to the New Channel icon in the Channels palette. Select the copied channel in the Channels palette. Then choose a filter, such as the High Pass filter, to bring out the edges of the image object you want to select. You can use a selection tool to define a mask using a particular channel color, or all channels combined together. The following steps show you how to use a copy of a channel to define a simple object mask.

1. Open an image file. Select a channel that emphasizes the edge of the object you want to mask. Drag the channel over the Create New Channel icon (the new document icon) in the Channels palette. If you want the edges of the image to stand out, try applying the High Pass filter located in the Filter, Other menu. Set the radius of the High Pass filter to 3-5 pixels.
2. Choose a selection tool from the toolbox. Click on the object you want to mask. Drag the selection tool around the edges of the image.

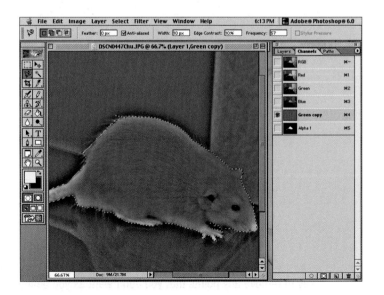

3. Once the selection tool highlights the image, click on the Save Selection as Channel icon (mask icon) in the Channel window. The mask icon resembles a white circle in the middle of a gray rectangle. An alpha channel mask appears in the Channels palette.
4. Select the mask channel you just created from the Channels palette. Use the Magic Wand tool to select the white area of the mask. Then choose Feather from the Select menu to smooth the edges of the masked area.
5. Press ~ to view the mask with the full-color image in the image window.

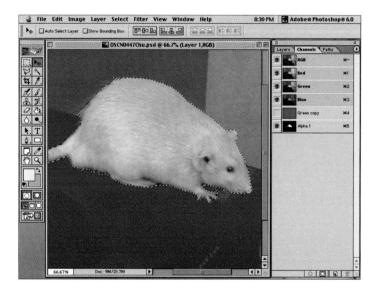

6. Press ~ once more to view the mask. Select the channel in the Channels palette. Ctrl/Command+~ to select the mask along with the red, green, and blue channels in the masked area.
7. Ctrl/Command+click and drag the image to a new image window. If you don't hold down the Ctrl/Command keys while dragging, you'll only see an empty selection area in the target image window. In order to move the masked image, hold down the Crtl key on a Windows PC, or the Command key on a Mac to move the image along with the selected area to the second image window.

 Using the Magnetic Lasso tool to select an image? Press the Delete key to remove any points that you don't want as you define the selection.

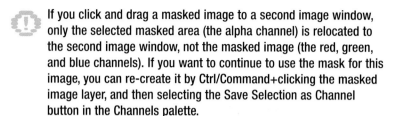 **If you click and drag a masked image to a second image window, only the selected masked area (the alpha channel) is relocated to the second image window, not the masked image (the red, green, and blue channels). If you want to continue to use the mask for this image, you can re-create it by Ctrl/Command+clicking the masked image layer, and then selecting the Save Selection as Channel button in the Channels palette.**

CREATING A MASK IN THE IMAGE WINDOW

Channel masks are the most dynamic kind of mask you can create and work with in Photoshop. To create a mask that blends in well with another image, you may need to spend quite a bit of time defining and fine-tuning the mask before it's ready for prime time. You may need to apply effects, combine a mask with adjustment layers, or blend two masks together. The previous section showed you how to create a channel mask using a copy of a channel. This section shows you how to apply a selection tool directly to the image window to create a channel mask.

First, a little more information about channels. Channels store the color information of an image file. Photoshop opens most images from digital cameras in RGB (red, green, and blue) mode, a 24-bit image. If you look at the Channels palette, you'll find a red, green, and blue (RGB) channel. Each channel stores one third of the image data— 256 shades of gray plus black and white—or eight bits of information. For more information about channels, see Chapters 10 and 13. The following steps show you how to define and create a mask in the image window.

1. Open an image file in Photoshop.
2. Choose a selection tool from the toolbox. (I've selected the Magnetic Lasso tool.)
3. Click on or near the edge of the object you want to select. Release the button and then drag the cursor over the edge of the area you want to select. (The Magnetic Lasso should cling to the edge of the image area you want to select. If it doesn't, simply click once to create a selection point.) Press the Delete key to remove a selection point created by the Magnetic Lasso tool.
4. Move the selection tool around the border of the image. Click once on the starting point to close the selected area.

5. Select the Channels tab and click on the Save Selection as Channel button (the mask icon) at the bottom of the Channels palette.
6. A masked image appears in a new alpha channel. Select the alpha channel to view the black-and-white mask.

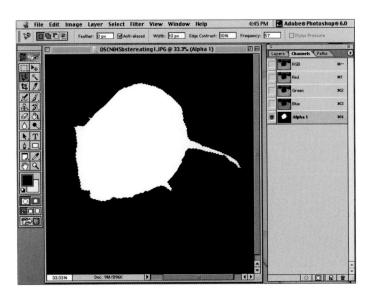

 Use the Magic Wand tool to select the white area of the mask. Then press Ctrl/Command+~ to view the selected area in full color.

 Once you've created a mask, you can modify it using the Pencil or Paintbrush tools. To modify a mask, first select the alpha channel containing the mask in the Channels palette. Click the eye icon next to RGB, or press ~ to view the masked image against the RGB image in the image window. The full-color image appears behind the mask, highlighted with a red hue. Use the Paintbrush tool combined with black to define the masked area and white to define the unmasked area of the image.

Another way to edit a mask is to set black as the foreground color, white as the background color. Press b to access the Paintbrush tool if you want to add to the mask. Press e to use the Erase tool to delete any part of the mask.

EXTRACTING AN IMAGE

If you want to mask an image that contains indefinable edges, try using the Extract command. The Extract command enables you to define the edges of your mask using the Highlighter and Paint Bucket tools in the Extract window. This command tries to separate the foreground object from the background image. It can take a while to create a mask. But it's a great alternative to manually defining a mask. The following steps show you how to extract an object from the rest of an image.

1. Open an image file.
2. Choose Extract from the Image menu.
3. Click on the Highlighter tool and draw an outline around the edges of the image you want to extract. Green is the default highlight color. The Extract command will analyze the pixels below the highlighted areas and find the differences between the edges of the mask and the rest of the picture.
4. Once you've surrounded the image you want to mask, click on the Paint Bucket tool. Click inside the highlighted area. It should fill with a blue color. Click on the Preview button to preview the extracted image. When you're ready to extract the image, click OK.

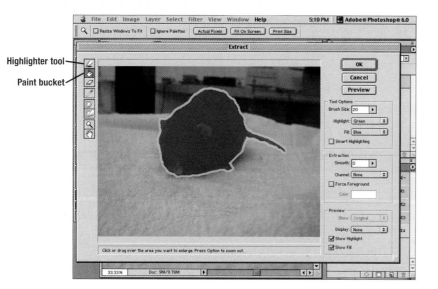

Highlighter tool
Paint bucket

5. The extracted image appears in the image window. Notice how much more precise the edges of this image mask are compared to those created in the previous sections.

COMBINING MULTIPLE MASKS

Once you've created a mask, you can move it to a new location in the image window or to a new layer or file. Moving the mask can help you see any rough edges or incorrectly colored pixels in the mask. Use the Feather menu command to smooth the edges of the mask, or the selection and paintbrush tools to refine the masked area before or after moving it to another image file.

When a masked image is moved to another layer or image window, Photoshop creates a new layer for the masked image. You can then layer masks by moving an image to the top of the Layers palette, or add effects such as a motion blur to a specific layer in the Layers palette. The following steps show you how to create more than one mask in the same image file.

1. Open an image file. I've chosen a picture of a location for this example. Choose one of the selection tools and create a mask in the Channels palette.
2. Use the Magic Wand to select the white area of a mask, and press Ctrl/Command+~ to switch to RGB mode and view the masked image in full color. Alternatively, you can press ~ to view the masked area in full color, with the unmasked area highlighted in red.

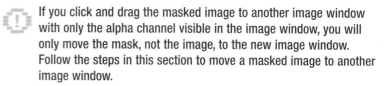

If you click and drag the masked image to another image window with only the alpha channel visible in the image window, you will only move the mask, not the image, to the new image window. Follow the steps in this section to move a masked image to another image window.

3. Photoshop surrounds the selected image with a marquee, a black and white line marking the border of the selected area. Ctrl/Command+click and drag the masked image to the target image window. Repeat steps 1 through 3 to add more masked objects to the target image file.

4. As each mask is added to the picture, a new layer is created in the Layers palette. Click and drag the layer within the Layers palette to change an object's layer order. (Images, masks, and layer effects located at the top of the Layers palette affect images below them.)

5. Add adjustment layers and fill layers to add effects and tweak the colors for a particular layer, or all layers in the picture.

MASKS AND LAYER SETS

You can stack masks or isolate matte effects and layer effects by grouping image elements in a layer set. Layer sets work similarly to regular layers, except that layers in a layer set are grouped in a folder. View layer sets in the Layers palette. Click and drag a layer set and move it above or below another layer in the Layers palette. Turn a layer set on or off, or turn any layer within a layer set on or off, by toggling its eye icon in the Layers palette. The following steps show you how to create a layer set and populate it with layers.

1. Open an image file.

2. Copy and paste several images into the image window.

3. Select a layer in the Layers palette, and then choose an Adjustment Layer command from the Layer menu. Add as many layers as you like to the Layers palette.

4. Click on the folder icon in the Layers palette. A layer set icon should appear in the Layers palette. Toggle the triangle beside the layer set folder icon so that you can view the contents of the layer set. Isolate effects by grouping masked images and layer effects into layer set folders.

5. Click and drag any layer into the layer set folder.

 The top-most layer in the Layers palette is also the top-most layer in the image window. Layers at the top of the Layers palette affect any layers located below them. In the preceding example, all layers in the Adjustments folder affect all layers in the Mouse folder in addition to the background layer. However, only the layers within the Mouse folder affect the mouse image.

PASTING MASKS INTO A PICTURE

When an image is pasted into another image window, Photoshop creates a new layer for the pasted object. An object in a layer floats above other layers, including the background image. To move a masked image into the selected area of a second image window, use the Edit, Paste Into command, as follows:

1. Open an image file. Choose a selection tool from the toolbox and select the area of the object you want to mask in the image window.
2. Create a mask and then choose Feather from the Select menu. Feather dithers the pixel edges of the masked image, creating an anti-aliased effect that helps blend the edges of the mask with its background or foreground images.

3. Use a selection tool such as the Magic Wand to select an area in a second image.
4. Return to the first image window. Choose Copy from the Edit menu, or press Ctrl/Command+C.
5. Switch to the second image window. Ctrl/Command+click on the layer containing the mask. This will select the masked area in that layer. Select Paste Into from the Edit menu.

6. The image from the first file appears in the second image window, but is masked to the selected area.

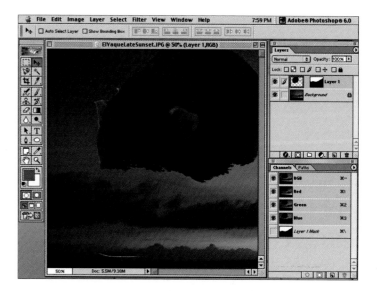

 Use the Paste Into command to paste an image into an irregularly shaped selection area of an image file. This is one way to blend the pasted image into the target image.

RECONSTRUCTING AND FREEZING PIXELS

You can apply filter effects to a masked image just as you would apply an effect to all or part of any non-masked image. You might have noticed that some effects must be applied to a layer or background image in order to be accessible, whereas other effects and filters, such as adjustment layers, can be toggled on and off in the Layers palette. Reconstruct and Freeze tools work similarly to adjustment layers, except that these tools are found only in the Liquify window. If you want to experiment with image distortion effects, you can apply several different distortion effects to an image in the Liquify window. Then undo any of them using the Reconstruct tool. The following steps show you how to apply distortion effects in the Liquify window, and revert them using the Reconstruct tool.

1. Open an image file. If the image file contains multiple layers, select a layer containing an image. If you want to liquify a masked area, Ctrl/Command+click the layer containing the mask.
2. Select Liquify from the Image menu.
3. Choose the Freeze tool and select the area you want to protect by clicking and dragging the mouse over it. The Freeze tool icon consists of a paintbrush with a white circle over a gray rectangle. Frozen areas of an image are covered in red.

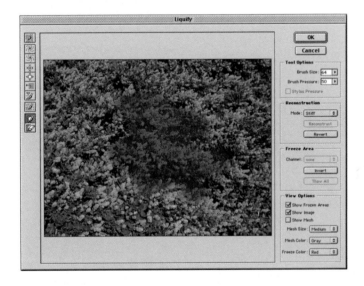

4. Click on an effect tool, such as warp, twirl, pucker or bloat, located on the left side of the Liquify window. Click and drag the cursor on the image to apply a distortion effect.
5. Select the Reconstruct tool from the toolbox. The Reconstruct tool icon is located right above the Freeze tool icon. The Reconstruct icon consists of a paintbrush over an ordered set of pixels surrounded by scattered pixels.
6. Click on any part of the image that is warped. The Reconstruct tool restores the image to its original, unwarped state.

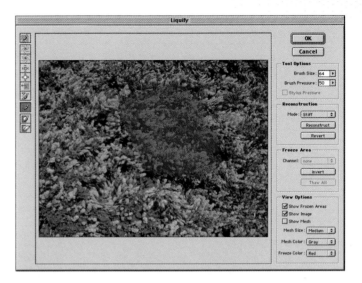

The settings on the right side of the Liquify window enable you to adjust the stroke size and effects of the Liquify tools in the toolbox.

CREATING COMPLEX MASKS

An image might be perfectly compelling when taken from a camera. However, you might want to make a totally different composition, or combine a set of great images all into one file. These image files can contain several masks, mattes, and alpha channels.

By now, you probably know what a mask and an alpha channel are. What's a matte? When an image is masked, pixels along the edges of the image may not match the pixel colors of the background image, such as the background of a Web page, or the background or foreground of another image layer in Photoshop. This difference in colors can create a fringe or halo effect around all or part of the masked image. You can apply the Defringe matte command to shrink the masked area to eliminate the halo effect. This section shows you how to work with layers of masks, create a gradient mask, and use matte commands on a mask.

CREATING LAYERS OF MASKS

Although you might be working with only one picture, you can create as many masks as you like. Use the selection tools to define any area of the picture as a mask, and then click on the Save Selection as Channel icon in the Channels palette. Ctrl/Command+click to select the mask in the Channels palette and then press Ctrl/Command+~ to bring the RGB channels into the mask. Press Ctrl/Command+J to copy the masked image into a new layer.

Use these steps to create multiple layers of masks within the same image:

1. Open an image file. Using a selection tool from the toolbox, select an object in the image window. Then choose Save Selection as Channel in the Channels palette to create a mask.

2. Hold down the Shift key and select a second or third object if you want.
3. Click on the Channels palette tab, and then click on the Save Selection as Channel icon (mask icon) at the bottom of the palette. Photoshop creates a mask channel.

4. Return to the Layers palette. Click on a layer. Use a selection tool to select one or more image objects.
5. Create another mask in the Channels palette.

6. Each masked channel appears in the Channels palette. To place the mask in its own layer, select it in the Channels palette, and then press Ctrl/Command+J.
7. When you've made you're final edits to the image file, save it first as a Photoshop file. If you want to see how the picture will look on a Web page, flatten the layers of the image. Select the Flatten Image command from the Layer menu to merge all visible layers into one background layer.
8. If file size is still an issue, you might want to try changing the image mode to condense the way the image stores its colors. Open the Image menu, choose Mode, and select Indexed Color.
9. Select Save for Web from the File menu to optimize the image for the Web. To find out more about how to prepare an image for the Web, see Part 4, "Publishing Pictures."

 One of the last things you can do to correct an image is to use the Unsharp Mask filter located in the Filter menu, under the Sharpen submenu. This filter adjusts the contrast of the edge detail in a picture, thus creating the illusion of a clearer, focused image.

 If you've created a fairly large sized image mask that you want to post to a Web page, consider using the Slice tool to break the mask into smaller files. Be sure to save a copy of the image file containing the mask before exporting the slices as GIF or JPG files. Then you can go back and edit the original image without starting from scratch.

CREATING A GRADIENT MASK

Recall that each alpha channel, or channel mask, contains eight bits of grayscale date: black and white, and 254 shades of gray. The black color in a mask represents uneditable areas, whereas any white part of the mask can be edited if the layer containing the mask is selected.

Shades of gray in a channel enable you to add a partial transparency to an image. You can add a gradient to a channel in the Channels palette to create a partial transparency within an image layer. The shades of gray in the channel act as a mask to the rest of the image in that layer. For example, select the white portion of a gradient channel combined with a mask. With the gradient channel selected, choose Load Channel as Selection from the Channels palette. If you change the color in the color well, you can create a nice fade effect in that image layer. The following steps show you how to create a gradient mask using a copy of the background image.

1. Open an image file. Create a new layer in the Layers palette. Then copy and paste the background image into the new layer. Select the new layer. Click on the Create a New Channel (new document icon) button in the Channels palette. In this case I named the channel 'gradient'.

2. Select the Gradient tool from the toolbox. Click on the gradient drop-down menu in the options toolbar, and choose the black-and-white gradient. The black and white colors of the gradient will map to the shades of gray supported by the alpha channel we created in step 1.

3. Click and drag the cursor vertically in the image window to define the gradient. A gradient is created in the selected alpha channel.

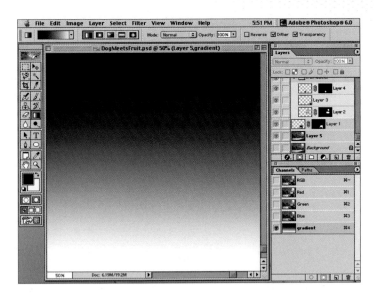

 If the image edges aren't clear enough, use a red, green, or blue channel to help find a better image to create the mask with.

4. Click and drag the gradient channel to the Load Channel as Selection (dotted circle) icon at the bottom of the Channels palette. A selection border should appear around half of the image.

5. Click the eye icon next to the RGB channel in the Channels palette. The color well changes to black-and-white colors, and the gradient mask is displayed with the full-color image.

6. Select a different background color. The default color is white. Press the Delete key to apply the background color to the gradient. If you don't see any changes, be sure the background layer is hidden. Click the eye icon for the background layer to hide it.

7. Click in the image window to deselect the gradient. The end result of this gradient mask is a gradual fade to a transparent, checkerboard background.

1. Open an image file. Create or add a mask to the image file following the steps in the first sections of this chapter.

2. Select the layer containing the masked image.

TWEAKING MASKS WITH MATTES

Although you can use the Feather command to smooth the edges of a mask, in some cases you can also use a matte. If you've created a masked image containing a border of pixels surrounding the mask, you may be able to shrink the edges of the mask, removing the halo surrounding the mask by using the Defringe matte command. Photoshop provides three different matte commands to help blend the edges of a mask with the rest of the picture: Defringe, Remove Black Matte, and Remove White Matte. The following steps show you how to defringe a mask and the Remove the Black Matte command to blend it into a white background image.

3. Choose the Layer menu. Select Matte, and then choose the Defringe command. If you created a masked image with a halo, or pixel border, try applying the Defringe command to remove the halo effect.

4. Type a number in the text box to determine how many pixels are removed from the edges of the masked image. Then click OK.

5. The edges of the masked image will be blended in with any contrasting colors in the background layer.

6. To blend the masked image with a black or white background, choose Remove Black Matte or Remove White Matte from the Layer, Matte menu. In this example, the masked image will be placed over a white background. Choose Remove Black Matte command from the Layer, Matte menus to blend the mask edges into a white background.

 Another way to smooth mask edges is to adjust its layer blending options for the masked layer and the layer directly below it in the Layers palette. For more information about layer blending options, see Chapter 11, "Experimenting with Layers."

EDITING A MASK

A good mask can take a lot of time to get just right, especially when the image being masked contains many detailed or fuzzy edges. A bad mask is generally a sloppy one, making the overall image look disjointed. One way to tell whether a mask is effective is to compare the masked image to its proposed background picture. Try to find the edges of the masked image, or any other characteristics of the image that might make the image look out of place in the picture. If you find a stray or incorrectly colored pixel, you can use the Pen, Paintbrush, or Pencil tools, plus some menu commands, to blend your mask into the rest of an image.

CHANGING THE SHAPE OF A MASK

Since you can modify a mask once it's created, the initial selection area you create does not have exactly match the object you want to mask. Try to capture the core shape of the mask the first time you apply the selection tools to an image window or channel when you create the mask. Once the mask is created, use the Pen or Pencil tools to fine-tune, or re-shape, the masked area. As you apply black or white to the masked or unmasked areas of the image, the shape of the mask changes. If you want to grow or shrink the size of a mask, see the following section, Scaling Masks. The following steps show you how to change the shape of a mask.

1. Open an image file. Select an area of the image. Then click on the Save Selection as Channel button (white circle in a gray rectangle icon) to create a mask.
2. Activate the eye icon for the RGB channel to view the mask with the rest of the unmasked image. A red hue should appear over the unmasked areas.

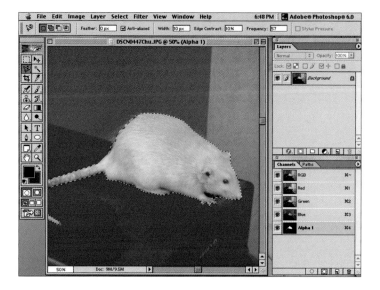

3. Use a Paintbrush or Pencil tool with black as the foreground color to define the areas you do not want to include in the mask. If you apply black around the edges of the mask, the size of the mask shrinks.
4. Click on the arrows in the color well to swap the foreground and background colors.
5. Use a Paintbrush or Pencil tool to define the masked area. If you apply white to the fringes of the masked image, the mask will grow in size. In this example, I use the Pencil tool to extend the whiskers on the mouse.

 In step 5, use the Paintbrush or Pencil tool even though the mask area is highlighted.

SCALING MASKS

After the masked image is created and feathered, you can move it to another image window. Press Ctrl/Command+click and drag the masked image to another image window. Chances are the masked image won't quite fit into the new picture. Fortunately, Photoshop has Transform commands that enable you to shrink or enlarge an image. You can also skew, rotate, distort, and flip an image using the Transform commands. The following steps show you how to scale a masked image that was moved to another image window.

1. Press Ctrl/Command+click on a layer to select the masked image in that layer.
2. Open the Edit menu, choose Transform, and select Scale.
3. A rectangular bounding box appears around the masked image. Click and drag the corner or side points of the bounding box to resize the selected image.

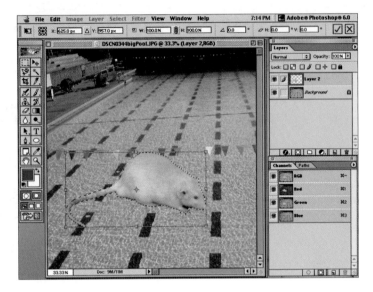

4. Use the Move tool to place the resized image in the background picture.
5. Repeat steps 1 through 4 with a second or third image. Use the Scale command to resize them. Similarly, use the Skew and Distort commands to adjust the image perspective to match the background image.

6. Adjust the opacity and image mode in the Layers palette to blend the masked image into the rest of the picture.

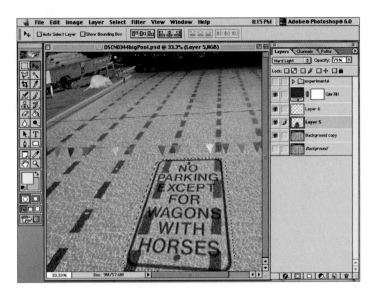

EXPORTING MASKS

You can use the magic combination of keystrokes of Ctrl/Command+click, Ctrl/Command+~, and Ctrl/Command+click and drag to move a full-color masked image to another image window. Ctrl/Command+click the image in the new layer to select the masked area. Then select the Save Selection as Channel button from the Channels palette to create a new mask in the second image file.

Since there is no easy way to export a mask out of Photoshop, the best way to preserve a mask is to save it along with its layers and channels as a Photoshop file. The following steps show you how to preserve alpha channel masks and layer masks when you save an image as a Photoshop file.

1. Open an image file. Create one or more channel masks and layers. Choose the Save As command from the File menu.

2. Choose Photoshop from the Format pop-up menu. If you choose a non-Photoshop file format, mask, channel, and layer information will be flattened. This means you create a smaller file size, but eliminate individual layers, stand-alone channels, or masks within layers. Save your masks by saving channels and layers as a Photoshop document.

3. Check the Alpha Channels check box if you want to save the file with its channels information.

4. Select the Layers check box to preserve any layers and layer sets. Otherwise, the layers will be flattened when the file is saved.

5. Click on the Save button to save the picture.

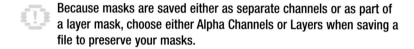 **Because masks are saved either as separate channels or as part of a layer mask, choose either Alpha Channels or Layers when saving a file to preserve your masks.**

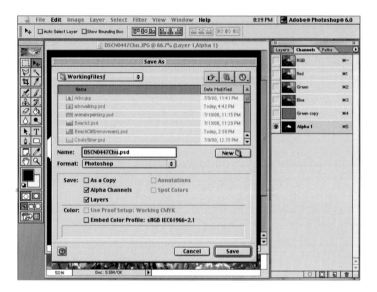

CHAPTER 13

EXPERIMENTING WITH
CHANNEL OPERATIONS

THE TERM CHANNEL OPERATIONS CAN CONJURE UP VISIONS OF REMOTE
CONTROLS AND TV SCREENS WITH PICTURE-IN-PICTURE. IN THE CONTEXT
OF PHOTOSHOP, HOWEVER, CHANNEL OPERATIONS REFER TO TASKS THAT
YOU PERFORM WITH CHANNELS, SUCH AS CREATING AND WORKING WITH
ALPHA CHANNELS. CHANNEL OPERATIONS CAN INVOLVE COMPOSITING
IMAGES WITH CHANNELS, LAYERS, AND MASKS USING THE CALCULATIONS
OR DUPLICATE COMMANDS.

ALL THE CHANNEL, LAYER, AND MASK EXAMPLES IN THIS BOOK REQUIRE
THE IMAGE TO BE IN RGB COLOR MODE. (AS MENTIONED BEFORE, RED,
GREEN, AND BLUE ARE THE CHANNELS THAT MAKE UP AN RGB IMAGE.)
OPEN THE IMAGE, MODE MENUS AND CHOOSE RGB COLOR TO CHANGE AN
IMAGE TO RGB MODE.

ONCE YOU'VE CREATED THE FINAL IMAGE, YOU CAN FLATTEN THE LAYERS
AND CHANNELS IN AN RGB IMAGE AND CREATE A SMALLER IMAGE BY
CHOOSING ANOTHER IMAGE MODE, SUCH AS INDEXED COLOR, OR BY
CHOOSING A FILE FORMAT SUCH AS JPEG OR GIF. IF YOU PLAN TO SHARE
YOUR PICTURE ON A WEB PAGE, SMALLER FILE SIZES DOWNLOAD FASTER
THAN LARGER FILE SIZES. YOU'LL WANT TO USE THE SMALLEST POSSIBLE
IMAGE THAT PRESERVES THE BEST IMAGE QUALITY.

CREATING A CUSTOM CHANNEL

You can select and copy image channels from the Channels palette. Select a channel and drag it to the New Channel icon to create a copy of a channel. Although an image might initially consist of RGB channels, when a channel is copied, it can be viewed individually or combined with other channels. The following sections show you how to customize a single channel or all three channels.

 If you have duplicate channels in the Channels palette, selecting the eye icon might make the image's colors a little too red or green in the document window. Click on the eye icon to hide a channel you don't want to view in the image window.

CONVERTING COLOR TO GRAYSCALE

One way to convert a color image to a grayscale image is to choose Grayscale from the Image, Mode menu. This menu command removes the color information from an image file. The Channel Mixer window provides a more dynamic way to convert a color image to grayscale. You can access this menu command from the Image, Adjust menu, or from the Layer, New Adjustment Layer menu.

The channel mixer window lets you convert either the red, green, or blue channel of an image into a grayscale image. You can also modify the red, green, and blue channels, and then convert the image to monochrome. Or switch from color to monochrome, modifying the monochrome image with color, then converting the image back to monochrome to create a custom grayscale, channel-mixed image.

There is an easy way to view an image in grayscale or color without losing any color information: Add a Channel Mixer adjustment layer to an image. Toggle it on or off to view an image in color or grayscale. The following steps show you how to create a grayscale image using its red channel.

1. Open an image file. Select a layer in the Layers palette. If you have multiple layers in an image file, the background layer is selected by default.
2. Open the Layer menu, choose New Adjustment Layer, and select Channel Mixer.
3. Check the Monochrome check box, and then click on OK. If you want to combine red, green, and blue channels to create the final mono-chrome image, choose each channel color from the Output Channel drop-down menu. Then adjust the slider controls for Red, Green, and Blue until you're ready to convert the image in the image window to grayscale. Finally click the Monochrome check box to create the grayscale image.

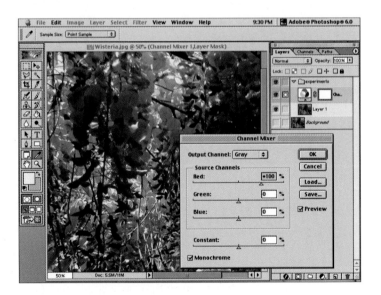

4. The image window displays a grayscale image based on the red, green, or blue channel settings you chose in the Channel Mixer window.

5. Click on the new channel, named Channel Mixer 1 Mask, in the Channels palette. Notice that the red, green, and blue channels remain with the image in the Channels palette.

6. View the image.

 It's okay to have duplicate channels in the Channels palette. When you flatten the image, any duplicate channels are merged with any other similar channels.

CREATING COMPOSITE IMAGES

An RGB image is made up of three 8-bit color channels, resulting in a 24-bit image. An 8-bit channel can either represent 256 color values of an image, or 256 shades of gray. An alpha channel is the latter, and as a result contains less information than any single red, green, or blue channel. When you create a mask, the image isn't converted to black and white; it's converted to black (represented by zero), white (represented by 255), and 254

shades of gray. The 256 shades of gray in an alpha channel are the core elements that define channel processing in Photoshop.

A *composite image* is an image that consists of two or more image elements, each with distinct characteristics, which, when combined, retain their uniqueness while contributing to the whole picture. Creating a composite image involves combining a foreground image (image above the selected layer) with a background image (image in the layer below the selected layer in the Layers palette). An 8-bit channel functions as a transparency layer to the rest of the image. For example, if a channel were only 1-bit, consisting of black and white colors, there would be no smooth transition to the second, or composite, image. Likewise, if you place a mask over a mask, the transition and transparency looks best when there is a smooth gradient between the images. The following steps show you how to create two channel masks, then use the Group command to create a composite image.

1. Open an image file in Photoshop. This will eventually contain the composite image.

DIGITAL DARKROOM

166

2. Choose the Magic Wand tool from the toolbox. Click on a small area of color in the document window.

3. Photoshop surrounds the set of pixels with a marquee (animated dotted line). Click on the Save Selection as Channel button in the Channels palette to save the selected area as an alpha channel.

4. Open a second image file. Choose a selection tool and select part of the image, or copy the entire image to a new layer.

5. Select the Channels palette, and then click on Save Selection as Channel (square with white circle icon).

6. Ctrl/Command+click on the mask in the Channels palette and then press Ctrl/Command+~. Then Ctrl/Command+click and drag the masked, selected image from the second image window to the first image window.

7. Return to the first image window (opened in step 1). Use the Move tool to select and place the image in the new layer in the first image window.

8. Select the new image layer in the Layers palette. Open the Layer menu and choose Group, or simply Alt/Option+click between the new layer and the layer containing the initial selected area (see step 2). This groups the two layers together.

DUPLICATING CHANNELS

You can use the Duplicate command to create a copy of all the layer and channel information in an image. The duplicate image can act as a backup to any additional experimental changes you might want to make. It can also provide an easy way to mimic any channels you created in one file and want to carry over to a second image file. The following steps show you how to use the duplicate command.

1. Open an image file.

2. Create several layers in the Layers palette, and several channels in the Channels palette.

3. Choose Duplicate from the Image menu. Type a name for the duplicate file. Then click on OK.

4. A new image window appears in the workspace.
5. The new image window contains the same layers and channels as its original. You can either save or toss the new image.

ADDING LIGHT AND SHADE ACROSS CHANNELS

You can add light or shade to a channel mask by applying a lighting effect (Filter menu) or layer style (Layer menu) to it. Unlike a layer style, a lighting effect cannot be toggled on or off. Layer styles enable you to experiment with shadows to hint at a subtle light source, or emphasize a masked image. The following steps show you how to apply a lighting effect to a masked channel image.

✓ It's a good idea to save a copy of your image containing layers as a full-blown (that is, having a large file size) Photoshop file. Although it's difficult to apply universal lighting effects to a layered image, it takes even more time to construct layers and layer sets for a complex image that has been prematurely flattened.

1. Open an image file. Copy and paste or click and drag an image from one document into another.

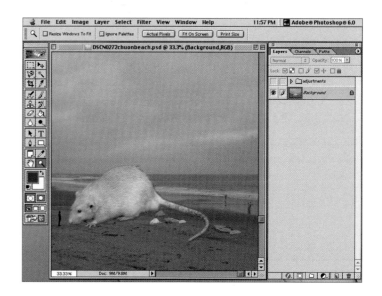

2. Deselect any images in the document window. Then, open the Filter menu, select Render, and choose Lighting Effects. The Lighting Effects window opens.

3. Click and drag the bounding box to set the light source for the entire picture.
4. Choose a light type from the pop-up menu, and adjust any properties to modify the light source. Click on OK to save your changes and apply them to the picture.

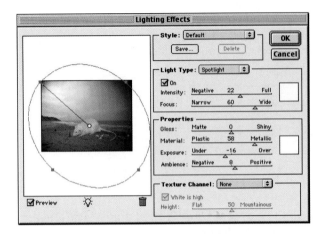

5. View the lighting effect in the image window.

 Move the sliders on the Lighting Effects window inward if there are no extreme dark or light values in the histogram in the Levels window. White space can make an image unnecessarily larger.

COMBINING CHANNELS AND IMAGES

Selecting and fine-tuning a single channel mask can be a time-consuming task. Working with several channels of masks can make a simple image instantly complex. To select masks from more than one alpha channel, Ctrl/Command+click in the alpha channel to select the masked object in the first channel. Then hold down the Shift key as you Ctrl/Command+click any other channel masks you want to select. You should see the dotted outline (marquee) for each mask appear in the image window as you Shift+Ctrl/Command+click each one. Once the channels are selected, press Ctrl/Command+~ to view the full-color image for those selected masks. Finally, press Ctrl/Command+J to place the selected masked images into a new layer.

ADDING MULTIPLE CHANNEL MASKS TO AN IMAGE

You can click and drag a selected channel mask to another image window. First, Ctrl/Command+click a channel mask in the Channels palette to select the masked area of that channel. Then press Ctrl/Command+~ to view the mask with the RGB color channels also selected. Ctrl/Command+click and drag as many channel masks as you like to an image window. Be careful not to run short on memory or disk space.

As you move masked images to a new image window, each mask is added to its own layer. You can continue to edit these masks by selecting the masked image from the Layers palette (Ctrl/Command+click on a layer containing the masked image). Then click on the Save Selection as Channel button in the Channels palette. An alpha mask is created in the Channels palette. Press ~ to edit the mask, or use the mask to create additional layers containing the same image. Create complex images by adding multiple channel masks to an image.

The following steps show you how to create a channel mask and copy the masked image to a new layer.

1. Open an image file. Copy and paste one or more images into an image window.
2. Ctrl/Command+click on a layer in the Layers palette. This key combination selects the masked image in the layer. You can also use a selection tool and select part of the image in the image window.
3. Select the Channels tab. Then click on the Save Selection as Channel icon to create an 8-bit alpha channel mask from the selection. A new alpha channel with the mask appears in the Channels palette.

4. With the masked area of the channel selected (hold Ctrl/Command and click on the alpha channel in the Channels palette), press Ctrl/Command+~ to bring the RGB channels into the channel mask. Then press Ctrl/Command+J to copy the selection to a new layer. The new layer appears in the Layers palette.

 Adjust the opacity of a layer to blend a layer containing a masked image with other layers.

BLENDING CHANNELS

You adjust the opacity and blend modes for selected layers to blend channel masks together or blend them into the larger picture. All layers except the background layer contain an opacity level that affects only the selected layer. Select two images, and then experiment with blend modes on a selected channel mask. You can use blending options to blend a masked image in a layer with the background layer image. Before beginning the following steps, open an image file, then select a masked image (Ctrl/Command+click on a layer to select its masked image). Add the RGB color channels to the selected mask (press Ctrl/Command+~). Now you're ready to move the image to a new image window by performing the following steps.

1. Open an image file. Ctrl/Command+click and drag a masked image or copy and paste an image object into a second image window.

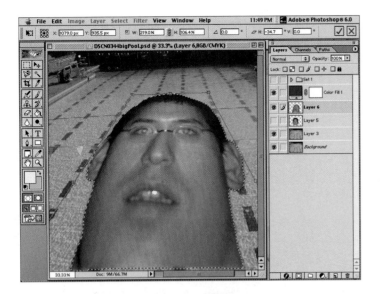

2. First make a backup of the layer you want to experiment with. Select the new layer and press Ctrl/Command+J to make a copy of the layer. Then de-activate the eye icon to hide the first layer.

3. Select the visible layer containing the masked image in the Layers palette. Then click on the right-arrow or f-icon pop-up menu in the Layers palette and choose Blending Options.

4. The Layer Style window appears. Click and drag the arrow beside the opacity setting, or type a number into the text box to change the opacity value. The selected image should blend with the background layer.

5. You can blend specific channels of the selected layer and the layer below it using the Blend If section of the Layer Style window. Hold down the option key to split the slider control. Any area between the sliders will be gradually blended into the other layer. Any values to the left or right of the sliders will be excluded from the blending process.

6. View the changes in the image window. Repeat steps 1 through 5 to blend other channel mask images with other image layers.

WORKING WITH CHANNELS AND LAYERS

In a nutshell, channels are stored in the Channels palette, and layers live in the Layers palette. Yet, both image elements exist in the same image window. If you have several channel masks and layers, use layer sets to organize the image layers related to the channel masks in the Layers palette. You can use commands to help blend mask channels with other layers in an image. This section shows you how to use the Feather and Calculations commands to help blend channel masks with other image layers.

ORGANIZING CHANNELS WITH LAYER SETS

You can use layer sets to organize layers of images, including alpha channels whose corresponding images reside in layers. Create layer sets to organize masked images. You can use layer sets to separate alpha channels from adjustment layers, group effects with an alpha channel, and so on. The following steps show you how to use layer sets to group masks and their adjustment layer effects.

1. Open an image file. Ctrl/Command+click and drag a masked image from a second image window to the first image window.
2. Add a fill layer or an adjustment layer to the new layer. I've added an orange fill layer to help blend the mechanical dog in with the background image.

3. Create a layer set and move the layer containing the image of the dog, plus any related effects, to the Layer set folder.
4. Click and drag a second image to the image window.
5. Apply any adjustment layers or fill layers to the document. Create a layer set and move the second image and any related layers to the layer set folder.

6. Click and drag the layer sets to a higher layer in the Layers palette to determine whether any of the global effects or fills are shared with any particular layer set folder.
7. Resize the images added to the image window, and use layer sets to experiment with channel and layer effects without losing any of the original elements in the background layer.

8. Select or de-select the eye icon to show or hide any layer sets of a particular document.

BLENDING A MASK WITH A LAYER

You should always smooth mask edges before or after adding a mask to another document. The Feather command is probably the easiest way to smooth rough edges on a mask. Select the mask and choose Feather from the Select menu, and poof, the mask edges are smoother.

The Feather command settings work with alpha channels similarly to the way the Gaussian Blur effect in the Filter menu blurs pixels in an image. If you plan to use a mask with different images, you may not want to apply the Feather command until after you've moved it to a new image file. You can use the Blur tool in the toolbox to soften pixels in part of an alpha channel as an alternative to apply the Feather command across the selected area of an alpha channel.

The following steps show you how to use the Feather command.

1. Open two image files. Copy and paste an image from one image file into another.
2. Use the Move tool to place the image in the image window.
3. If the background image is hidden, try adding a Fill layer to bring the two image elements together.

4. Ctrl/Command+click on a layer in the Layers palette. This key combination selects the image in the selected layer. Choose Feather from the Select menu.
5. Type a number, for example 5, into the text edit box to determine the number of pixels to be softened or blurred on both sides of the selection. For example, a feather of 50 (which I used to exaggerate this effect) softens the selected area 25 pixels inward and 25 pixels outward. Click on OK.

6. View the feathered mask in the image window.

USING CALCULATIONS WITH CHANNELS

You can blend masked or unmasked images without touching a pixel using the Calculations command in the Image menu. The Calculations command can apply blend modes to single channels between two source image files, resulting in a single grayscale channel. If you want to create a color result, use the Apply Image command. For more information about the Apply Image command, see Chapter 10, "Making Images Stand Out with Alpha Channels."

The Calculations window enables you to control inter-channel operations between layers and channels including alpha channels in the selected source images. You can apply this command to a single image file, or across two image files. Both images must be the same size (both images in this example are 1,600×1,200 pixels), and it might take a little time to determine the right combination of blending modes and calculation settings. However, the Calculations command can create some of the most unique

channel effects in Photoshop. The following steps show you how to use the Calculations command to combine channels with a blending mode, creating a new, grayscale image.

1. Open an image document, and then choose Calculations from the Image menu.
2. Select a source 1 and source 2 image. If you already have other image files open, Photoshop shows any of those images with the same dimensions in the drop-down menu.
3. Select the layer you want to use with the Calculations settings.
4. Choose Gray, Red, Green, or Blue from the Channel pop-up menu.

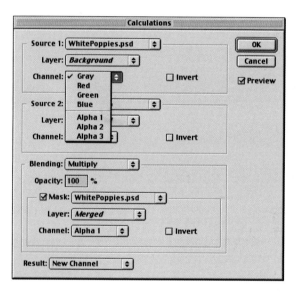

5. Pick a blending mode from the Blending pop-up menu. The blending modes available are Normal, Multiply, Screen, Overlay, Soft Light, Hard Light, Color Dodge, Color Burn, Darken, Lighten, Add, Subtract, Difference, and Exclusion. All of these blending modes are available to layers added to the Layers palette. For more information about blending modes, see Chapter 8, "Combining Images with Layers."
6. Finally, choose Selection, New Channel, or New Document from the Result pop-up menu. Then click on OK.

You can save the result of a calculation as a channel, a new file, or as a selection in the current document window. You simply choose one of the three output formats from the Result pop-up menu in the Calculations window.

7. If you chose to save the result in a channel, the image is saved to the Channels palette.

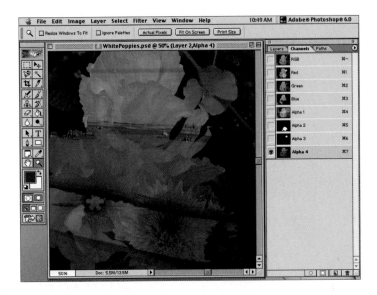

 Create a calculation between a layer and channel from the same image. Then save the result as a channel or selection to continue working with the image in progress.

ADDING EFFECTS TO CHANNELS

Choose a red, green, or blue channel and apply any effect from the Filter menu to it. Generally, the High Pass and Find Edges filters can be helpful to isolate the image's edges and thus facilitate creating a channel mask. Alternatively, use calculations to combine images, layers, or channels and save the result to a new channel in the Channels palette.

ADDING EFFECTS TO A SINGLE CHANNEL

Copy a channel or select an alpha channel if you want to apply an effect to a specific red, green, blue, or alpha channel. Once the effect is applied, you probably won't be able to use the other two channels to create a full-color image. Apply an effect to a single channel as you would to a full-color image. First copy the channel you want to use with the effect. Pick a selection tool from the toolbox, and then select all or part of the image in the image window. Choose a filter from the Filter menu and apply it to the selected image. View the effect in the image window. The following steps show you how to create a grayscale effect by applying the Find Edges effect to a channel.

1. Open an image file. Select a channel from the Channels palette. Click and drag the selected channel over the Create New Channel button (new document icon) to create a copy of that channel.
2. Click on the copy of the channel in the Channels palette. Choose an effect from the Filter menu. For example, I chose Find Edges from the Stylize submenu.

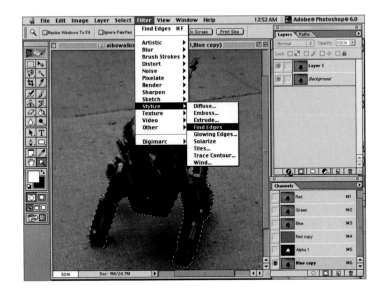

3. View the effect in the image window.

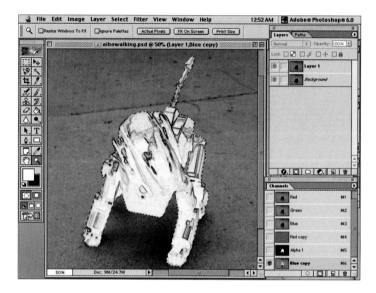

4. Press Ctrl/Command+Z to undo the filter effect, or choose Save from the File menu to permanently apply the effect to the channel.

ADDING EFFECTS ACROSS CHANNELS

If you choose one of the default red, green, or blue channels in the Channels palette, you can apply an effect to the full color image in the image window. Click on the RGB channel, or on any of the original red, green, or blue channels in the Channels palette. Then apply an effect from the Filter menu. The following steps show you how to apply two different effects, plastic wrap and trace contour, to the red, green, and blue channels of an image.

1. Open an image file. Select RGB, or one of the red, green, or blue channels in the Channels palette, and then choose a filter from the Filter menu.

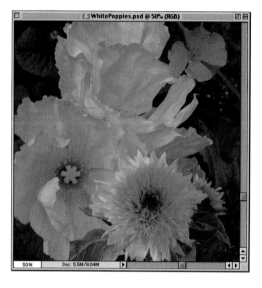

2. Choose a filter from one of the Filter sub-menus. For example, I opened the Filter menu, chose Artistic, and selected Plastic Wrap. Adjust the stroke and effect settings in the Palette Knife window. Click on OK to apply the effect. In this example, I set the stroke size to 15, the stroke detail to 2, and softness to 1.
3. View the effect in the image window. If you don't like the effect, choose Undo from the Edit menu to remove the effect from the image window.

4. Try applying a different filter to the image. Open the Filter menu, choose Stylize, and select Trace Contour.

5. Preview the effect in the document window. You can modify the effect by adjusting the level and edge settings in the Trace Contour window. Click OK.

CHAPTER 14

COMBINING IMAGES TO
CREATE ANIMATION

DIGITAL IMAGES ARE GREAT TO LOOK AT AS A SINGLE PHOTOGRAPH, BUT THEY CAN ALSO HELP YOU CREATE SOME GREAT ANIMATION. YOU SIMPLY HAVE TO OPEN A PHOTOSHOP FILE IN IMAGEREADY, ADD A FEW FRAMES, EDIT A FEW LAYERS, AND APPLY SOME EFFECTS. THEN YOU VIEW YOUR ANIMATION! IF YOU'RE CREATING ANIMATION FOR THE WEB, YOU THEN FLATTEN THE FRAMES INTO LAYERS AND EXPORT THE FILE AS AN ANIMATED GIF.

ANIMATING WITH FRAMES

ImageReady uses frames to create animation. Each frame appears in the Animation palette and can have its own set of layers in the Layers palette. You can create keyframes to define the motion path of the animation. Then use the Tween command to add frames between two keyframes. You can adjust the timing of a frame by assigning a delay to it in the Animation palette. Use the VCR controls at the bottom of the Animation palette to view and step back and forth through the animation.

RESIZING WITH THE IMAGE ASSISTANT

Although this chapter shows you how to create animation with ImageReady, you can resize an image in Photoshop before opening the file with ImageReady. Resizing a digital picture to a smaller size can help an animation play back faster, as well as require less memory for ImageReady to display it, and reduce the final size of the animation.

One way to resize an image is to open the Image menu and choose the Image command. If you're uncomfortable typing pixel or other dimensions into the Image Size window, use Photoshop's Resize Image Assistant. The following steps show you how to resize an image file using the Resize Image Assistant.

1. Open an image file you want to resize in Photoshop. Choose Resize Image from the Help menu.
2. Select the Online radio button. I chose the Online radio button because I want to use the resized image with a Web page. Choose the Print radio button if you plan to print the resized image. Click on Next.

3. Type the desired width and height of the image, and then click on Next.

4. Wait for the image to be resized. If this is the size you want, click on Finish. Otherwise, choose Back and type in a new width and height.

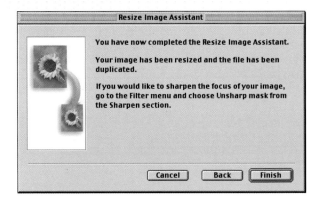

 You can use the Fit Image command to resize an image file to a specific pixel width and height. Open an image file, then choose the Fit Image command from the File, Automate menus. Type the width and height of the image into the Fit Image window, then click OK. Choose the Fit Image command after selecting the Batch command to resize a folder full of images.

DEFINING THE FIRST AND LAST FRAMES OF THE ANIMATION

You begin designing an animation by creating keyframes. The first and last frames in the Animation palette define the beginning and end keyframes of your animation. Once you define the start and end frames of the animation, you can add intermediate keyframes to define any middle animation points. Then you can use the Tween command in the Animation palette to generate any number of frames that you want to add between any two keyframes. The following steps show you how to create the first and last frames of an animation in ImageReady.

1. Open a Photoshop image file in ImageReady. This particular image should contain several layers of images. The Animation palette opens at the bottom of the workspace. If the Animation palette is not visible, open the Window menu and choose Show Animation.
2. Click on the first frame of animation in the Animation palette, and then click the Duplicates Current Frame icon (the document icon).

Duplicates Current Frame icon

3. Select the last frame of animation from the Animation palette. The last frame is the right-most frame in the Animation palette. With the last frame selected, make some of the layers visible to compose the final frame of the animation.
4. Use the Move tool to place the layer objects in the last frame of the animation in the image window.

5. Select the first frame. Make a different set of layer objects visible in this frame of animation.

6. Adjust the opacity levels to blend the layered images with the background image.

7. Click the Play button at the bottom of the Animation palette. Watch the animation play back and try to identify any particular intermediate keyframes that you can add to smooth the playback of the animation. If you want to track a specific image object across frames, Ctrl/Command+click its image layer. A dotted line will surround the selected image as each frame appears in the image window.

 The paradox of creating animation is that more frames are required to sustain fluid motion. If you're creating animation for the Web, however, smaller files are better. In a nutshell, use as few frames as possible to create your Web animation. If you're working with large image files (1,600×1,200 pixels or larger) ImageReady might move more slowly as the file grows bigger with more layers, masks, channels, and animation frames.

Select a larger icon view for the Layers palette to help you visualize the image in each layer. Choose Palette Options from the Layers palette pop-up menu to view three thumbnail image sizes. Click on a radio button to select an icon view. Being able to view each layer might help you figure out how the animation should flow across frames.

CREATING A KEYFRAME ANIMATION

The first frame of the animation is the original image we opened in ImageReady. You created the last frame of the animation in the previous section. The following steps show you how to create an intermediate keyframe and in-between frames in the Animation palette. Create as many intermediate keyframes as you like between the first and last frames of an animation. After you've created all the keyframes of the animation, use the Tween command to generate in-between frames of the animation.

Be sure to keep track of the amount of disk space available on your computer as you work on your animation. Most of all, remember your audience. If this animation is for a Web page, will the person viewing your animation want to wait for a long or short period of time before he or she can actually view it?

As you play back the animation in real time or step through each frame, you need to become familiar with the copy, paste, and selection tools in order to create additional keyframes and tweak or edit the frames of an animation. The following steps show you how to add intermediate keyframes and use the Tween command.

1. Click on the first frame of the Animation palette. Then click on the Duplicates Current Frame icon to create the second frame, an intermediate keyframe. Click on the second frame to select it.
2. Click on a layer in the Layers palette to select the masked image along with its layer.
3. Select the Move tool from the toolbox and move the masked image in the image window. If the selected image is also in the previous or next frame, place it in the motion or directional path of one of the other frames. This second frame will be the keyframe between the first and last frames of this animation.

4. Select the first frame, and then choose Tween from the pop-up menu in the Animation palette.

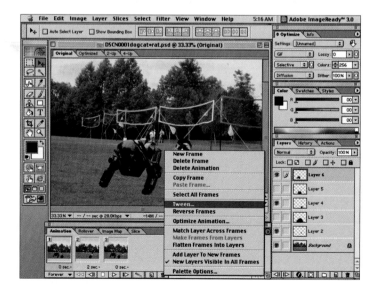

5. Click on a radio button to choose whether all layers or only a selected layer should have in-between frames created. In this example, I chose all layers.

6. Mark any check boxes to select the parameters of the Tween frames, such as position and opacity. Determine the number of frames to add in the Frames to Add text box.

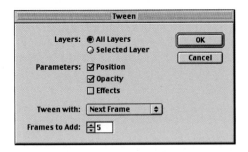

7. Choose Next Frame from the Tween with drop-down menu. Choosing this setting tells the Tween command to create tween frames between the first and second keyframes in the Animation palette. Click on OK. Wait for ImageReady to render each frame.

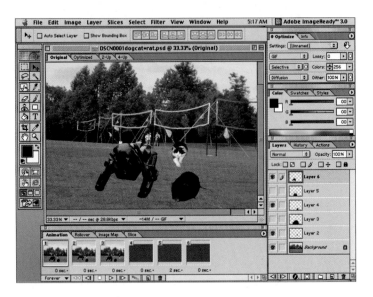

VIEWING ANIMATION

The Animation palette contains a fully functional set of VCR control buttons. You can play, stop, pause, and step through an animation in the same way you control a videotape in a VCR. Choose the number of times you want the animation to loop from the pop-up menu in the lower-left corner of the Animation palette. Play the animation several times and take some quick notes if you see anything you want to change.

1. Click on the Play button in the Animation palette.
2. View the frames as they change in the image window.
3. Click on the Stop button to stop the animation playback.
4. Click on the Step Forward or Step Backward buttons to view the animation forward or backward manually, frame by frame.

Animation playback might be slower if each image contains many layers, channels, or channel masks. Also, if the image is several megabytes in size, it might take ImageReady a little time to process each frame of animation.

ADDING ANIMATION EFFECTS

The previous sections showed you how to add frames to create an animation. You can manually add an effect to an image layer across several frames of animation. You can also add effects using the Transform commands to distort the shape of the object at the beginning and end frames of an animation sequence.

In traditional animation, these distortions are called squash and stretch techniques. The squash motion flattens the image as it impacts a solid surface. The stretch motion pulls the object up or down as the image moves toward or away from the solid surface. This section provides brief examples of how you create a composite image for video in Photoshop and distort an animation in ImageReady.

WORKING WITH BLUE AND GREEN SCREENS

Blue and green screens refer to the chroma-key effects commonly used in television. *Chroma-key* works by using a single key color such as blue in one screen, for example, behind an actor, and then replacing the color with a different background. If any of the live actors or still-image elements in the picture contain the color of the chroma-key, that area of the live image will also show the second image. This creates a hole through part of the image you actually want the viewer to see.

You can add video to a digital image by creating alpha channels that can be used with chroma-keyed video. The alpha channel shares a common color with the chroma-keyed video. The resulting composite image can display full-motion video within a still-motion digital picture.

Use any color you like to create a composite image. As mentioned in Chapter 10, "Making Images Stand Out with Channels," and Chapter 13, "Experimenting with Channel Operations," a composite refers to two distinct elements that retain their uniqueness, but contribute to the whole image. Composite images bring two images, masked or unmasked, still or video, into a believable single picture.

The following steps show two different examples of how you can combine a masked image with a chroma-key color to combine a second image or video with an image.

1. For the first image in this example, create a new image file in Photoshop or ImageReady.
2. Press Ctrl/Command+A to select the entire window.
3. Select the Paint Bucket tool. Choose a blue foreground color in the color well. Click in the image window to fill it with the blue foreground color.
4. Copy and paste a full-color image or Ctrl/Command+click and drag a masked image into the image window. The masked image should appear as the foreground image with blue as the background color. If you apply the masked image to each frame of video, the resulting composite image will show the masked image in front of the video footage.

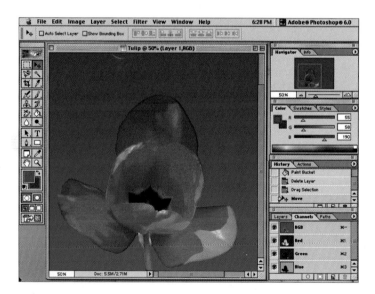

5. For the second example, create a mask of an image. Ctrl/Command+ click the alpha channel in the Channels palette to select the mask in the alpha channel. Then press Ctrl/Command+~ to bring the RGB channels into the mask. Press Ctrl/Command+click to put the image into copy mode, and then drag it to the image window containing a green background. Composite the still image with a different background layer or image. The background layer can also contain video.

6. Alternatively, invert the mask and use a fill color in the masked area. Click and drag the masked image and place it in the image window to complete the final composite image.

 Combine animation, still images, and video using composite imaging. If the image's edges tend to stand out, create a mask and feather the edges.

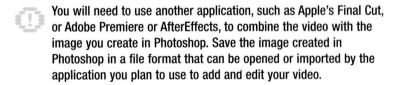 You will need to use another application, such as Apple's Final Cut, or Adobe Premiere or AfterEffects, to combine the video with the image you create in Photoshop. Save the image created in Photoshop in a file format that can be opened or imported by the application you plan to use to add and edit your video.

SCALING AND DISTORTING IMAGES

You can use the Transform commands in Photoshop or ImageReady to distort an image, image layer, or masked image in an animation. The following steps show you how to use the Transform commands to distort the shape of an image in Photoshop. This example only shows a single image being distorted. Depending on the animation you want to create, you may need to distort up to a dozen image files to create a smooth, flowing squash or stretch effect. Edit several images in Photoshop, then open them in ImageReady to create the animation.

1. Ctrl/Command+click and drag a masked image to the target image window. If the target image window contains fewer pixels (for example, if the source image is taken from a 2,000×1,500-pixel image, but is being moved to a 640×480 image), the source image will appear disproportionate to the target image.

2. Select the image layer in the Layers palette.
3. Open the Edit menu, choose Transform, and then select Scale. Or press Ctrl/Command+T.
4. Click and drag a point on the boundary box to resize the image.

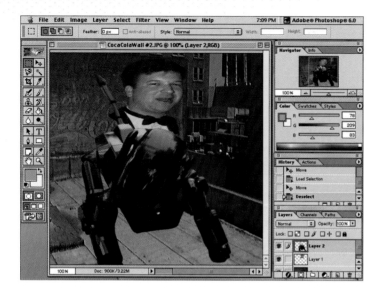

5. Add a second masked image to the target image window. Select the second image layer.
6. Open the Edit menu, choose Transform, and select Distort.
7. Adjust the image to match the perspective of the background picture.

 An easy way to create a simple animation is to use the Flip Horizontal or Flip Vertical commands located in the Transform submenu of the Edit menu.

For some animation, such as making a character jump or walk, you can use the Transform commands to create a squash and squish effect across the frames of an animation. Once you create the keyframes in Photoshop, save the image as a Photoshop file. Then create the in-between frames in ImageReady.

EXPORTING ANIMATION

The final phase of creating animation is to prepare it for another application, or for the World Wide Web. The following sections show you how to prepare an animation for the Web. Choose Animated GIF as the file format to

export from ImageReady. You can use other applications, such as Adobe AfterEffects, Macromedia Flash, Fireworks, or a Web-editing tool, to add more effects or elements to your GIF before sharing the final results on a Web page.

FLATTENING FRAMES INTO LAYERS

You need to save two copies of any image you work on in Photoshop or ImageReady. Save one as a Photoshop file to retain any layers, masks, channels, and animation frames. Then, using ImageReady, flatten the image in the second copy, save it as an animated GIF file, and import it into another application, or post it to a Web site. The following steps show you how to flatten animation frames into layers with ImageReady.

1. Open a Photoshop file containing animation frames.
2. Preview the animation by using the Play and Stop buttons in the Animation palette. Save the image as a Photoshop file so that you can continue to edit it after you've exported it as an animated GIF.

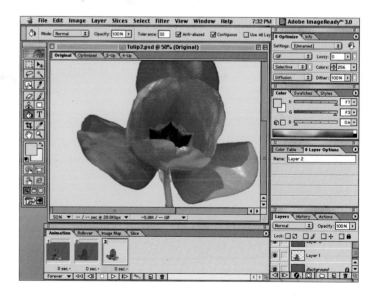

3. Choose Flatten Frames Into Layers from the pop-up menu in the Animation palette.

4. ImageReady converts the animation frames into layers, which appear in the Layers palette. The new layers are marked as visible in the Layers palette and any layers that existed prior to flattening frames are marked as hidden.

5. Select GIF from the Optimize palette. Choosing this file type enables you to save the visible layers as an animated GIF. An animated GIF is a single file containing an animation.

6. Choose Image Size from the Image menu and resize the animation so that it will have a reasonable download time on a Web page. I chose 400×267 for my animation.

7. Click on the drop-down menu in the lower-left corner of the Animation palette. Choose Once, Forever, or Other to set the number of times the animation will loop, or repeat itself, once it starts playing.

8. Preview the image by choosing the Optimized tab in the image window. View the download time of the resized image. Click on the drop-down menu at the middle-bottom of the image window to view a different download time for the animation.

Photoshop files are the only files that can save Photoshop-specific features, such as layer styles and layer sets. Be sure you have plenty of disk space if you plan to create and save several animation files, especially when they contain lots of layers, masks, and channels.

OPTIMIZING AND EXPORTING ANIMATION

Preview each frame of your animation using ImageReady's Web-savvy optimization tools and file formats. You can preview frames before or after flattening frames. You may want to save two different versions of the same animated GIF to compare different optimization settings. The animated GIF is saved as a single file that can be embedded in an HTML file and posted to your Web site. If you're not sure which optimization settings to use, you can create a separate Web page for each animated GIF to compare them.

Continuing from the previous set of steps, the following steps show you how to optimize and save the animation as an animated GIF file.

1. Select an Adaptive, Perceptual, or Selective palette from the Color Reduction drop-down menu in the Optimize palette to ensure colors are consistent across frames.
2. Select the 2-Up or 4-Up tab from the image window to compare the original image to the settings in the Optimize palette. For example, compare the image using an adaptive palette with the same image using a selective or perceptual palette.
3. Review the quality of the GIF image compared to the original, and note the file size and download time in the bottom-right panel of the document window.

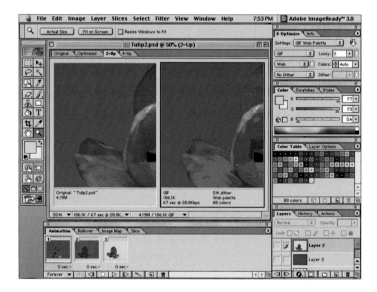

4. Choose Save Optimized As from the File menu. Select Save Image Only from the drop-down menu in the Save As window. The file name in the text box should end in .gif, indicating you'll be saving an animated GIF file. Click on Save to create the animated GIF.

5. Type a name for the animated GIF file and then click on the Save button.

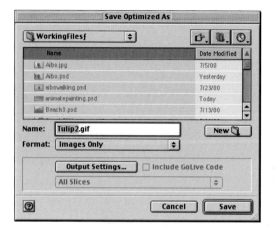

6. ImageReady creates a single GIF image containing the animation.

Try to choose the shortest possible download time, with the largest possible image size for your animation. If you think the person viewing the animation will have a broadband or T1 Internet connection, you can save larger image sizes. However, most people browsing the Internet have a 28.8 or 56k connection. If you want to download a large animation to your Web page, add a text message to let your Web visitors know that they should expect to wait a certain amount of time before they can view your animation.

If your target audience is most concerned with file download time, create the smallest possible file, or break up the animation into smaller pieces, if possible. If your target audience wants to view animation containing, keep the image at its full size and choose GIF with a 128-color palette.

CHAPTER 15

COMBINING IMAGES WITH TEXT

IN THIS CHAPTER, YOU LEARN HOW TO ENHANCE A PICTURE WITH A FEW WORDS OF TEXT, OR CREATE A MONTAGE CONTAINING TEXT AND IMAGES. PHOTOSHOP 6 ENABLES YOU TO EDIT TEXT DIRECTLY IN THE IMAGE WINDOW. YOU THEN USE THE CHARACTER AND PARAGRAPH PALETTES TO FORMAT AND VIEW TEXT SETTINGS.

ADDING TEXT TO IMAGES

Choose the Type tool and type in the image window to add text to any image file. When the Type tool is selected, the toolbar at the top of the workspace displays all the Type tool options, such as font, font size, and font style. Quickly change text settings by changing the text settings in the Type options bar.

FORMATTING TEXT

If you don't plan to create a design-oriented multimedia masterpiece by adding text or line art to a photographic image, you might be perfectly happy with the default font and formatting settings. If you change your mind, font size, styles, and other character and paragraph settings can be right at your fingertips. The following steps show you how to format text and access the Character and Paragraph palettes.

1. Open an image to which you want to add text in Photoshop.
2. Select the Type tool from the toolbox, and click in the image window at the location where the text should start.
3. Select the proper font, font size, and font style from the options bar at the top of the workspace.
4. Click in the image window and type some text. Photoshop displays the text in the image window and creates a text layer in the Layers palette.
5. Click on the layer containing text in the Layers palette. This key combination selects the text as well as its layer.
6. Use the Move tool to arrange the text in the image window.
7. Change the font size by typing a number into the text box in the options bar, or by selecting a font size from the pop-up menu.
8. Select Show Character from the Window menu. The Character and Paragraph palettes appear.

9. Click on the Paragraph tab to view the Paragraph palette. Click on a button to adjust the alignment or formatting options of a selected block of text.

10. Click outside the selected text area to de-select the text in the text layer, or click on a different layer in the Layers palette.

Another way to select text is to click on the text layer in the Layers palette, and then click and drag the Type tool. Click and drag the cursor over the text you want to select in the image window.

WARPING TEXT

Hidden in the right end of the Type options bar is an amazing tool that can warp text in over a dozen ways: the Warp Text tool. You can also access the Warp Text command by clicking on the Layer, Type menus. You can customize each warp form by adjusting slider settings, or by typing percentage values for horizontal or vertical effects. The Warp Text window enables you to quickly create text effects. The following steps show you how to warp text.

1. Open an image file. Choose a text layer in the Layers palette, and select the text in the image window by holding the mouse button while dragging the cursor across the text.
2. Click on the Type tool in the toolbox. Then click on the T button on the right side of the tool options bar to open the Warp Text window.
3. View the list of styles in the Style drop-down menu of the Warp Text window. Click on a style in the drop-down. Click on a slider control to customize the warp effect. Click on OK.

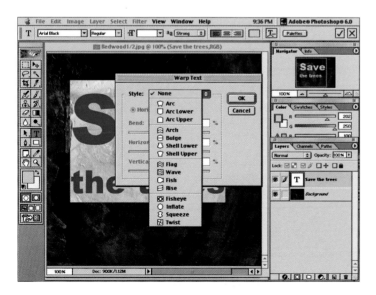

4. View the warp effect on the selected text.
5. Select the text layer and press Ctrl/Command+J to duplicate the layer.
6. Click on the newly created layer, choose the Type tool from the toolbox, and then choose Character from the Window menu to open the Character palette. Double-click the color box and select a new color from the palette. Then place the changed text below the first layer to create a 3D effect. You can use the Move tool to create a slight offset of the text in either of the layers to heighten the effect.

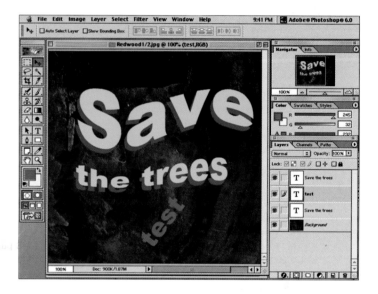

RASTERIZING TEXT

Text, also referred to as type, is added to an image as vector graphic objects in a layer. Each character is resolution independent, and can have its own font size, or style, independent of any character beside it. However, in order to apply an effect to text, it must be rasterized, or rendered into a bitmap. Once text is rasterized, it can no longer be edited with the Type tool. However, you can still use selection tools, such as the Magic Wand, to select text bitmaps. The following steps show you how to convert vector type into rasterized, or bitmap, type.

1. Open an image file that contains a newly added text layer (that is, one that has not been rasterized).
2. Click a text layer in the Layers palette.
3. Select an effect from the Filter menu. A dialog box appears informing you that you must rasterize the type before proceeding. Click on OK.

⚠ **This type layer must be rasterized before proceeding. Its text will no longer be editable. Rasterize the type?**

[Cancel] [**OK**]

4. Click the OK button, the text will be rasterized and the Filter will be applied.

❗ Click on the text layer to apply an effect only to the text in the image. Conversely, click on the background image to apply an effect specifically to the background layer.

VIEWING IMAGES INSIDE TEXT

Sometimes adding text can enhance an image by reiterating a visual message. Use the Type tool to add two-dimensional text characters to an image. Then convert that text to a mask or blend another image into the text to create a more complex image.

CREATING A TEXT MASK

You can place an image inside some text to give the text a little more substance. To create this effect, first create a text mask. Most text is added as a solid color to an image window, making it easy to convert to a mask. Paste an image into the selected text, or group the layers together in the Layers palette to create a unique text effect. The following steps show you how to create a text channel mask.

1. Open an image to which you want to add text in Photoshop. Choose the Magic Wand tool.
2. Hold down the Shift key and select each letter you want to use to create the mask.

3. Select the Channels tab in the palette window.
4. Click on the Save Selection as Channel button in the Channels palette to create an alpha channel.
5. Click on the alpha channel to view the black-and-white mask.

 If you plan to move or resize text, remember to remove any channels that contain masked text. This helps to avoid mismatched effects and reduce confusion when experimenting with layers and masks.

 You can create a single text mask by clicking a text layer. Then select each letter of the mask using the Magic Wand tool. If you applied the Magic Wand tool to the alpha mask channel, press Ctrl/Command+~ to bring the RGB channels into the selected mask area. Then press Ctrl/Command+J to create a new layer containing the text mask.

BLENDING TEXT ACROSS LAYERS

In this section, you select an image from a different picture and combine it with a text mask to buffer the edges of each letter with a sophisticated or colorful image. You can use the text mask created in the previous section to complete this task. This effect can help merge the text with the big picture. The following steps show you how to use the Paste Into command to complete the effect described in the previous section.

1. Open an image file containing two or more text layers.
 2. Choose a selection tool from the toolbox to select part of the image. I chose the Rectangular Marquee selection tool.

3. Select the Copy command from the Edit menu.
4. Ctrl/Command+click the text layer in a second image window.

5. Select Paste Into from the Edit menu. The image appears in the text layer. Notice that a mask is created with the new image layer in the Layers palette.

 Try creating multiple layers of text combined with different layer styles and adjustment layers to find the best combination of text and images.

MASKING TEXT WITH AN IMAGE

You can also combine text with an image mask. Bigger fonts will obviously show more of the image than smaller fonts. Select an image mask that is larger than the text image window. When you group the image with the mask, the text layer will show the masked image instead of its default text color. You can move the image mask and place it anywhere over the text in the image window to customize the effect. The following steps show you how to combine an image mask with text.

1. Open an image file containing a text layer.
2. Ctrl/Command + click and drag an image mask from a second image window into the image window containing the text mask. Click and drag the image mask layer and place it above the text mask layer.

3. Open the Layer menu and select the Group with Previous command to mask the image with the text.

4. The masked image appears over the text in the image window. Use the Move tool to place the masked image over the text.

LAYER STYLES AND TEXT EFFECTS

In order to apply an effect to text, you must convert the vector graphic text into bitmapped, or rasterized, text images. Once text is rasterized, it can be treated like any other image layer in the Layers palette. You can add a drop shadow or an inner glow. You can also apply effects to your heart's content and experiment with layer styles to create unique text effects.

ADDING DROP SHADOWS AND EFFECTS

Compared to working with picture images, it's a little easier to determine where a drop shadow should fall when working with text. You can add any layer effect to make a letter or word stand out in a picture. The following steps show you how to add a drop shadow adjustment layer to bitmap text.

1. Open an image file and add text to it using the Type tool. Select the text layer, open the Layer menu and choose Rasterize Type to convert the vector text to bitmap text. Ctrl/Command+click the text layer. This keyboard combination selects all text characters in a layer. Select the text you want to apply a drop shadow effect.

2. Open the Layer menu, choose New Adjustment Layer, and select Drop Shadow.

3. Adjust the angle of the shadow by typing a value in the Angle section of the Layer Style window, or by clicking and dragging the directional line in the Angle circle. Try to approximate the lighting direction in the background image to give a more realistic effect.

4. Click in the color square next to the Blend Mode pop-up menu to change the color of the drop shadow.

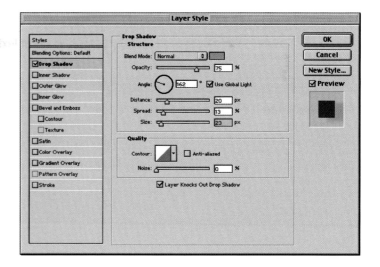

5. Click on OK to save your changes. View the drop shadow in the image window.

6. Turn the drop-shadow effect off by clicking on the eye icon in the Layers palette.

7. Select the effect, and then choose Change Layer Content from the Layer menu to edit the drop shadow.

 You can duplicate a layer of text and place it a layer below or above the first text layer to create a multi-colored drop-shadow effect.

ANIMATING TEXT

You need to open a Photoshop file containing text layers in ImageReady to animate text. You then work with the frames, text layers, channels, and masks in ImageReady to create animation. Take the first frame and create new key frames. Move text around in each key frame to create a motion path across the key frames. Then generate in-between frames with ImageReady's Tween command. To find out more about how to animate images, see Chapter 14, "Combining Images to Create Animation." The following steps show you how to create a simple text animation with ImageReady.

1. Open a Photoshop file in ImageReady.

2. The image is selected as the first frame in the Animation palette. Click on the Duplicates Current Frame button in the Animation palette at the bottom of the workspace.

3. Select the second frame. Move the text objects to a different position than the first frame.

4. Click on the first frame. Choose Tween from the pop-up menu and wait for ImageReady to generate the in-between frames.
5. Click on the Play button to watch the animated text.

CHAPTER 16

AUTOMATING TASKS

A FEW DOZEN YEARS AGO WHEN COMPUTERS WERE BEGINNING TO TAKE ON
THE FORM OF A DESKTOP MACHINE, A FEW WRITERS WROTE ABOUT A DAY
WHEN COMPUTERS MIGHT TAKE OVER THE WORLD. TAKE THIS SAME PREMISE
AND VIEW IT FROM ANOTHER PERSPECTIVE, AND YOU MIGHT THINK
SOFTWARE WOULD BE EASY TO USE IF IT COULD RUN REPETITIVE TASKS ON
ITS OWN, WITHOUT THE HELP OF SOMEONE TO SIT THERE AND CLICK THE
MOUSE TO MAKE THE SOFTWARE GO.

THE ACTIONS PALETTE TOOLS ENABLE YOU TO RECORD AND PLAY BACK
MOST TASKS IN PHOTOSHOP. THE AUTOMATE COMMANDS ALLOW YOU TO
AUTOMATICALLY RUN TASKS SUCH AS RESIZING IMAGES OR CREATING A
CONTACT SHEET. THE FOLLOWING SECTIONS SHOW YOU HOW TO USE THE
BUILT-IN ACTIONS AND AUTOMATION SCRIPTS IN PHOTOSHOP.

CREATING AN AUTOMATED TASK

Photoshop includes a default set of actions. However, you can easily create your own, share them with friends, and of course, watch Photoshop do your work for you. You record and play actions from the Actions palette.

USING THE ACTIONS PALETTE

Like the other Photoshop palettes, the Actions palette has the same pop-up menu and toolbar. Choose an action or an action set from the Actions palette pop-up menu. Once an action or action set is loaded, actions are listed in the palette window. Each set of actions is preceded by two selectable boxes, one for toggling each item on or off, and the other for toggling its dialog box on or off. The following steps provide a brief tour of the Actions palette.

1. Select the Actions palette from the floating window.
2. View the list of action categories available to you.
3. View the Stop, Record, Play, folder set, and action script icons at the bottom of the window. Click on the triangle icon to view the actions for each category. Click on the right-arrow drop-down menu to view a list of menu commands for the Actions palette.
4. Click on the pop-up menu in the upper right corner of the Actions palette. Choose another set of action scripts from the bottom portion of the pop-up menu.

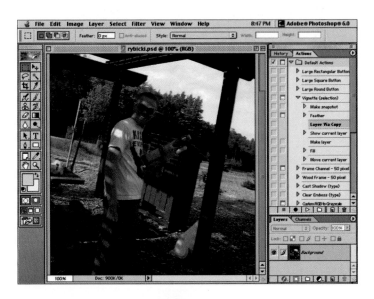

 If the Actions palette is empty, choose Load Actions from the pop-up menu and navigate to the Photoshop 6 Required folder. Double-click on the Default Actions document.

5. Click on an action to select it.
6. Expand a triangle for an action. You should see a description for that action. Double-click on an action in the Actions palette. If an item in the Actions palette has a collapsible triangle below it, double-clicking this kind of action will only display its Action Options window. In this example, a copy of the background image is created in the Layers palette.

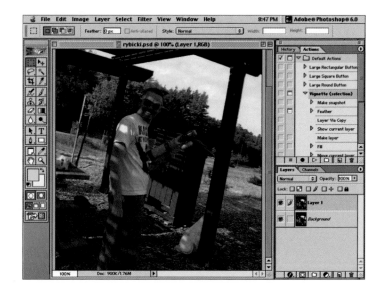

CREATING ACTIONS

Most tasks in Photoshop can be recorded with the Actions palette VCR control buttons. This enables you to repeat tasks with a click of the mouse. The following steps show you how to use the Record button to create a script in the Actions palette.

1. Open an image file. Click on the Record button in the Actions palette.
2. Select an effect from the Filter menu.
3. Adjust the filter settings. Click on OK to apply the filter to the document window.

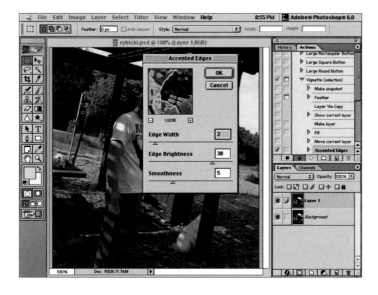

4. View the effect in the image window. Then click on the Record button a second time to stop the recording.
5. The new action appears in the Actions palette. Select the action, and then click on the Play button to execute the action.

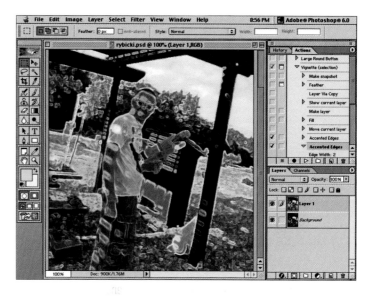

Photoshop can't record everything you do as an action. Try to record small actions to verify that they can be automated in Photoshop. This is better than running through long combinations of tasks, only to find out that one or two of them cannot be recorded as an action.

PLAYING AN ACTION SCRIPT

You can run a Batch command on a set of open files in Photoshop in order to automatically add an effect or filter to all the files at once. The following steps show you how to apply an effect action for applying an effect. Then use the Batch command to automate adding that effect to a folder of images.

1. Choose Image Effects from the Actions palette pop-up menu.
2. Open an image file. Double-click an effect in the Actions palette.

3. Adjust any settings for the effect (this step applies to effects that are associated with their own effect window) and then click OK.

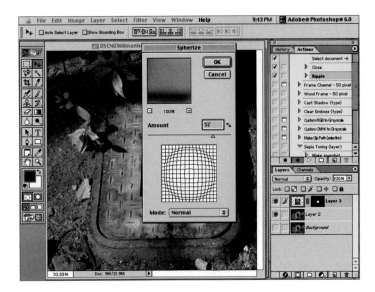

4. View the effect added to the selected area of the image.

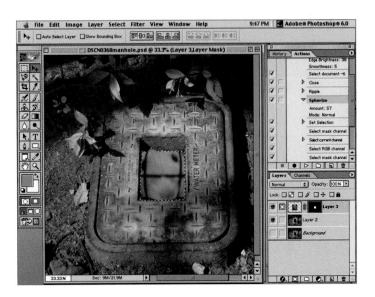

5. Choose Batch from the File menu. Click on the Set drop-down menu and choose Image Effects.atn. Click on the Action drop-down menu to choose the effect you want to apply on the selected image files.

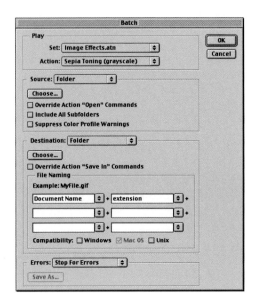

6. Click on the Source and Destination buttons to select the folder you want to apply the script on, and the folder where you'd like to save the resulting images to. Click OK to run the Batch command. The Batch command will process each file in the selected folder and apply the effect to each image.

 Use the Record and Stop buttons in the Actions palette to create your own effects scripts. As you create new scripts, one should appear in the Batch window. Each script is saved with the action set that was open when the task was recorded.

 For more information about Photoshop plug-ins and effects, see Chapter 6, "Enhancing Images with Filters and Effects."

USING AUTOMATED TASKS

You can change the image mode of a picture, resize the images, generate a contact sheet, or create a Picture Package using the scripts in the Automate menu. You can use the Conditional Mode Change script to change an image from RGB mode to Indexed color mode. The Fit Image script enables you to resize the width and height of an image. The Contact Sheet II script can take a folder full of image files and create a thumbnail of each picture in a contact sheet enabling you to view or print pages of pictures from Photoshop. If you want to view an image at one or two different sizes in the same image window, use the Picture Package script to automatically resize and lay out the image in a new image window. Choose Batch to perform an action on a folder full of files.

RESIZING IMAGES AUTOMATICALLY

Most 2- and 3-megapixel cameras create large files ranging from 640×480 pixels to 1,600×1,200 or 2,000×1,500. Choose the Fit Image automation script to let Photoshop resize your pictures for your Web site.

 Resizing a large image to a smaller one works great if you're trying to add graphics to a Web site. However, if you have a 50×50-pixel image, resizing it to 640×480 will only enlarge the pixels, and the image might not be recognizable.

The following steps show you how to resize images using the Fit Image script.

1. Open an image file that you want to resize.
2. Open the File menu, choose Automate, and select Fit Image.
3. Type a value for the width and height of the image in the Fit Image dialog box. I chose 320×240. Then click on OK.

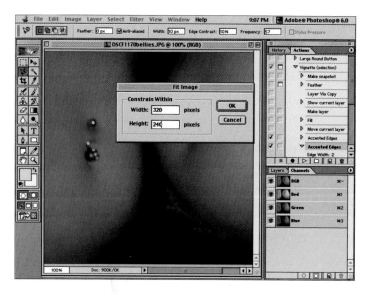

4. The image is resized within the selected document window. Save the file with its new dimensions, or select Undo from the Edit menu to revert the image to its original size.

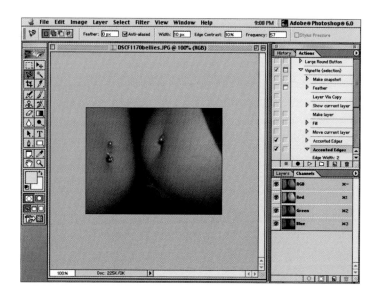

CHANGING IMAGE MODES

You can run a script to switch the image mode of an image file. For example you can change an image open in RGB mode to another image mode, such as grayscale or CMYK mode. This kind of script can be helpful if you have a folder full of images you want to print, or convert to grayscale before editing them. The following script shows you how to run the Conditional Mode Change script on a folder to change the files to indexed color mode. This example uses Indexed Color as the target mode, but you can choose from Bitmap, Grayscale, Duotone, CMYK, Lab, and Multichannel modes, too. Saving an image in Indexed Color mode can reduce the image file's size while preserving most of the image quality. The following steps show you how to change an image from RGB to Indexed Color mode using the Conditional Mode Change script.

1. Open an image file. The image mode of the image appears in the title of the image window. For example, if the image opens in RGB mode, you should see RGB following the name of the image file at the top of the image window. Open the File menu, choose Automate, and select Conditional Mode Change.

2. The Conditional Mode Change window opens. Select Indexed Color from the Target Mode drop-down menu. Click on OK.

3. The Indexed Color window opens. Adjust the settings for Indexed Color mode.

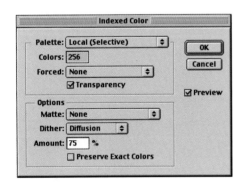

4. Click on OK and wait for Photoshop to switch image modes for the selected file.

5. View the image in Indexed Color mode.

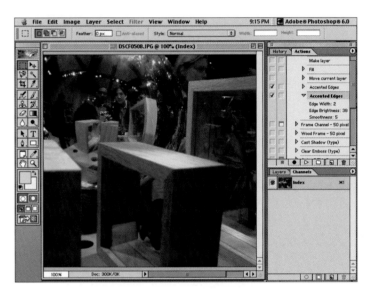

 Most images produced from digital cameras open in RGB mode in Photoshop. Unless you need to work with the image in CMYK or another image mode, I suggest saving the file in RGB mode as a Photoshop file until it is ready to be optimized and saved for the Web.

USING BATCH PROCESSING

Turn actions into automation scripts by choosing Batch from the Automate menu. The Batch command enables you to use an action script on a folder full of files as opposed to applying an action to the image window. Customize play, source, destination, and error settings for the action from the Batch window. The Batch command is probably the easiest to use, and the most powerful menu command you'll find for automating tasks in Photoshop. The following steps give you a brief tour of the Batch window.

1. Open the File menu, choose Automate, and select Batch.
2. Choose an action set from the Set drop-down menu (located at the top of the Batch window) if you want to run a particular action on a folder full of image files. If you have an action set loaded in the Actions palette, it will appear in the Set drop-down menu. Choose another action set from the Set drop-down menu if you want to use a different action script with the Batch command.

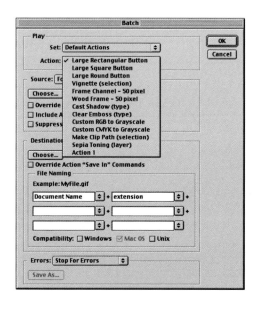

3. Select the type of source you want to use with the Batch process.
4. Click on the Choose button to select the folder on which you want to run the batch process.

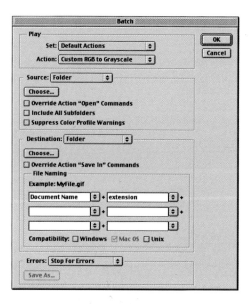

 Although using a Batch process can be a great time saver, you should still take time to review all the images generated by the automation script before posting them to a Web site. Remember that software can make mistakes, too.

CREATING A CONTACT SHEET

Let Photoshop put a folder of pictures onto a contact sheet. Contact sheets can be printed and used to catalog all the digital pictures you take, create, or convert from a 35mm camera. You can then preview the layout and adjust the settings for the contact sheet in the Contact Sheet II window. The following steps show you how to create a contact sheet using the Contact Sheet II script.

1. Open the File menu, choose Automate, and select Contact Sheet II.
2. Click on Choose and navigate to the source folder you want to use with the contact sheet. The source folder is a folder on your hard drive or network server that contains the images you want to put on the contact sheet. Click on the Choose button to select the folder containing the image files. Review the Document and Thumbnail settings in the Contact Sheet II window and customize any settings as you like. Then click on OK to run the script.

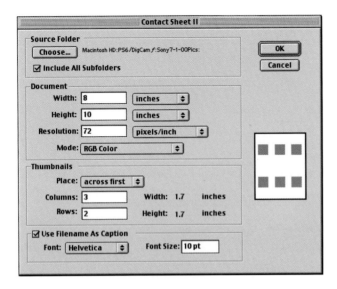

3. Wait for the images to be resized in the selected folder. Photoshop will automatically create a new image window for each contact sheet until all images in the source folder have been processed.

4. View the contact sheet(s) in the image window(s).

 It may take a while to create a contact sheet. If you decide you want to stop the contact sheet script, press the Escape key.

 Check the Use Filename as Caption check box to attach the file names to each picture on the contact sheet. Being able to associate the picture with the file name on your hard drive can prevent you from hunting for a picture in vain.

USING THE PICTURE PACKAGE SCRIPT

Choose the Picture Package script to view a color image at different sizes in one image window. Use the current image in the image window with the Picture Package script, or select an image file from your hard drive. Choose from two different pages sizes: 11×17 and 8×10, plus a wide range of photo sizes, from four 4×5 or two 5×7 images on a page, or a combination of sizes, such as two 4×5 and four 2.5×3.5 images. The page layout you choose appears on the right side of the Picture Package window. The following steps show you how to use the Picture Package script to layout a picture as two 5×7 images.

1. Open the File menu, select Automate, and choose Picture Package.
2. Click on Choose, select a source file, and then pick a layout from the pop-up menu. For this example, I chose two 5×7 images. Click on OK.

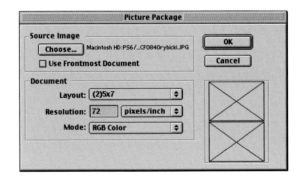

3. Wait for the automation script to run. Photoshop creates a new window and re-sizes the picture to match the criteria selected in the Place Picture window.

4. View the Picture Package window. Save it if you like it, or discard it.

Although I did not provide an example, you can easily automate the image slicing process. You can use the Slice tool to break an image up into smaller files, or slices. Slicing an image file can help graphics load more quickly on a Web page. To automate slicing, you can create an action in the Actions palette to automate creating a slice. Then use the Batch command to run the slice action on a folder of image files.

PART 4

PUBLISHING PICTURES

ONE OF THE ADVANTAGES OF TAKING PICTURES WITH A DIGITAL CAMERA
OR WORKING WITH ANY DIGITAL PICTURE IS THAT YOU CAN SHARE THEM
ON THE WEB WITH RELATIVE EASE. OF COURSE, IT HELPS TO HAVE YOUR
OWN WEB SITE. HOWEVER, MANY WEB SITES, SUCH AS SHUTTERFLY.COM
AND OFOTO.COM, WILL HOST YOUR WEB PHOTO ALBUMS FOR FREE. THE
FOLLOWING SECTIONS SHOW YOU HOW TO OPTIMIZE YOUR PICTURES FOR
THE WEB AND CREATE A WEB PHOTO ALBUM.

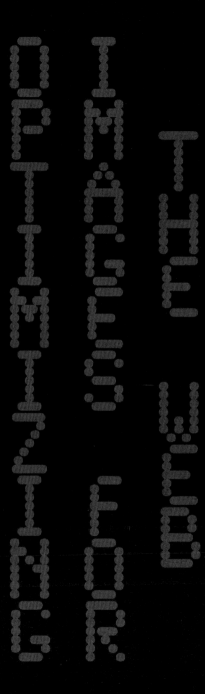

OPTIMIZING IMAGES
FOR THE WEB

OPTIMIZING AN IMAGE FOR THE WEB WITH PHOTOSHOP OR IMAGEREADY
INVOLVES THE PROCESS OF REDUCING THE SIZE OF AN IMAGE FILE WHILE
RETAINING AS MUCH OF THE IMAGE'S QUALITY AS POSSIBLE. THIS
CHAPTER FOCUSES ON USING THE OPTIMIZATION SETTINGS IN THE SAVE
FOR WEB WINDOW IN PHOTOSHOP. HOWEVER, IMAGEREADY HAS MANY
SIMILAR FEATURES IN ITS OPTIMIZE PALETTE AND IMAGE WINDOW. AN
IMAGE WITH LOTS OF SOLID COLOR AND STATIC IMAGES IS EASIER TO
OPTIMIZE THAN AN IMAGE CONTAINING A BROAD RANGE OF COLORS AND
LOTS OF SMALL, BRIGHT, OR ANIMATED ELEMENTS. SINCE PHOTOS TEND TO
FALL INTO THE LATTER CATEGORY, YOU'LL PROBABLY BE OPTIMIZING AN
IMAGE AS A JPEG OR GIF 128 FILE FORMAT. THIS CHAPTER SHOWS YOU HOW
TO PREVIEW AN IMAGE, USE THE SLICE TOOL TO BREAK UP AN IMAGE IN
PHOTOSHOP, AND OPTIMIZE COLORS AND WORK WITH TRANSPARENCIES TO
CREATE WEB-READY IMAGES.

ANALYZING WEB ELEMENTS

Previewing different file formats is the key to optimizing an image for a Web page. Of the file formats available for the Web, JPEG usually can create the smallest image because it uses file compression. However, the quality of the image can vary depending on whether you choose to save the image as a low, medium, or high quality image.

A GIF image with 128 colors is another alternative for saving a Web image, especially if it contains transparency settings. JPEG does not support transparency settings, so if an image needs to blend with a background image, you must save is as a GIF. Additional Web elements to consider when optimizing an image are download time and image quality.

OPTIMIZING FILE SIZE

Optimized files can be previewed in the Save for Web window before they are actually saved to the hard drive. Choose JPEG, GIF, or PNG file formats, which support different numbers of colors in their corresponding color palettes. Choose 2-Up or 4-Up modes to compare optimized files with the original picture.

 If you plan to post several images to a Web page, open several windows and place them side by side onscreen to compare the final optimized images for each picture.

The following steps show you how to change an image file from RGB mode to Indexed Color mode.

1. Open an image file in Photoshop. View the file size of the image by choosing Document Sizes from the drop-down menu in the lower left corner of the image window. In this example, the image file size is 900k. It is a 640×480 pixel image.
2. Open the Image, Mode menus and choose Indexed Color.
3. Adjust the settings in the Indexed Color window. Choose either Selective, Perceptual, or Adaptive from the palette drop-down menu. If you want to force the colors in the image to a Web, Primary, or Black and White palette, select the palette from the Forced drop-down menu. In this example, I've chosen None. Check the Transparency box if you want to preserve any transparency settings in the image.
4. Click on OK to apply the changes to the image window.

5. Wait for Photoshop to process the file.
6. View the new file size in the lower left corner of the image window.

REVIEWING IMAGE SETTINGS

Before you optimize an image, view its current settings, such as its file format, file size, and the number of colors in the image. Some optimization settings, such as those in the Settings drop-down menu in the Save for Web window in Adobe Photoshop, are tied to specific color palettes and default values. The following steps show you how to change the color palette for an image and preview the changes in the Save for Web window.

1. Open an image file in Photoshop. Open the File menu and choose Save for Web. The Save for Web window opens.
2. Choose Selective from the Color reduction algorithm drop-down menu (second drop-down menu on the left side of the Save for Web window). Then wait for Photoshop to generate a preview image. Click on the 2-Up tab to compare the new set of colors with the original image.
3. View the number of colors, file sizes, and download times in the preview pane, and compare the new image with the original one.

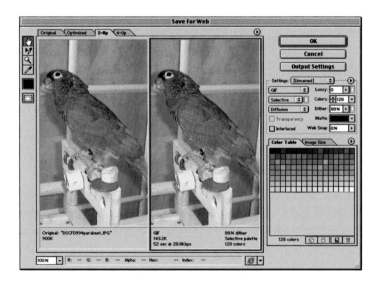

4. Choose Web from the same selection box.
5. Wait for Photoshop to generate the preview image. Note the number of colors, file sizes, and download times in the preview pane, and then compare the new image to the original.

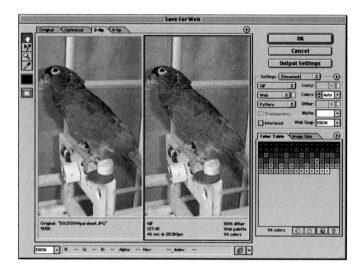

Changing the number of colors or changing to the GIF file format changes the Settings pop-up menu to an Unnamed state.

If you want to compare the Web and Selective color palettes to the original image in one preview window, choose the 4-Up tab.

EVALUATING IMAGE QUALITY

The baseline for measuring image quality is to use the original source image taken by a camera or generated by a scanner. This may be difficult to do if you've sliced an image or combined several images into a single picture. You may need to save an image (or slice) in a particular file format and then open the original to compare the two separate images.

Image quality can be measured by the comparing the clarity of the image and color accuracy to other images or to the original image. When evaluating an optimized image, try to see if the optimization settings retain image clarity and color compared to its original. The following steps show you how to compare different Web images in the Save for Web window in Photoshop.

1. Open an image file in Photoshop. Choose Save for Web from the File menu. The Save for Web window opens.
2. Click on the 4-Up tab. Select a file format from the Settings selection box.
3. Repeat steps 1 and 2, but choose a different file format for each pane.
4. Wait for Photoshop to update the preview panes in the Save for Web window.
5. Use the Hand tool to drag the image in the selected pane. Pick a complex part of the picture and compare the three file formats to the image quality of the original. The image with the best quality should look as close to the original picture as possible.

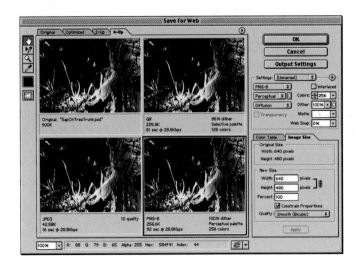

 You can resize a Web image directly from the Save for Web window. Simply type the new (preferably smaller) dimensions of the image in the Image Size palette. In most cases, making an image smaller retains the image quality of the picture while shrinking the overall file size.

WORKING WITH ROLLOVERS

Rollovers are actions you can add to a button graphic on a Web page. A Web page button is a fancy looking link that takes you to another Web page or another location on the same Web page. A rollover button can have a more dynamic behavior. For example, you can swap the image of the unpressed button with a glowing button when the mouse is over the button graphic. Or when the button is pressed, you can show an image of a pressed button instead of an unpressed, glowing button. These behaviors are called rollover states. You can use an image as the button graphic and create rollovers in ImageReady. Create each rollover state in the Rollover palette, storing each image state in the Layers palette.

Preview each rollover state in a browser window, and then save the HTML and image files to your hard drive. Add these files to a new or existing Web page, and then move the finished Web pages to your Web server.

CREATING A ROLLOVER

You can add up to five different rollover states to an image or create your own custom rollover state in ImageReady. Choose a photo you want to use as a button on a Web page. Copy the button image to new layers in the Layers palette and edit a layer for each rollover state. The following steps show you how to create a rollover with ImageReady.

1. Open an image file with ImageReady.
2. Select the Rollover tab in the palette window located at the bottom of the screen to view the Rollover palette. The open image represents the Normal state of the rollover button.

3. Click on the Creates New Rollover State button (document icon) at the bottom of the Rollover palette. The rollover state appears above the thumbnail picture in the Rollover palette window. Copy and paste an image into a new layer. Hide any other layers to assign the visible layer in the Layers palette to the selected rollover state in the Rollover palette.
4. Click on a rollover thumbnail image in the Rollover palette that you want to edit. Choose a layer in the Layers palette. Use the Selection, Draw, and Fill tools to change the picture in the image window for each rollover state.

5. Click on the Play button to cycle through each rollover state. When you've created each rollover state, open the File menu and select a browser from the Preview In menu. Drag your mouse over the button graphic in the browser to see if the rollover states behave as they were designed in ImageReady.

 Add animation to a rollover by adding images to the animation palette in ImageReady. Select the thumbnail for the rollover state you want to assign to the animation, and then make the layer containing the first frame of the animation visible in the Layers palette.

SAVING ROLLOVERS

After you've previewed your rollover in a browser window, make any additional changes to each rollover state. When you've finished creating your rollover, save the image and HTML files to your hard drive. Choose the Save Optimized As command from the File menu to select the current optimization settings. You can optimize rollover images the same way you optimize other Web graphics. When you click on Save in the Save Optimized As window, ImageReady generates a separate image file for each rollover state, as well as JavaScript code, which is then saved as an HTML file. The HTML code tells a browser how to create each rollover state using the rollover image files you created in ImageReady. The following steps show you how to save your rollover files to your hard drive.

1. Open an image file containing a rollover in ImageReady.
2. Select different optimization from the Optimize palette. Preview and compare different file formats to the original. In this example, I chose GIF 128 Dithered.
3. Choose Save Optimized As from the File menu.
4. Type a name for the image files, and select HTML and Images from the Format drop-down menu.
5. Click on the Save button to save the rollover to your hard drive.

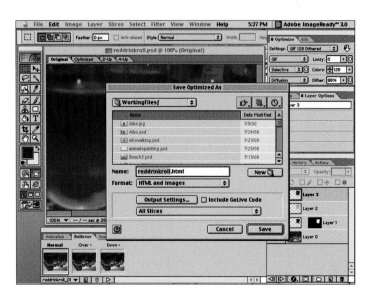

This process might seem a little confusing if you've never worked with Web pages before. In order to put information on a Web page, you must create an HTML file, which will eventually reside on a Web server. You will also need to upload each image file to the Web server. To update an existing Web page with the rollover, you have to add the HTML code created by ImageReady to a Web page and then post the images and HTML file(s) to your Web server. You can use an HTML editor application, such as Notepad or SimpleText, or Microsoft FrontPage or Bare Bones BBEdit software to create or edit a Web page.

SLICING UP AN IMAGE

You can use the Slice tool (K is the shortcut to select this tool in the toolbox) to break a big image into smaller pieces. Then re-assemble the slices with HTML code to view the full image on a Web page, Photoshop and ImageReady can create two kinds of slices: user slices and layer slices. The following sections show you how to create user slices. To create a layer-based slice, click on a layer in the Layers palette. Then open the Layer menu and choose New Layer Based Slice. The image in that layer will be changed into a slice. In ImageReady you can assign a URL, add rollover behaviors, and optimize an image slice.

An alternative to creating slices is to preserve the full image size with an image map (P). You can add links and rollover functions to an image map. The Image Map tool, which is only available in ImageReady, can be used to create a layer-based or user image map. Although the image map tool is not covered in this book, you may want to experiment with this tool in ImageReady to compare it with images created with the Slice tool (K).

Slices enable you to break up a large image so that it will load faster in a browser window. You can create a single slice or slices on top of other slices. A secondary or tertiary slice (a slice below a slice) can also be called a sub slice. When you save an image file that contains slices, each slice is saved as a separate file. A sliced image can be made up of different image file formats. For example, one slice can be saved as a GIF, and the rest of the slices as JPEG files. Open the File menu and choose Save for Web to save your slices in Photoshop. Open the File menu and choose Save Optimized As to save your slices in ImageReady. Both applications can generate the HTML code to position each slice on a Web page. You can save the slice HTML code as a table or as a cascading style sheet. Add the HTML code from ImageReady or Photoshop to your own Web page, and then upload the image files and HTML files to your Web server to add the sliced image to your Web site.

CREATING SLICES

Both Photoshop and ImageReady have a Slice tool (K) in their toolboxes. You can create a sliced image in Photoshop or ImageReady. The tool works the same in both applications.

Select the Slice tool from the toolbox. Click and drag the cursor in the image window to create a slice. When you create a slice, you draw a single rectangle in the image window. Photoshop breaks the rest of the image up into corresponding slices in the image window, assigning a unique number to each slice image.

Try to create a slice that breaks the image into equal sized parts. Alternatively, if there is one particular area of the picture that should load more quickly than the others, create a smaller slice around that image to allow it to load faster. The following steps show you how to use the Slice tool in ImageReady.

1. Open an image in Adobe ImageReady.
2. Choose the Slice tool (K) from the toolbox.
3. Click and drag the tool in the window to create a square or rectangle.
4. The number of the slice appears in the upper-left corner of the rectangular slice. Each shaded slice area also contains a slice number.

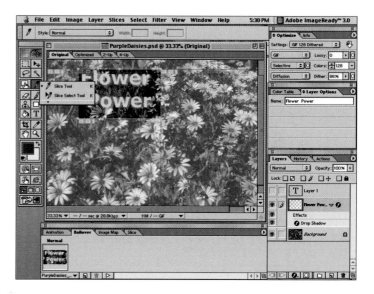

5. Click and drag the mouse in a different location in the window. A second slice is created.

6. To edit the slice, select the Slice tool from the toolbox. Then hold down the Ctrl/Command key and place the cursor near the edge of a slice. Click and drag the cursor in the image window to resize the slice. You can only edit slices that are highlighted in the image window. Slices that are automatically generated by Photoshop or ImageReady change as the main sliced image changes.

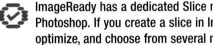 A slice affects all the layers, masks, and channels in an image. You can view additional information about a slice in ImageReady's Slice palette.

ImageReady has a dedicated Slice menu that you won't find in Photoshop. If you create a slice in ImageReady, you can duplicate, optimize, and choose from several menu commands to edit your image slices.

LOCKING SLICES

If you're working with several image layers or don't want any of the slices to be edited after you've chosen the optimization settings, choose Lock Slices from the View menu in Photoshop. When you lock slices, you will not be able to select or edit any slices in the image window. ImageReady does not have a lock slice feature, although it has a dedicated Slice palette and Slice menu. The following steps show you how to lock slices in the image window in Photoshop.

1. Open an image file in Photoshop.

 2. Use the Slice tool (K) to create a slice in the image window. Each slice has a unique number in the upper-left corner. The slice you create appears as a highlighted slice in the image window.

3. Choose Lock Slices from the View menu.
4. The slices in the image window remain unchanged. If you try to adjust a slice, Photoshop will bring up a dialog box telling you that the slices are locked.

5. Choose Lock Slices again (from the View menu) to unlock all slices (a check mark appears when slices are locked).

OPTIMIZING PALETTES

Color plays a big roll in determining the quality and clarity of an image. In some cases, color is the subject of the picture. In most cases, preserving the original colors of an image is the most important part of creating high-resolution photos for the Web.

Digital cameras create high-resolution images that can capture millions of colors. Depending on the resolution of your computer monitor, you may or may not see the full bandwidth of color captured by the camera, yet it will look great on your computer screen. If you put that same image on a Web site, however, it might take a long time to load. Although an image can be sliced or resized and still be accessible on a Web site, another way to optimize an image is to reduce the number of colors available to it. Conversely, if your computer screen is set to a lower color resolution, such as 256 colors, you may not see any difference after reducing the number of colors. The following sections show you how to optimize an image file's colors. Although these steps use Photoshop, you can perform many of these steps in ImageReady using the Optimize palette.

CHOOSING THE COLOR PALETTE

Naturally, if you choose only 32 colors to display a GIF file, the image won't look as good as if it had 128 colors (unless, of course, the subject in the image contains fewer than 32 colors). You can view the colors that are actually used in an image file by choosing the Color Table tab in the Save for Web window. The following steps show you how to choose a color palette in the Save for Web window in Photoshop.

1. Open an image you want to post to a Web site. Open the image with Photoshop.
2. Choose Save for Web from the File menu.
3. Click on the 2-Up tab in the Save for Web window. If you've created slices, the Settings area of the Save for Web window will be empty. Choose Optimize to File Size from the Settings pop-up menu (located on the right side of the Save for Web window). Type the file size that appears in the right pane in the Desired File Size text box in the Optimize to File Size window. Choose Autoselect GIF/JPEG and Total of All Slices, and then click on OK. In this example, the image window contains a slice. I had to choose Optimize to File Size to optimize the selected slice.

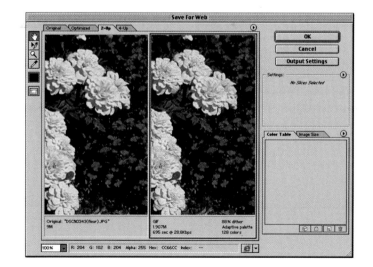

4. Choose a file format from the Settings drop-down menu. Click on the Colors drop-down menu and select the number of colors for the image palette in the Settings area of the Save for Web window. View the image in the right panel and compare the color palette and resulting image in the Save for Web window. In the following figure, I chose a GIF image to compare with the original (without slices). Notice the colors for the GIF image are not quite the same as the original.

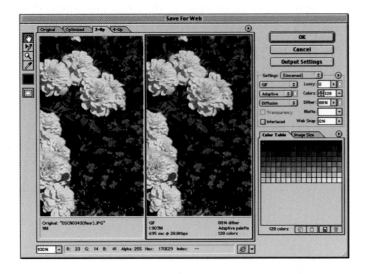

JPEG images do not have color palettes. Because most digital cameras create JPEG files, you will not see a color palette for the original image if the Original tab is selected in ImageReady, or in the Save For Web window in Photoshop.

OPTIMIZING THE COLOR TABLE

Web file formats appear with different numbers of colors in the Settings selection box in the Save for Web window. For example, you can choose a GIF file format with 128 colors or a GIF file format with only 32 colors. Depending on how you want viewers to see an image, you may want to choose a smaller color palette over a larger one. Some images might look better with fewer colors than with more colors.

The colors for each file format appear in the Color Table in the Save for Web window. You can edit each color in the Color Table. Use the Eyedropper tool to extract specific colors in an image. Double-click on a color to view its color information in the Color Picker window.

Web browsers use a 216-color palette on any computer platform. You can force one or all colors in the Color Table to use these Web safe colors. If you choose a Web safe color in Photoshop or ImageReady, the color you selected will appear the same in a browser application running on a Windows, Mac OS, or Linux computer.

The following steps show you how to view the Color Table information in the Save for Web window in Photoshop.

1. Open an image in Photoshop.

2. Choose Save for Web from the File menu.

3. Click on the Settings drop-down menu to select a Web image file format and color palette. In this example I've chosen PNG-8 128 Dithered. PNG-8 is a Web graphics file format. The number 128 indicates how many colors are available in the color palette for the PNG-8 image file.

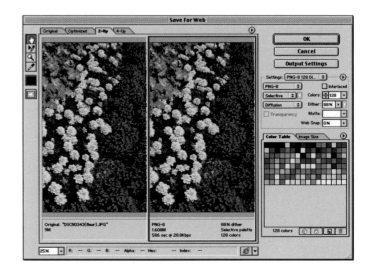

4. Click on the Eyedropper tool in the Save for Web window toolbar (on the left side of the window). Click on a color in the image. The color appears highlighted in the Color Table. Double-click a color to change it.

5. Click on the Settings drop-down menu and choose a different file format. Click on the Colors drop-down menu to select the number of colors for the Color palette. The colors appear in the Color Table. Compare the image in the right panel to the image in the left panel. If the image is a GIF or PNG 8, compare the color tables. Fewer colors generally indicate a smaller image file. However, fewer colors can also affect the quality of the image.

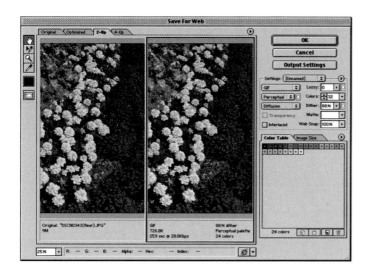

 You can convert (or snap) the color palette for an image to a Web safe color palette to reduce the probability that viewers of your Web site can't use the custom color palette.

 Press the Escape key to exit the Save for Web window.

OPTIMIZING IMAGE QUALITY

You can preview file formats and image settings in the Save for Web window in Photoshop and in the Optimize, 2-Up, and 4-Up tabs in the image window in ImageReady. You can use Photoshop or ImageReady to try to improve the quality of specific objects in the image. For example, you can experiment with adjustment layers in Photoshop or optimize a rollover in ImageReady. With both applications, if there is no limitation to the size of an image file you can create, try to preserve as much of the original image's quality as possible in the optimized image. The following sections show you how to optimize size and quality with Photoshop.

REDUCING IMAGE SIZES

You can choose a lower quality image with a smaller file size to make an image download faster and take up less disk space. Photoshop provides the Fit Image automation script, the Resize Image wizard, and the Image Size menu command to change the dimensions of an image. You can also resize an image in the Save for Web window in Photoshop. Here's how:

1. Open an image file in Photoshop and then choose Save for Web from the File menu.

2. Type a new width and height in the Image Size section of the Save for Web window. Click on the Apply button and wait for Photoshop to process the image.

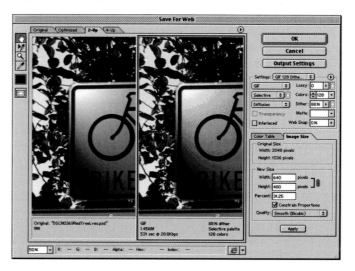

3. Choose JPEG Low from the Settings pop-up menu.
4. Wait for Photoshop to render the image in the newly selected file format.
5. Review the file size and download time at the bottom of the JPEG pane in the Save for Web window.

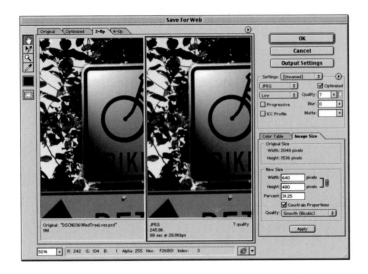

IMAGE QUALITY AND FILE FORMATS

GIF and JPEG image files are the most commonly used file formats for Web graphics. Photoshop offers three color-palette sizes for GIF images: 32, 64, and 128. GIF compression usually works best with images that contain chunks of solid color and that support transparency. Higher quality JPEG images tend to have very little loss of quality to the original image. However, lower quality JPEG images can have a considerable amount of data loss, resulting in a lower quality image. As computers and networks grow faster, the PNG file format is starting to grow in popularity.

PNG is a relatively newer file format for Web graphics. It's an acronym for Portable Network Graphics. Photoshop and ImageReady enable you to optimize or save an image as either PNG-8 or PNG-24 file format. The PNG-8 file format is not supported by many browsers, so you may

want to put this file format on the bottom of your list of things to try when optimizing an image. The PNG-24 file format supports 24-bit color and can save lossless images, similar to the JPEG lossless compression file format. PNG-24 files can also store up to 256 levels of transparency, enabling you to blend many image elements together. However, multiple levels of transparency is not supported by many browsers.

The following steps show you how to use the Optimize to File Size window to find the best optimization settings for an image you want to put on the Web.

1. Open an image file in RGB mode in Photoshop. Then choose Save for Web from the File menu.
2. Choose Optimize to File Size from the pop-up menu.
3. Click on Auto Select GIF/JPEG and then click on OK to enable Photoshop to choose the best file format for the selected image. Compare the image on the right with its original on the left in the Save for Web window.

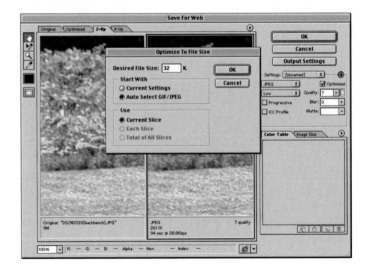

 Use the Hand tool to move the image in the selected panel in the 2-Up or 4-Up views. This enables you to view the image quality of any part of the picture.

WORKING WITH TRANSPARENCY SETTINGS

It might not be apparent, but adding transparency to an image can enable you to create some nice effects. However, sometimes images with transparency settings don't optimize easily, especially when the transparency relies on an unknown background image or is mixed with other images containing transparency settings. This section explains how to export transparency settings for an image and how to reduce halo effects when the Web image is combined with a background image.

EXPORTING TRANSPARENCY SETTINGS

Transparency settings are important if you want to blend a Web graphic with a background image on a Web page. For example, if you don't want the edges of a graphic to appear over the background color on a Web page, you can assign transparency settings to a color so that it won't appear in the browser window.

 If an image contains transparency settings, ImageReady and Photoshop automatically select the Transparency check box in the Save for Web and optimization windows.

The following steps show you how to save transparency settings for an image using the Export Transparent Image Assistant in Photoshop.

1. Open an image file containing a mask in Photoshop.
2. Select the background layer and press Ctrl/Command+J to create a copy of it as a new layer.
3. Clear the background layer and fill it with a foreground color from the color well.
4. Adjust the opacity level of one of the layers from the Layers palette. Click on the slider control beside the Opacity text box and drag it to the left to blend the image in the selected layer with other image layers. In this example, the opacity setting is set to 100%.
5. Choose Export Transparent Image from the Help menu.
6. Choose the radio button that best describes your image, and click on Next.

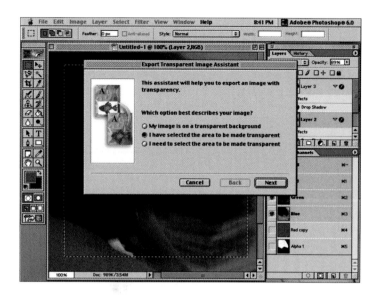

7. Choose the Online radio button and then click on Next.
8. Select a file format from the Format pop-up menu.
9. Click on the Save button to save the image with a transparency setting. Flatten the image, and then adjust any settings in the Indexed Color window (the Assistant opens it automatically). Click on Finish to complete the process.

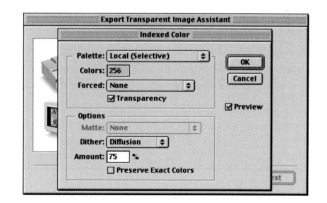

AVOIDING HALO EFFECTS

A halo effect can appear around an image containing transparent areas when it is placed against a background. If you create anti-aliased text or a gradient that contains a color that's marked as transparent in the image's color table, the colors in the image may appear incorrectly when the image is placed over the background color or background image of a Web page. You have to adjust the optimization settings for an image containing transparency settings in order to reduce the likelihood of accidentally creating a halo effect. The following steps show you how to select the transparency settings for an image file.

1. Open an image file in Photoshop. Create a mask, and press Ctrl/Command+J to copy the masked image to a new layer.
2. Select the new layer. Open the Image menu, choose Mode, and select Indexed Color. Hide the background image in the Layers palette so that only the masked image appears in the image window. The gray and white checkerboard represents the transparent areas of the resulting image, which surrounds the masked image.
3. Review the settings in the Indexed Color window and select the Transparency check box. Then click on OK.
4. Choose Save for Web from the File menu.
5. Check the Transparency box in the Save for Web window. Choose the GIF color palette you want to use with the image, and then click on OK. The file will be saved to your hard drive.

6. Open the GIF image in Photoshop. Open the Image menu, choose Mode, and select Color Table.
7. If the background color of the Web page is also in the image, click on the Eyedropper tool in the Color Table window. Then click on a color in the image window. The color in the Color Table becomes transparent in the Color Table and in the image window.

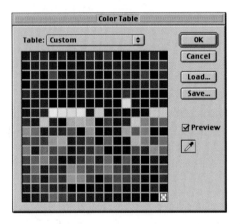

 To blend an image with the background color of a Web page, you first need to know what the background color is. Then you can change add that color to your Web image so that the image and background color will blend together.

 Each color in an image file is represented as a hexidecimal value on a Web page. If you're not sure if you've selected the right color to mark as a transparent, double-click the color in the Color Table (in the Save for Web window) or Color Palette (in the Photoshop workspace) and view the hexidecimal value for the selected color in the # text box.

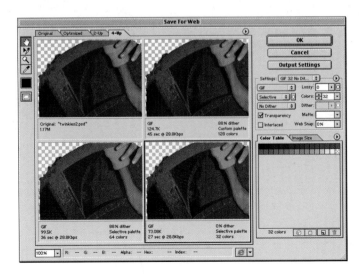

PREVIEWING COLOR FOR MAC AND WINDOWS BROWSERS

Gamma settings correspond to the monitor used with your computer. Brightness and midtone values generated by a monitor are measured in gamma. Windows computers use a higher gamma value than Macintosh computers. High gamma values create darker images.

Gamma settings on Windows PCs tend to have more of a red tint than the Macintosh gamma settings. If you want the image to appear correct on both Macintosh and PC computers, you should save two copies, each with the gamma-specific settings. Then you have to add the HTML code that tells the Web page to show the correct picture to the client computer.

SETTING MACINTOSH GAMMA

Before saving an image, choose the Standard Macintosh Color setting from the Save for Web drop-down menu to determine whether any of the colors will look differently on a Mac. If the Mac colors are different, choose the gamma settings that most accurately represents the colors in the image. You can also adjust the colors in the Color Table and then save a copy of the image to your hard drive. The following steps show you how to view an image with Macintosh gamma settings.

1. Open the image you want to use on your Web page in Adobe Photoshop.
2. Choose Save for Web from the File menu. Then choose Standard Macintosh Color from the drop-down menu on the upper right corner above the image in the Save for Web window.

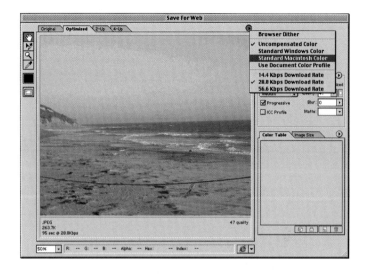

3. The colors in the image should change slightly. View the adjusted colors for the Macintosh. To adjust the Color Table, click on the Eyedropper tool and click on a color in the image. Its corresponding color becomes selected in the Color Table. Double-click a color to view or change it from the Color Picker window.
4. Click on OK to save the file to your hard drive.

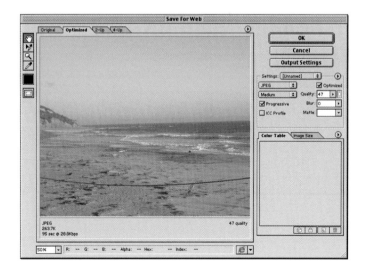

VIEWING WINDOWS GAMMA

Alternatively, you can view or save the same image with Windows Gamma settings to preserve color settings for Windows browsers. If you do not want to save two separate images for each computer platform, try replacing differing colors with colors that are more compatible with both platforms. The following steps show you how to save an image with Windows gamma settings.

1. Open the image you want to use on your Web page in Adobe Photoshop.
2. Choose Save for Web from the File menu. Then choose Standard Windows Color from the pop-up menu.

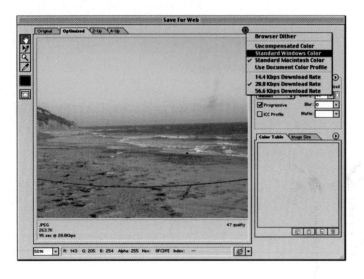

3. View the image in the Optimized tab of the Save for Web window. To adjust the Color Table, click on the Eyedropper tool and click on a color in the image. The selected color is highlighted in the Color Table. Double-click a color to view or change it in the Color Picker window.
4. Click on OK to save the file to your hard drive.

CHAPTER 18

SAVING IMAGES FOR THE WEB

IT'S EASY TO SCOFF AT WEB GRAPHICS THAT LOAD QUICKLY BUT ARE DIFFICULT TO RECOGNIZE OR TO GET GRUMPY BECAUSE AN IMAGE TAKES FOREVER TO LOAD. A WEB PAGE LOOKS EVEN WORSE WHEN THE BROWSER TIMES OUT BECAUSE IT CAN'T LOAD ALL THE GRAPHICS. SURE, THE NETWORK AND THE WEB SERVER CONTRIBUTE TO MAKING WEB GRAPHICS LOAD PAINFULLY SLOW. BUT ALL THE NETWORK MECHANICS ASIDE, YOU NEED TO FIRST CREATE SMALL, GOOD-LOOKING GRAPHICS TO SPICE UP YOUR TEXT-BASED WEB SITE. PHOTOSHOP AND IMAGEREADY ENABLE YOU TO SAVE AN IMAGE FILE IN ITS NATIVE PHOTOSHOP FILE FORMAT OR ONE OF SEVERAL DIFFERENT, COMMONLY USED WEB GRAPHIC FILE FORMATS, SUCH AS JPEG AND GIF. THIS CHAPTER SHOWS YOU HOW TO SAVE SLICED IMAGES OR A GIF OR JPEG IMAGE.

SAVING FILES

If you edit an image file, you can open the File menu and choose the Save command to save your changes to the original image. You save files to preserve any changes you made to it. When you're resizing an image, saving a file can be very simple. Press Ctrl/Command+S, and your changes are saved. In most cases, you're probably going to save the file in the same format it was created in: either a JPEG or Photoshop file. If you're saving the file for the Web, the image's file format will most likely be JPEG or GIF.

When I save a file, I like to keep a copy of the original image. If I edit an image, I use the Save As command in the File menu and re-name the file to reflect the changes I made to it. For example, if I resized an image, I'll add the new dimensions to the end of the file name. You can check the Save as Copy check box in the Save As window if you want to preserve the original image file and save all your changes to a new file.

If the image file contains layers, masks, rollover states, or animation, I'll save the image as a Photoshop file, and then optimized as a JPEG or GIF file. You can use the Photoshop file to continue editing the image, slices, rollover, or animation without having to re-create layers or masks. The following sections show you how to save a file as a GIF image and how to save a sliced image in Photoshop.

SAVING FOR THE WEB

When you open the File menu and choose Save As, you can save an image file in 18 different file formats in Photoshop. Click on the Format menu in the Save As window to view the available file formats. You can add a plug-in to Photoshop to add support for additional file formats, too.

As mentioned before, use the Photoshop file format if you want to preserve any layers, masks, or channels in an image file. You can save, open, and edit a native Photoshop file in Photoshop or ImageReady. The following is a list of the file formats Photoshop can use to save a file. Each item on the list contains a brief description of the file format.

* BMP. This is the standard Windows image format. Create a BMP file by saving an image using Internet Explorer 5.0 on a PC. Edit or view BMP files in RGB, indexed-color, grayscale, or bitmap color modes.
* GIF. GIF is an acronym for Graphics Interchange Format. It is the most commonly used file format for Web graphics. The GIF file format employs LZW compression to minimize file size, which in turn enables a Web graphic to download faster to a browser window. Transparency in indexed-color images is preserved. However alpha channels are not supported.
* EPS. EPS is an acronym for Encapsulated PostScript, a language file format created by Adobe. Photoshop converts EPS vector graphics into pixels when the file is opened. EPS files can also be saved as PDF (Portable Document Format) files. Use the Import command to open a PDF file in Photoshop. View or edit EPS or DCS files in CMYK, RGB, indexed-color, duotone, grayscale, and bitmap color modes. The EPS file format does not support alpha channels or clipping paths. However, DCS 2.0 formats support spot channels and single alpha channels. EPS TIFF and EPS PICT Preview formats can be opened but are not supported by Photoshop. EPS PICT Preview is available only on Mac computers.
* JPEG. JPEG is an acronym for the Joint Photographic Experts Group format, which is another commonly used Web graphics file format. View and edit files in RGB, CMYK, and grayscale color modes. The JPEG file format does not support alpha channels but retains all color information. Depending on the JPEG compression level chosen for the file, some image data might be selectively discarded to create the final, compressed file.
* PCX. Another common file format for Windows PC graphic images. View and edit files in RGB, indexed-color, grayscale, or bitmap color modes. The PCX file format does not support alpha channels.
* PDF. The Portable Document Format is commonly used to share files across applications and computer platforms. It is based on the PostScript imaging model (see the EPS file format for more information about PostScript files). View and edit PDF files in RGB, indexed-color, CMYK, grayscale, bitmap, or Lab color modes. Alpha channels are not supported. PDF files can only be saved in the Photoshop PDF file format. However, you can open Adobe Acrobat and generic PDF files with Photoshop.
* PICT. Most Macintosh graphics applications can view PICT files. View and edit PICT files in RGB, indexed-color, grayscale, single alpha channel, and bitmap file formats that do not contain alpha channels. A PICT file can be saved in 16- or 32-bit pixel resolution.

✳ PICT Resources. A PICT resource is a PICT file stored in the resource fork of a Mac OS file. The PICT resource format supports the same formats as a PICT file. However, you must import a PICT resource in Photoshop in order to open this particular file format.

✳ Pixar. This file format is specifically designed for exchanging files with Pixar computers that work with high-end graphics applications. View and edit these files in RGB mode or in grayscale mode with a single alpha channel.

✳ PNG. Portable Network Graphics is a patent-free Web graphics file format designed for displaying high-quality images on Web pages. View and edit files in grayscale or RGB mode with a single alpha channel or files in indexed-color mode that do not contain alpha channels. Transparency can be preserved in the single alpha channel of a file, and the PNG file format supports up to 24-bit images.

✳ Raw. Raw files consist of a stream of bytes that describe the color information in a file. A single pixel is described in a binary format, where 0 equals black and 255 equals white. This format can be used to transfer files between applications and computer platforms. View and edit files in CMYK, RGB, and grayscale files with alpha channels as well as multichannel, Lab, indexed-color, and duotone files without alpha channels.

✳ Scitex CT, or Scitex Continuous Tone format. This is used by Scitex computers for processing high-end images. Although alpha channels are not supported, you can view and edit CMYK, RGB, or grayscale files.

✳ Targa, or TGA. These files are used with the Truevision video board on MS-DOS applications. View and edit 32-bit RGB files with single alpha channels, indexed color, grayscale, or 16-bit and 24-bit RGB files that do not contain alpha channels.

✳ TIFF. The Tagged-Image File Format can be used in digital cameras to store large, raw image files. It is also a common file format that can support LZW compression and can be used to exchange files between applications or computer platforms. Most desktop scanners can create TIFF images that in turn can be read by most paint, image-editing, or page-layout applications. View and edit files in CMYK or RGB modes or in grayscale mode with alpha channels.

✳ Amiga IFF. Image files created by Amiga computer systems or with the Video Toaster can be saved as Amiga Interchange File Format files. This format does not support alpha channels, but it is compatible with many Windows PC applications such as Deluxe Paint by Electronic Arts. View and edit this format in RGB, indexed-color, grayscale, and bitmap color modes.

✳ Photoshop DCS 1.0 and 2.0. See EPS.

You can save an image file as a GIF, JPEG, or PNG file in the Save for Web window in Photoshop. You can also choose these Web file formats in ImageReady from the Optimize palette and then open the File menu and select Save Optimized As. The following steps show you how to use the Save for Web window in Photoshop to save an image file.

1. When you're ready to save an image to be posted to a Web site, open the File menu and choose Save for Web.

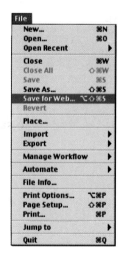

2. Click on the Settings drop-down menu to select a file format. In this example, I chose GIF 128 dithered. Click on the Optimized tab in the Save for Web window to view the file with the settings selected in the Save for Web window. The settings appear on the right side of the Save for Web window.

3. View the file format, file size, and download time in the bottom-left corner.

4. If this is the image you want to share on your Web site, click on OK.

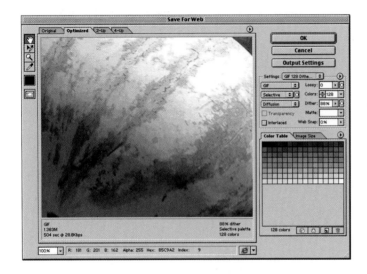

5. Type a name for the file and navigate to a folder on your hard drive where you want to save it. Then click on Save.

SAVING IMAGE SLICES

Visitors to a Web site rarely remember the name of the Web page, much less the name of the Web graphics. However, if you plan to update your Web images regularly, it's much easier to navigate through all the HTML and graphics files when they have names that reflect their contents. Whether you're saving a single image file or several image slices, choose a name that reflects the image in the file. You can give a custom name to image, slice, and HTML files in Photoshop or ImageReady. You can access slice naming options in ImageReady by selecting File, Output Setting menus, and then choosing Slices. The following steps show you how to save slices in Photoshop.

1. Open an image in Photoshop.

2. Use the Slice tool (K) in the toolbox to create a slice in the window.

3. Choose Save for Web from the File menu.

4. Click on the Output Settings button.

5. Choose Default Settings from the Settings drop-down menu. Select Slices from the drop-down menu on the Output Settings window. Define how the slices are named by changing the Default Slice Naming settings. For example, if you do not want to use the document name (doc.name), you can type a more descriptive name in the text box, replacing doc.name (the default setting).

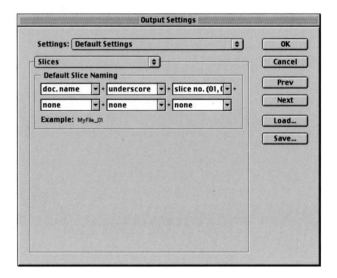

 Choose Saving Files from the unnamed drop-down menu in the Output Settings window to define how files are named when saved by Photoshop.

SAVING GIF AND JPEG FILES

Photoshop and ImageReady can save an image file with the same JPEG and GIF file formats. Photoshop can also save an image as a GIF89a file. This file format exists as a Photoshop plug-in in the Plug-Ins folder. The GIF89a Export command enables you to set the color palette and assign transparency before saving a GIF image. This process is different than using the Save for Web window in Photoshop or the Optimize palette in ImageReady. The following sections show you how to save an image as a GIF or JPEG in Photoshop.

EXPORTING A GIF89A IMAGE

JPEG and GIF files are the most common file formats used on Web sites. See Chapter 17, "Optimizing Images for the Web," for more information about JPEG and GIF files. Another variation of the GIF file format is the GIF89a file format. The following steps show you how to use the GIF89a file format to save a file for the Web. The GIF89a Export option enables you to save a file using the standard GIF file format. If you use this file format, any other computer platform with a browser will be able to view this type of file. If GIF89a does not appear in the Export menu, you may need to move this file from the Photoshop CD into the Photoshop Plug-Ins folder on your hard drive.

1. Open an image in Photoshop. In this example, I opened a JPEG image file.
2. Open the File menu, choose Export, and then select GIF89a Export.

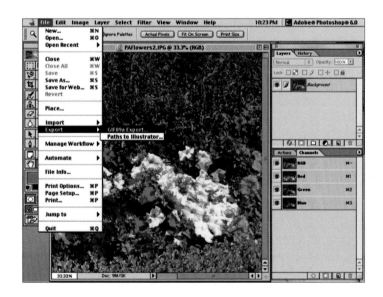

3. The GIF89a Export window appears. Select the type of palette from the Palette pop-up menu. Choose from Exact, System, or Adaptive palettes. In this example, I chose Adaptive.

4. Type the number of colors to be used with the image. The default setting is 256, which is what I've chosen in this example. Click on the Preview button to view the color palette and the image as it will appear if you save it with the selected settings. If you are working with a file saved with the CompuServe GIF or GIF89a file format, you will see a similar preview window. However, you can also modify the color palette and toggle the Interlaced option for the GIF image. Click on OK.
5. Type a name for the exported file, and then click on the Save button.

 If you own an earlier version of Photoshop, drag the GIF89a plug-in into the Photoshop 6 folder.

SAVING A JPEG IMAGE

You need to choose a specific JPEG compression level for images you want to use on your Web page. High-quality JPEG images lose little pixel information, yet are compressed versions of the original. If you select a lower level of compression, the JPEG encoding and compression algorithms remove certain pixels in order to make the file smaller. The following steps show you how to preview and save JPEG image files.

1. Open an image in Photoshop. Then choose Save for Web from the File menu.
2. Select JPEG from the second tier selection box in the Settings section of the Save for Web window.
3. Select an option from the Quality selection box (below the one you just used), or type a value into the text box to set a specific level of JPEG compression.
4. Preview the changes by choosing the 2-Up tab. Compare the image size, download time, and quality with that of the original image. Click on Save to save the JPEG image.

 Try comparing custom PNG settings to JPEG and to the original image.

USING IMAGEREADY TO EXPORT FILES

You can open a Photoshop file in ImageReady to apply a broader range of optimization tools to your Web images. ImageReady supports the same Web file formats as Photoshop, plus a few more optimization settings. You can convert images or masks to rollover buttons or image maps in ImageReady, and then save the images as optimized for the Web instead of returning to Photoshop to run similar menu commands. The following sections show you how to optimize and save an image with ImageReady.

OPTIMIZING WITH IMAGEREADY

ImageReady opens each image in its own image window. The image window has four document views, which you can access by clicking on its tab at the top of the image window: Original, Preview, 2-Up, and 4-Up. You can preview optimization settings in the Optimize palette. Choose different Web file formats to find the best combination of colors, image quality, and file size for each Web graphic. The following steps show you how to use the 2-Up tab to preview images in ImageReady.

1. Open an image in ImageReady.
2. Choose a file format from the Settings pop-up menu in the Optimize palette.

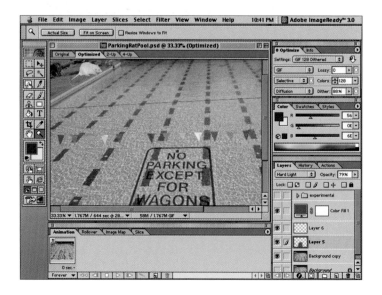

3. Click on the 2-Up tab in the window to compare the optimization to the original image.

4. Select a different file format and compare it to the original.

CHOOSING A FILE FORMAT

Try previewing two or three GIF or JPEG files settings of each Web graphic in order to compare the file size and image quality of each. Then review the download times for each file format. The size of a file directly affects its download time. Although some people have high-speed Internet connections, such as cable modem and DSL, they are still the minority; most people dial into the Internet with 28.8- or 56Kbps modems.

Try to keep an image's download time to 5–10 seconds at 28.8Kbps. If an image is too large, use the Slice tool to break it into smaller files, thus enabling the image to load faster when viewed by a browser. The following steps show you how to compare file formats before saving the file in ImageReady.

1. Load an image into ImageReady.
2. Choose three different file formats from the Settings drop-down menu in the Optimize palette. Preview the file size and image quality of each in the 4-Up window by selecting the 4-Up tab.
3. Click in the document window of any of the four documents to select it and to change its optimization settings in the Optimize palette.

4. Choose Save Optimized As from the File menu.

5. Type a name for the file and choose a format from the Format pop-up menu. Click on the Save button to save the file to your hard drive.

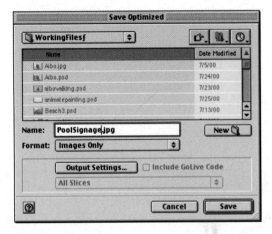

 Although JPEG files can ultimately be smaller than GIF or PNG file formats, GIF128 files can store transparency layers as well as 128 colors and often produce a better Web image. Use the Magnify tool to take a closer look when comparing GIF to JPEG files for the Web.

CHAPTER 19

PUTTING IMAGES ONLINE

ONE OF THE MOST DREADED TASKS I FACE AFTER TAKING DOZENS OF
DIGITAL PICTURES IS FIGURING OUT HOW TO PUT THEM ALL ON MY WEB
SITE. MY IDEAL PHOTO ALBUM WEB PAGE CONTAINS 100×100 PIXEL
THUMBNAIL IMAGES OF EACH IMAGE THAT, WHEN CLICKED, BRINGS UP A
640×480 OR LARGER IMAGE. MY FIRST PROBLEM WAS THAT I DIDN'T WANT
TO SPEND TIME RESIZING EACH IMAGE, CREATING A THUMBNAIL AND
640×480 IMAGE OF EACH DIGITAL PICTURE TAKEN FROM A CAMERA. MY
SECOND PROBLEM WAS TRYING TO FIGURE OUT HOW TO CREATE HTML
CODE FOR THE IMAGE FILES. FINALLY, I HAD TO FIGURE OUT IF I HAD
ENOUGH DISK SPACE TO HOLD ALL THESE IMAGES AND WEB PAGES ON MY
WEB SERVER. FORTUNATELY, WITH PHOTOSHOP YOU CAN USE THE BUILT-IN
WEB PHOTO GALLERY AUTOMATION SCRIPT TO MOVE YOUR DIGITAL
PICTURES TO THE WEB. I WAS ABLE TO TAKE 70MB OF JPEG IMAGE
FILES AND TURN THEM INTO A 13MB WEB PHOTO GALLERY ON MY WEB
SITE (HTTP://SURFIN.SPIES.COM/ LISALEE/GALLERIES/DDGALLERY/
FRAMESET.HTM).

CREATING A WEB PHOTO GALLERY

The last item in the File, Automate menu is the Web Photo Gallery script. You can turn folders full of images into a Web Photo Gallery using this Automate command. The resulting HTML files and images can be uploaded to a Web site. Then you can navigate the gallery images with a browser application. You can customize HTML in the Web photo gallery before you run this script in Photoshop. Or you can edit the HTML files using an HTML editor application after Photoshop has created all the photo gallery files on your hard drive. Although the Web Photo Gallery window looks deceptively simple, it provides a wide range of flexibility, enabling you to choose from several styles, options, and image sizes. The following sections show you how to create a vertical frame and simple Web photo gallery.

GENERATING A WEB PHOTO GALLERY USING AUTOMATED TOOLS

Each automated tool in the File, Automate menu contains a corresponding dialog box that enables you to customize settings for the automated task. You can have Photoshop create a Web Photo Gallery with your image files using the Web Photo Gallery command in the File, Automate menu. Choose from one of four different layout styles for your photo gallery. Each style, or Web page layout uses a thumbnail image of a resized original image. If you click on the thumbnail image, its link takes you to another Web page containing some banner text and the full-size image. Click on OK in the Web Photo Gallery window to create the photo gallery using the settings selected in the dialog box.

Photoshop resizes each image in the source folder and stores the resulting files in a Thumbnail and Images folder on your hard drive. An index and, if applicable to the style, a FrameSet HTML file are generated by Photoshop. Then Photoshop opens your default browser and loads the frameset or index html file in a browser window so you can preview your Web photo gallery.

The following steps show you how to create a Web photo gallery in Photoshop.

> An alternative to creating your own Web Photo Album pages is to use a Web site, such as **http://www.ofoto.com**, **http://www.snapfish.com**, **http://www.shutterfly.com**, or **http://www.myfamily.com**. These Web sites offer a variety of photographic services ranging from converting traditional pictures to digital pictures, printing digital pictures to traditional photographic paper, and hosting your Web photo album.

1. Open the File menu, choose Automate, and select Web Photo Gallery.
2. Simple is the default photo gallery style. You can choose from Horizontal Frame, Table, or Vertical Frame. In this example, I've chosen Vertical Frame.
3. Choose Banner from the Options drop-down menu. Type a name for your gallery in the Site Name text box, and choose a font and font size for the site. This information will appear on the right (larger) side of the generated Web page. Choose another option, such as Gallery Images, Gallery Thumbnails, or Custom Colors to choose the settings for those components of the Web gallery. Each of the settings in these options windows will appear in the final, generated Web photo gallery.

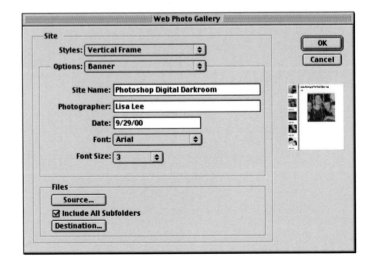

4. Click on the Source button to choose a folder containing image files that will be used to create the photo gallery. Double-click a folder to view the contents of that folder in the navigation window. In this example, I selected a folder containing about one hundred image files. Click on the OK/Choose button to designate the highlighted folder as the Source folder.

5. Click on the Destination button to choose a folder where the photo gallery images will be saved. In this example, I created a new folder (click on the New folder button in the navigation window) on my Desktop. Click on the folder you want to use to store the files generated by Photoshop. Then click OK/Choose to save your choice and return to the Web Photo Gallery window.

6. Click on OK and wait for the script to run. Photoshop may take a few minutes to process the images for the photo gallery. When the script is finished, you should see your Web photo gallery in a browser window.

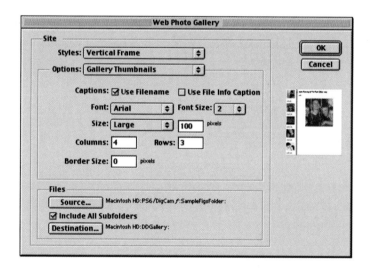

 Make a backup of your source images before running an automation script. If for some reason changes are made to an image when the script is run and Undo doesn't apply, it's nice to have a backup to return to instead of starting over again.

CREATING A SIMPLE PHOTO GALLERY WITH THUMBNAIL IMAGES

The simple photo gallery is another photo gallery style you can use to create a Web photo gallery. Like the other photo gallery styles, the main page of the photo gallery contains thumbnail images. If you click on a thumbnail image, a larger image appears in a new Web page.

Although there are four styles of Web photo galleries, I only cover the vertical frame and simple styles in this chapter. However, the Horizontal Frame style is similar to the Vertical Frame style, and the Table style photo gallery is similar to the simple gallery. The following steps show you how to create a simple Web photo gallery.

1. Open the File menu, choose Automate, and select Web Photo Gallery.

2. Choose Simple from the Styles drop-down menu. The simple photo gallery layout appears on the right side of the Web Photo Gallery window. Select Gallery Thumbnails from the Options drop-down menu.

3. Check the Use Filename check box, and then click on the Font to choose a font for the name text that will appear below each thumbnail image. Select a size for the Thumbnail in the Size drop-down menu. Click on the Source button to pick the folder containing the images you want to use for the image gallery. Select the Destination drop-down menu to create a new folder or choose an existing folder where Photoshop will store the Web photo gallery image and HTML files. Click on OK to start the script.

4. View the thumbnail images in the browser window opened by the Photoshop script.

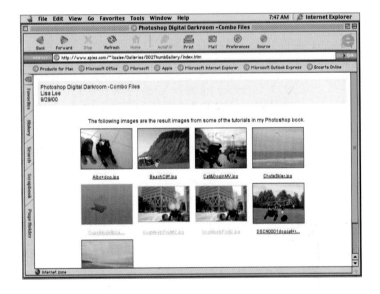

CUSTOMIZING SETTINGS

The Web Photo Gallery window contains many customizable settings. If you prefer to use a larger thumbnail image, or want to show the full 2,000×1,500 pixel image on a Web page, you can do this by changing a few settings in the Web Photo Gallery window. The following steps show you how to choose custom thumbnail and image sizes in the Web Photo Gallery window.

1. Open the File menu, choose Automate and select Web Photo Gallery.

2. Choose Gallery Thumbnails from the Options drop-down menu. Then click on the Size drop-down menu and choose Custom. Type a number in the text box to create a custom thumbnail image for your photo gallery.

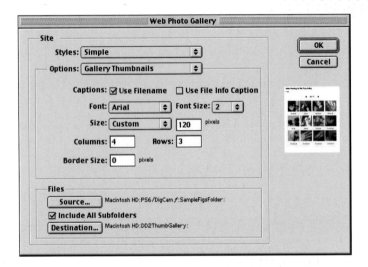

3. Choose Gallery Images from the Options selection box.

4. Choose Custom from the Resize Images drop-down menu. Type a number to set the width of the gallery image. Adjust the image quality and file size of the JPEG image by clicking and dragging the slider control in the middle of the Web Photo Gallery window.

5. Click on OK and wait for the script to run. Then view the results in a browser window.

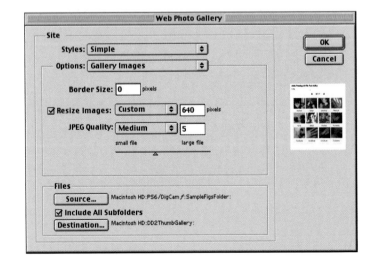

PUTTING PHOTOS ON THE WEB

Although the biggest hurdle to creating a Web photo gallery can be generating HTML code that works, there are several additional steps you need to follow before you can access a Web site. This section assumes you already have login and password information to an Internet service provider's (ISP) Web servers, and that the Web files have already been tested and posted to a working Web server. If you are not the administrator of your network, you might need to give your Web files to a network administrator before they can be posted to the Internet. If you're not sure how to post Web pages to your Web server, contact your ISP, or refer to a book that's dedicated to configuring or working with a Web server (like Apache).

A Web server is not required if you want to make changes to your Web photo gallery. You can customize your HTML code using an HTML editor (a simple text editor, or more advanced Web page editing application) and view the results in a browser window. The following sections deconstruct a Web photo gallery created with the vertical frame style. The last section shows you how to upload a file to your Web site using an FTP application.

 Try the Resize wizard located in the Help menu. Choose the Resize Image command to walk through a group of screens that help you resize images for print or online viewing.

EMBEDDING IMAGES WITH HTML CODE

You can add an image to a Web page by using the IMG src HTML tag. HTML code is made up of a series of tags. Each tag has a bracket on each side. For example the bold face text tag <B> is placed to the left of the text you want to format, and its closing tag </B> is placed to the right of the text.

When you embed an image, you use the IMG src HTML tag and then add the file name of the picture to the Web page. For example, you might use the following line of code to add the image file SCBeachUmbrella to a Web page.

```
<IMG src="thumbnails/SCBeachUmbrella.jpg" border="0"
alt=SCBeachUmbrella align="BOTTOM">
```

You can use a simple text editor, like Notepad (on a Windows PC) or SimpleText (on a Mac) to create or edit a Web page. In order for a Web server to recognize a Web page, the HTML file name must end in .htm. For example, Photoshop creates an index.htm file containing all the file names in the photo gallery.

However, you don't need to create a Web page to see how this works. One way to find out how an image has been added to a Web page is to load a Web page containing an image. Then view its source code in the browser application. If the page is using HTML to display an image, you can view the HTML code to see which tags are used to make a picture appear on the Web page. The following steps show you how to identify an embedded image in the Web photo gallery's HTML code.

1. Visit a Web page that contains an image file. In this example, I chose a photo gallery posted on my Web site.

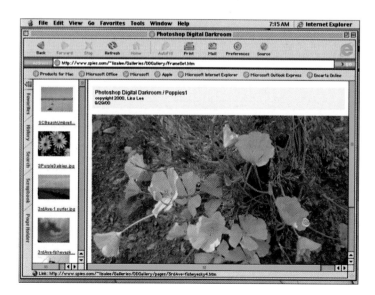

2. Choose Source from the View menu if you're using Internet Explorer. If you're using Netscape, open the View menu and choose Page Source. Since this Web page contains a frame, you'll need to hold down the Right-mouse button (on a PC) or Ctrl key (on a Mac) and choose View Frame Source from the drop-down menu in the browser window.

3. A window opens containing the HTML code for the current Web page. Look for the image file name in the source code. For example, look for the image file name from the source folder you chose for the Web photo gallery. You can also look for the IMG src tag in the HTML code to see if you can find the image's file name used with this HTML tag.

TABLES AND FRAMES

Organize one or several pictures in a defined layout by using tables or frames. Tables and frames are commonly used elements in Web pages. Tables organize text and images in rows and columns, which are defined by unique HTML table tags. Frames divide a Web page into sub-pages. For example, you can load another Web page into a frame, even if it's on a totally different Web site than yours. Embedding an image into a table or frame is similar to embedding an image into any Web page. The following steps show you how to identify the HTML tags for tables and frames in the Web photo gallery.

1. Drag and drop the FrameSet.htm file over a browser window. Wait for the pages to load in the browser window. Then open the View menu and choose Source.

2. Look for the TABLE tag to identify where the table begins in the HTML page. In this example, it's the eighth line from the top of the Poppies1.htm file. The TR tag is used to define the beginning of a table row. The TD tag is used to define the beginning of a table cell. In this example, the banner text for Poppies1.htm is stored in the same table row and table cell.

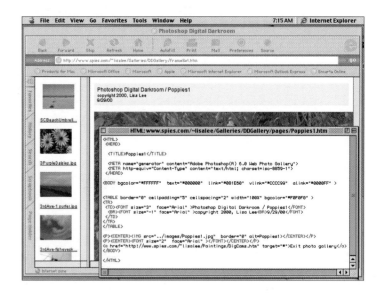

3. On a Mac, Ctrl+click on the right frame of the Web photo gallery in the browser window. If you're using a Windows PC, right-click on the frame. Choose View Frame Source from the drop-down menu.

4. The FRAMESET tag is used to define the frame elements in the browser window. In this example, the frameset has a border size of 1 and two columns, the left one is 20 percent of the size of the one on the right.

5. The FRAME tag is used to define each frame in the frameset. In this example, there are two frames, LeftFrame and RightFrame. The LeftFrame opens index.htm, which contains a list of all the images in the Web photo gallery, stored in the Thumbnail folder on your hard drive. The RightFrame opens the Poppies1.html file, located in the Pages folder on your hard drive.

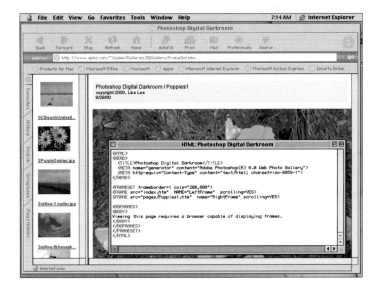

WORKING WITH FTP AND WEB SERVERS

When your photo gallery is complete, you can post it to your Web server. One way to update your Web site with new Web pages is to use an FTP application to access your Web server. There are many File Transfer Protocol (FTP) applications available for download on the Web. Whether you have a Mac or PC, one place to find reliable, virus-checked downloadable FTP applications is **http://www.download.com**. However, you can use any application that supports uploading files to a server using FTP. The following steps show you how to use Fetch on a Mac to upload files to a Web server.

1. Install Fetch on your Macintosh, or any FTP application to your PC.
2. Start the FTP application and log in to your Web site.
3. In the FTP application, navigate to the Web files you want to copy from your hard drive to the Web server. Click on the Put button on the FTP application window. The Put command enables you to copy files to the ftp server. Choose the file you want to upload to the Web server. Then click on Open to upload the file. Alternatively, you can click and drag a file on your Mac and drop it in the Fetch window to copy the files to the Web server.
4. Start a browser and type the URL to the Web page to see if it loads successfully in a browser window.

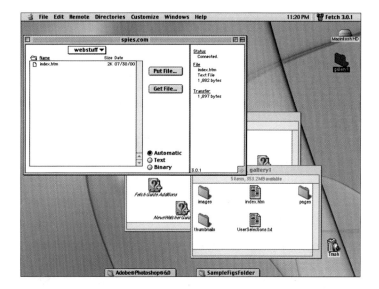

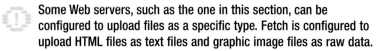

Some Web servers, such as the one in this section, can be configured to upload files as a specific type. Fetch is configured to upload HTML files as text files and graphic image files as raw data.

You can click and drag a file from the Fetch window onto your desktop to copy it from the Web server to your computer.

CREATING A DROPLET TO RESIZE IMAGES

A droplet is a small application that you can create in Photoshop. You can use a droplet to apply an action to a folder full of image files. For example, if you create an action to resize an image to a 100×100 pixel thumbnail image, you can save it as a droplet. You can use droplets to resize images and hand-tweak HTML files as an alternative to running the Web photo gallery automation script to create a photo gallery. The following steps show you how to create a droplet.

1. Click on the Create New Set icon in the Actions palette to create a new folder.
2. Click on the Create New Action icon in the Actions palette to add an action to the set. Click on the Record button. Perform a task in Photoshop. In this example, I chose Image Size from the Image, Adjust menus and resized this image to 640×480. Click OK in the Image Size window. Then click on the Record button in the Actions palette to stop recording the action.

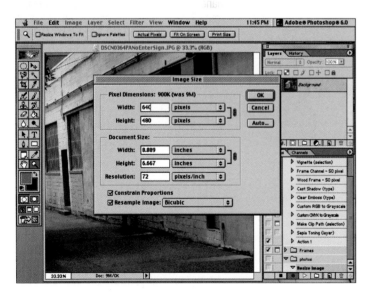

3. Click on the new action in the Actions palette. Then choose Create Droplet from the File, Automate menu.
4. Photoshop creates a droplet icon on the Desktop. To test the droplet, create a new folder and place a few image files into it. You can drag and drop one or several files over a droplet to repeat the action on all selected files.
5. Drag and drop the folder over the droplet icon. Photoshop starts and resizes each of the files in the folder.

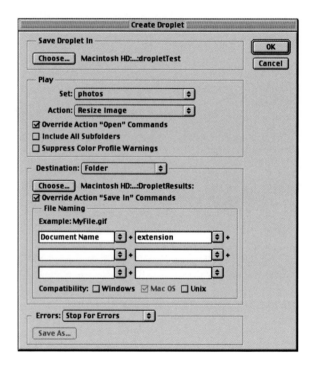

 On a Macintosh, you can create an AppleScript script to automate posting a folder or file to a Web server. Pick an FTP application that supports AppleScript. Write the script, and then test it with a sample folder on your hard drive.

CUSTOMIZING YOUR WEB PHOTO GALLERY

You really like the automated Web Photo Gallery tool included with Photoshop, but it doesn't always have the capability to create the Web page you envisioned. Don't worry. With a little time and HTML code, you can customize the Web Photo Gallery with little changes that can make a big difference. The following sections show you how to adjust the frame size and add banner text to the vertical frame style photo gallery.

CHANGING FRAME SIZES

If you chose Horizontal or Vertical Frame from the Styles drop-down menu in the Web Photo Gallery window, Photoshop will create your Web photo gallery with two frames; a left and a right frame. You can adjust the frame sizes in the Web Photo Gallery window by clicking and dragging the scroll bar on the right side of the left frame. The default proportions for the two frames are 20/80 percent. The frame on the left is 20 percent of the overall size of the browser window, and the frame on the right is 80 percent of the window. The following steps show you how to change the frame sizes for your Web photo gallery.

1. Navigate to the Photo Gallery folder on your hard drive and double-click the FrameSet.htm file. On a Mac, SimpleText will open this file. On a PC, Notepad or your designated HTML editor opens the html file.
2. Select the 20 percent, 80 percent text in the FrameSet.htm window in the text editor. This example shows the html source code being edited in SimpleText. Change 20 percent, 80 percent to 30 percent, 70 percent.

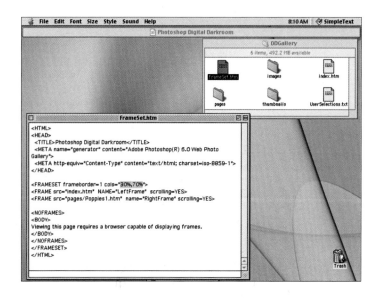

3. Press Ctrl/Command+S, or open the File menu and choose Save.
4. Click and drag FrameSet.htm to a browser window. The photo gallery Web pages should load. You should see a wider left frame in the browser window.

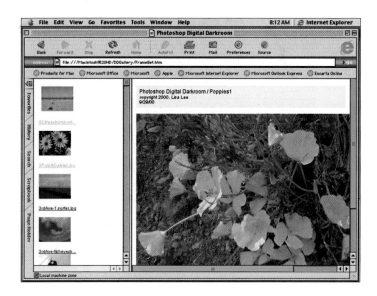

ADDING BANNER TEXT

Photoshop enables you to create a custom banner for your Web Photo Gallery. You can type a name, photographer, and date in the Web Photo Gallery window. Photoshop converts this text into HTML code and adds it to each page in the photo gallery. If you have a Web editor, you can add more detailed information to the banner section of each image's Web page, such as the copyright date for an image. Here's how:

1. Drag the FrameSet.htm file from your Web Photo Gallery photo and drop it in a browser window. Notice the banner title appears in the right frame, above the gallery image.

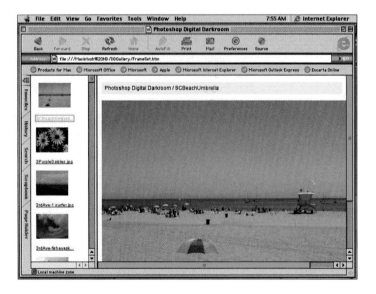

2. Open an HTML editor application. In this example, I've chosen BBEdit. Navigate to the Pages folder and open an HTML file for one of your images in the photo gallery. The file will be the name of one of the images in your image folder with htm as the file extension. In this example, I've opened the SCBeachUmbrella html file and highlighted the code that displays the banner and the image in a browser window.

3. Add or modify the HTML code. For example, I added copyright information next to my name. You can simply type additional text into the HTML editor. I chose to format the text by adding a font size.

```
<BR><FONT size="-1" face="Arial" >copyright 2000, Lisa
Lee<BR>9/29/00</FONT>
```

4. If you want to add a link to another Web page, you can add HTML code that creates a link on this Web page. In this example, I've added a link to take the browser to my main Photoshop Web page. You can replace the URL with your own custom URL.

```
<a href="http://www.spies.com/~lisalee/Paintings/DigCams.htm"
target="#">Exit photo gallery</a>
```

5. Open the File menu in the HTML editor and choose Save. Drag and drop the FrameSet.htm file over a browser window and navigate to the image file you just edited. You may need to refresh the image. On a Windows PC, press F5 to refresh Internet Explorer's browser window. On a Mac, press Command+R, or choose Refresh from the View menu. View the new banner text at the top of the browser window.

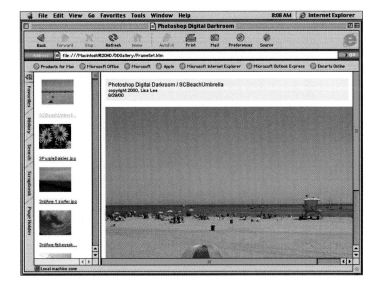

CREATING CUSTOM SCRIPTS

Although Photoshop can create slices and perform some Web-related tasks, the bulk of the Web features, such as rollovers, and exporting HTML code are only available in ImageReady. If you have enough memory to run both Photoshop and ImageReady on your computer, you can easily switch between the two applications by clicking on the Jump To button in the Toolbox. If you only want to access a particular action in ImageReady, you can record an action and save it as a droplet.

COPYING HTML CODE

You can create actions in ImageReady following the same steps as you would to create an action in Photoshop. You can use actions to automate tasks in ImageReady that are not available in Photoshop, such as exporting HTML code for an image file. Save these actions as droplets and use them anytime you like. A droplet is an application. To use it, drag and drop a file or folder of files over the droplet. The action will start ImageReady and play the action stored in the droplet. The following steps show you how to record an action to export HTML code from ImageReady. Then turn it into a droplet.

1. Open ImageReady. Click on the Create a New Action icon in the Actions palette.
2. Type a name for the action and then click on OK. Press the Record button in the Actions palette.
3. Open the Edit menu, choose Copy HTML Code, and select For All Slices (or For Selected Slices).
4. A new action should appear in the Actions palette. Click on the Record button to stop recording the action.
5. Choose Create Droplet from the Actions pop-up menu. Drop a file or folder over the droplet to copy the HTML code from the file (if any exists).

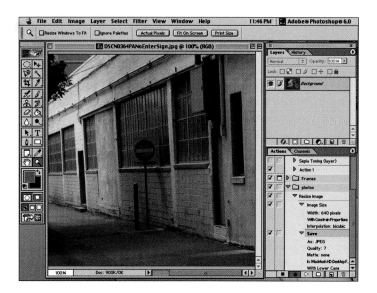

If you like digital photos and HTML code, visit **http://www.photo.net**. Many Web savvy photographers, amateur and professional, post helpful information to this Web site.

VIEWING PHOTOS WITH A WEB BROWSER

Take the time to view all your Web pages in a real browser window before posting them to a Web site. Make sure each image looks presentable and recognizable after being run through the script. If the pictures and Web pages look good enough to you, they're ready to share with the world. ImageReady has a Preview in Browser feature that enables you to view an image open in ImageReady in a browser window. You can view an image in Internet Explorer, Netscape Navigator, or the browser application of your choice.

USING IMAGEREADY

You can use the built-in menu commands to preview images with HTML code-in-progress within the ImageReady application using the latest version of Internet Explorer or Netscape Navigator. (Unfortunately, you can only preview images in browsers directly from ImageReady; Photoshop does not offer this feature.)

 Click on the Jump to Photoshop button in the toolbox in ImageReady to switch from ImageReady to Photoshop. You can also press Ctrl/Command+Shift+M to switch between the two applications.

 Preview images with two or three browser applications. I recommend previewing with Internet Explorer, Netscape Navigator, and America Online's browser. Even though an image may look fine with one browser, it may look differently with another.

The following steps show you how to use the File, Preview In command in ImageReady.

1. Open the File menu, choose Preview In, and select a browser from the submenu.

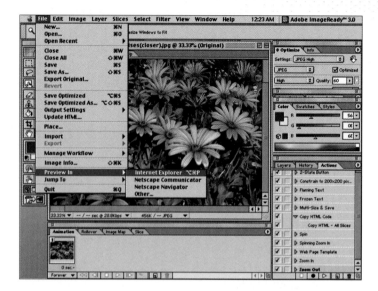

2. ImageReady switches to the browser application window and displays the selected image. In this example, I chose to view the image in Internet Explorer 5. Select a different browser by choosing File, Preview In, and select Other. Navigate your hard drive to locate the browser application of your choice.

GLOSSARY

A

Adaptive Palette A custom palette derived from actual colors in an image.

Align Orientation of one or more objects. Open the Paragraph palette to align selected type to the left, right, or center of the image window.

Alpha Channel Mask Also known as a channel mask or mask. 8 bits of grayscale information used to define the masked area of an image.

Angle Bracket A character used with HTML to identify a tag: < and >.

Animation Two or more images or text objects that play back and forth to create the illusion of motion. Animate digital pictures in ImageReady.

Anti-alias The process of smoothing the edges of an object or text so that it blends with the background color.

AppleScript The name of Apple's built-in scripting technology for automating simple tasks such as copying or moving a file to the Trash.

Application Also known as an executable or a program. An application such as Photoshop or ImageReady embodies all the code and features that enable you to create image files on a computer.

Archive Also known as a backup. A folder, compressed file, disk, or CD-ROM containing a set of files and folders for a particular project, day, and so on.

ATM An acronym for Adobe Type Manager, it is Adobe's software for enabling operating systems and applications to work with Adobe's font technologies.

Automate The technique of making an iterative or redundant task automatic. Choose an Automate command from the File menu, or create one or a combination of actions from the Actions palette.

B

Background The bottom layer of an image file.

Background Color The color of the background of the image window in the Photoshop workspace. It can also be the background color of a Web page.

Bit Depth Also known as the number of colors assigned to each pixel, and visible on a computer screen. Most images created by digital cameras contain millions of colors per pixel. Images created for the Web usually contain anywhere from 256 to thousands of colors per pixel.

Bitmap Graphics A matrix of pixels that form an image. Digital pictures are created as bitmap graphics. Photoshop generates bitmap graphics. See also *vector graphics*.

BMP A standard bitmapped file format supported by Windows PCs.

Brightness The luminance of a color across pixels in an image.

Browser An application that can read Hypertext Markup Language (HTML) documents.

Button A user-interface element that can be used on a Web page to perform a specific action, such as rollover to another Web page, or bring up a dialog window. If clicked, a button indicates a transition to a unique set of information on the same or different Web page.

C

Canvas Actual workspace area of an image file. Non-canvas areas of an image window are marked with a gray color.

CCD An abbreviation for Charge Coupled Device. CCDs are used with most popular digital cameras. CCDs translate light into digital data, which is in turn stored as a file on the camera's storage media. CCDs are also used in scanner peripherals and video cameras.

CD-ROM An abbreviation for Compact Disc Read-Only Media. Can store up to 600MB of data. Most software is distributed on CD-ROM, as well as most music albums. DVD-ROM can store up to 14GB of data. They can also read CD-ROM discs.

CD-RW An abbreviation for Compact Disc Read/Write. If you take a lot of digital pictures, you can use a CD-RW drive to archive the images. CD-RW drives also let you write more than once to the disc. CD-R drives allow you to write only once to a recordable CD-R disc.

There are also DVD-RW and DVD RAM drives, which enable you to archive up to 10GB of data per disc.

Channel 8 bits of grayscale information, which can be used to define red, green, and blue channels of an image file in RGB mode, or a channel mask.

Channel Mixer A menu command in Photoshop. Mix a percentage of a channel with part of another channel of an image in RGB mode. This command is available in the Image, Adjust menus and the Layer, New Adjustment Layer menus.

Check Box A user-interface element that can be used on a Web page to indicate that a particular feature is on or off.

Clone Stamp Tool A tool located in the toolbox that enables you to copy part of a bitmap image and apply it elsewhere in the image window.

CMYK An acronym used to express Cyan, Magenta, Yellow, and Black color values. Each color component has a value between 0 and 255. Some applications and printers do not use the black channel of a CMYK image file.

Color Picker Color palette and color selection system available in Photoshop. Choose between Photoshop's color picker window or the operating system's color picker window (for example Apple's color picker in Mac OS).

Color Table A table or group of colors associated with a particular graphic file. The color table is located in the Save for Web window in Photoshop. Add, lock, or snap a color to a Web palette in the Save for Web window.

Commands A menu or task performed in Photoshop. View each executed from the History panel.

Compositing The process of combining multiple images together. For example, if you combine multiple images into multiple layers and channels in a Photoshop image file, you are compositing images. The resulting single image is called a composite image.

Contrast The difference between light and dark pixel values in an image or object.

Convert Usually refers to changing the format of an image file from one file format to another.

Crop A tool that enables you to retain the subject of a photo, but remove unselected image areas. In Photoshop, you can crop an image as well as an object or path.

D

Digital Camera A consumer electronic device, similar to a traditional analog camera, that can capture digital images and store them to a removable card. High-end digital cameras can capture images directly to a computer's hard disk.

Display To make a layer, frame, or graphic object visible in the image window. Display is a direct result of selecting something in the Photoshop or ImageReady toolbox, palettes, or image window.

Display Modes Display modes affect how a document appears on the computer screen. ImageReady can display an image in Original or Optimized modes.

Download To copy a file or archive from another computer on a network or from the Internet. For example, if you want to edit your Web pages, you can log in to your Web site and download a file to your computer using a network connection.

DPI An abbreviation for dots per inch, which defines printer resolution.

E

Edge Border of a selected graphic text object.

Edit To change, adjust, or reorganize text or image objects.

Editor An application or feature in an application that edits text or graphics.

Effect Also referred to as a filter. One or more ways to adjust the way an image appears in the image window. Some effects can be added as layer styles or as an adjustment layer. Each effect in a layer style can be turned on or off in the Layers palette. All effects are accessible from the Filter menu. Each effect installed with Photoshop is stored as a plug-in file in the Plug-Ins folder on your hard drive.

Embed An HTML tag used to add a sound or media file to a Web page. See also *IMG SRC*.

Eraser This tool erases pixels from an image. Photoshop has three different kinds of erasers: eraser, background eraser, and the magic eraser tools.

Export A command used to convert a native image file format to a non-native file format.

Eyedropper A tool that can capture a color from an image and move it to the foreground or background color in the toolbox.

F

File Format A generic term for describing the way a file is saved. GIF, PSD, JPEG, and PNG are all different types of graphic file formats.

Filter Photoshop includes image-editing filters that adjust contrast, brightness, and other types of filters to improve your images.

Font A character set of a specific typeface, type style, and type size. Some fonts are installed with the operating system on your computer.

Foreground The front-most layer of objects or images in an image window.

Foreground Color The upper-left color in the toolbox. If the Pen, Pencil, Paintbrush, or other drawing tool is selected, the foreground color is used with the selected tool.

Frames A feature of HTML that can be used to divide a Web page, enabling you to view and navigate more than one page in a browser window. ImageReady uses frames to create each frame of an animation.

FTP File Transfer Protocol. Available in some browsers. Can be used to upload or download files to the Web or network server that has an FTP server.

G

Gamma Also known as the gamma correction setting. Adjusts an image to avoid midtones from appearing too dark on a computer screen. Switch gamma settings to view your Windows graphics on a Mac or your Macintosh graphics on a Windows platform.

GIF Pronounced "jif," the Graphics Interchange Format is one of the two most common graphic file formats used on the Web. The GIF format is most effective at compressing solid-color images and images with areas of repetitive color. In addition to supporting background transparency (which is great for animation), up to 256 colors can represent a GIF image. Best used with illustrations, text, and line art.

Gradient A progression of colors that gradually blend or fade into each other. Create a gradient within an object or across frames and layers.

Grayscale Represents a percentage of black where 0 is white and 100 is black and intermediate colors are shades of gray.

GUI An acronym for graphical user interface; pronounced "gooey." It represents all the buttons, windows, and menus you see if you're using Mac OS or Windows operating systems and any applications that support their correlating user interfaces.

Guides Visual interface element that indicates where a particular area begins and ends or enables you to position a selected object. In Photoshop, you can use slice guides, grid, or ruler guides to work with design elements.

H

Halo An off-colored ring of pixels that appears around borders of a graphic. Most noticeable around the edges of a mask or around the border of an image.

Hard Disk A hardware component commonly used in computers to store files and folders of data.

Hexadecimal A term to express red, green, and blue color values. Each component value is represented by a hexadecimal value, such as FF-FF-FF for white.

Highlight Color The color used as a visual interface to identify selected text or graphics.

History A command or action that has been performed on a Photoshop document. View a log of executed commands in the History palette.

HSB Hue, Saturation, and Brightness values. Hues range from 0 to 360 degrees. Saturation and brightness values range from 0 to 100%.

HTML An abbreviation for Hypertext Markup Language, which is the language used for most Web pages.

Hue/Saturation Hue is an adjustable range of colors from 0 to 360, or plus or minus 180. Saturation values encapsulate color intensity within a range of 0 to plus or minus 100.

I

Image A bitmapped matrix of pixels that represent a picture.

Image Map An image map is an image file broken up into slices. You can use the Slice tool to create an image map in Photoshop or ImageReady. Each slice is saved as a separate file on your hard drive.

Image Window The window containing the contents of an open image file in the Photoshop workspace.

IMG SRC HTML tag used to define the location of an image file on the Web server.

Import The command used to convert a non-Photoshop supported document into Photoshop.

Info Panel Displays the location, size, and colors of a particular object or document.

Inspector A floating panel containing settings and controls for Photoshop objects. Also synonymous with the terms *panel* and *palette*. See also *Panel*.

Integrate The process of combining two or more objects, components, or features.

Interpolation The process for calculating color when pixels are added or removed from an image during transformations. Bicubic interpolation creates the best results, but is usually the slowest method of interpolation.

ISP An abbreviation for Internet service provider. To access the Internet, a computer needs to have a connection to an Internet service provider. An ISP provides phone or network access to the Internet.

J

JavaScript A scripting language created by Netscape to add complex Web features to Web pages.

JPEG Created by the Joint Photographic Experts Group, JPEG is a popular graphic file format used on the Web. The JPEG file format preserves broad color ranges and subtleties in brightness and image tones and supports up to millions (24 bits) of colors. JPEG uses a lossy compression format that can remove some of the image data when a file is compressed. Best used with images and photographs. See also *PNG*.

K

Kerning Increases or decreases the spacing between specific pairs of letters. Used to improve the appearance of text.

Kilobyte Abbreviated KB; is equivalent to 1,024 bytes.

L

Lasso A selection tool that enables you to select a freeform set of pixels. Photoshop has three types of lasso tool: Lasso, Polygonal Lasso, and Magnetic Lasso.

Layer A particular plane in a document window that can create simple or complex graphics. Rearrange, add, remove, hide, and lock any layer in Photoshop.

Lossy compression An image file compression format that can be used to compress a JPEG image. Lossless JPEG compression preserves the original image without losing any image data. Lossy compression can lose image data when compressing a file. Photoshop lets you choose between 10 levels of JPEG compression.

M

Marquee Rectangular or ellipse tool that enables you to select an area of pixels in an image.

Mask A mask consists of two grouped objects. The mask itself is a sort of "cut-out" image that sits on top of the image being masked.

Megabyte Abbreviated MB. Equivalent to a million bytes, or more exactly 1,048,576 bytes.

Memory Also known as RAM. Refers to the amount of physical memory (in chips) installed on your computer. Virtual memory is the amount of memory or hard disk space allocated for use by the operating system and applications on a computer. Memory, in regards to an application like Photoshop, represents the amount of space required for an application to run its routines and functions.

Menu A user-interface element originating from the operating system and containing commands for an application.

O

Object Consists of one or more paths and points. Create and edit vector graphic objects with the Pen tool.

Onionskin View the contents of a previous or following frame in addition to the current frame with onionskinning turned on. Previous and following frames are slightly dimmed so that these images are easy to distinguish from the current image. This feature is only available in ImageReady.

Opacity The degree of transparency applied by a blending mode onto an object.

Optimize To reduce the size or image quality of a document in order to decrease the loading time for a Web page.

Optimize Window A tab in the ImageReady image window that enables you to see what an image will look like before you save or export it to your hard drive. Use this window to preview an image and compare it with other Web file formats to find the smallest, best-looking image for your Web page.

Options Bar Contains additional settings for tools in the toolbox. It is located at the top of the Photoshop workspace.

P

Paintbrush A drawing tool selectable from the toolbox window. Can be used to define the masked or unmasked areas of a channel, layer, or quick mask.

Paint Bucket A fill tool selectable from the toolbox window. Works with the color well to fill a selected object with a particular color.

Palette Also similar to the term floating palette and is synonymous with panel. See also *Panel*.

Panel A floating panel containing settings and controls for Photoshop objects. Also synonymous with the term inspector.

Path Comprised of two or more points, a path object, also referred to as a vector graphic, can be one or more lines of an open or closed object. View paths in the Paths palette.

Pen A drawing tool located in the toolbox. Can be used to create vector graphics.

Pencil A drawing tool located in the toolbox. Draw with a single pixel of color in the image window.

Pixel An atomic element of color that can be grouped together to form a picture or an image.

Plug-In A special type of file that can be placed in a folder on your hard drive. If the plug-in preferences are configured correctly, all plug-ins will appear in the Filter menu.

PNG The Portable Network Graphic is a newer graphic file format growing in popularity on the Web. Effectively compresses solid-color images and preserves details. The PNG format might require a plug-in to be added to a browser, but can support up to 32 bits of color, in addition to transparency and alpha channels. It uses a lossless form of compression. It is best used for creating high-color graphics with complex live transparency, and general low-color graphics. See also *PSD, GIF, JPEG,* and *Lossy.*

Preferences Application and document-specific settings that you can customize to increase your productivity in Photoshop.

Process A set of steps that, when followed, complete a task.

Processor The central processing unit of a computer. A faster processor will display graphics more quickly than a slower processor. Photoshop can take advantage of computers containing more than one processor.

PSD Photoshop's native file format. Preserve layers, layer sets, channels, and masks by saving them in a Photoshop file.

R

Radio Button A user-interface element found in applications and Web pages that has an on or off state.

RAM See *Memory.*

Resolution The number of horizontal and vertical pixels that make up a screen of information.

RGB Red, Green, and Blue values used to express a color. Each value can be within a range of 0 to 255.

Rollover Essentially a button that can have up to four unique appearances: up, over, down, click, and out.

S

Save A command used to convert an image stored in memory into a file on the hard drive.

Scale A term used to indicate the size—larger or smaller—of an original object or image.

Scroll Bar A set of window controls consisting of directional arrows, a scroll button, and a horizontal or vertical bar that navigate an image window.

Size Usually refers to the file size of an image file. Pages created for the Web should be less than 1MB in size, if not closer to a few hundred KB.

Slice Created using the Slice tool. Use slices to break a large image into smaller images so that the image can load faster in a browser window.

Slice Guides Slice guides show you where Photoshop will split the image into separate files when the image is exported. Slice guides are created when you apply the Slice tool to an image window.

Styles Store or load default or custom layer styles in the Styles palette. Create type, shapes, or select part of an image and apply a style from the Styles palette. Or choose a style and start drawing. Photoshop will apply the style as you draw.

Submenu Also referred to as a hierarchical menu. A secondary menu containing a list of menu commands.

Swatches Panel Can be used to store or load a custom group of colors created with the Color Mixer.

T

Tag A building block of HTML, such as <HEAD>. Tags work with a browser to determine how HTML content appears on a Web page. Tags usually appear in twos. For example, the <HEAD> will eventually be followed by the </HEAD> tag.

Text Also referred to as Type. Alphabetic, non-alphabetic, and numeric characters that define the characters in a font. Use the Type tool to add text to an image window.

Transform A set of tools that enable you to scale, rotate, flip, distort, or skew all or part of an image in the image window.

U

Undo A menu command that enables you to reverse a previous command in the image window. Set the number of undo levels in the General Preferences window.

Update To make current. Photoshop automatically updates all windows whenever you change a value in one window or panel.

Upload The process of copying a local file or folder to another computer.

URL An abbreviation for Uniform Resource Locator. Type a URL (such as http://www.adobe.com) into a browser window to go to a Web site or Web page on the Internet.

V

VCR Controls A set of buttons in the image window that enable you to navigate layers and interact with an image. ImageReady uses VCR control buttons to enable you to navigate image frames of an animation.

Vector Graphics Comprised of paths and points. They are used to create easily scalable drawings or graphic objects in Photoshop.

W

Web Also referred to as the World Wide Web. A group of computers running Web server software connected to an extended network around the world.

Web Client A computer connected to the Internet and configured with a browser and plug-ins to enable users to surf the Web.

Web Server A computer connected to the Internet and configured with server software to enable it to host one or more Web sites.

Wizard A type of application that provides a step-by-step method of configuring, installing, or converting files or programs on a computer. For example, choose Image Assistant from the Help menu to resize the image in the image window.

Z

Zoom Tool A tool that enables you to magnify the contents of the image window. Use with the Hand tool (H) to move the page while it is magnified. Press the Z key as a shortcut to select the zoom tool from the toolbox. Press the Ctrl/Command plus or minus keys to zoom into and out of an image in the image window.

INDEX